Faulkner and Twain

Edited by

Robert W. Hamblin

&

Melanie Speight

Faulkner and Twain

Edited by

Robert W. Hamblin

&

Melanie Speight

Published for the Center for Faulkner Studies
by Southeast Missouri State University Press • 2009

Faulkner and Twain
Edited by Robert W. Hamblin and Melanie Speight

Published for the Center for Faulkner Studies by
Southeast Missouri State University Press
MS 2650, One University Plaza
Cape Girardeau, MO 63701
www6.semo.edu/universitypress

ISBN: 978-0-9798714-74

Cover design: Thomas Marrone and Mandy Henley

Acknowledgments

The editors express sincere appreciation to Katie Carson, Jessica Copous, Leslie Loyd, and Matt Turner, research assistants in the Center for Faulkner Studies, for their indispensable aid in corresponding with contributors, managing and editing electronic files, and reading page proof.

We are grateful to Susan Swartwout, director of Southeast Missouri State University Press, and her assistants, Mandy Henley and Donna Essner, for their encouragement, guidance, and editorial expertise.

Our largest debt of gratitude is to the contributors for their engaging and thought-provoking treatments of two of the world's greatest writers.

"Mark Twain was the first truly American writer, and all us since are his heirs."

—William Faulkner

Contents

Introduction

The fifteen papers included in this volume were presented at the Faulkner and Twain Conference hosted by Southeast Missouri State University's Center for Faulkner Studies in Cape Girardeau, October 19–21, 2006. This Missouri town situated on the bank of the Mississippi River seemed to the organizers of the conference an ideal location for an event devoted to these two great American writers with Missouri connections.

Faulkner's great-grandfather, W.C. Falkner, migrated to northern Mississippi from Ste. Genevieve, Missouri, another Mississippi River town, in the mid-1800s; and Southeast Missouri State University owns the Louis Daniel Brodsky Faulkner Collection, one of the world's great collections of Faulkner materials. Missouri and the Mississippi River figure prominently in Faulkner's novels and stories. In *Light in August* and *The Unvanquished*, Faulkner recounts how the Burden family migrates from Missouri to Mississippi during Reconstruction—where two of them are murdered for their efforts on behalf of the freed slaves. The murderer, incidentally, is the character modeled on Faulkner's great-grandfather. In *A Fable*, the Missouri Bootheel is one of the backwoods places where the groom takes the stolen thoroughbred to run races to entertain the local populace. And the story "Old Man" is Faulkner's treatment of the 1927 Mississippi River flood.

Twain's connection with Missouri, of course, is stronger and better known. Born in the small town of Florida and raised in Hannibal, Twain became a steamboat pilot on the river and took his famous pen name from the rivermen's vocabulary. His *Life on the Mississippi* includes a not-altogether flattering description of Cape Girardeau, and some scholars think the setting of *Pudd'nhead Wilson*, Dawson's Landing, is modeled on Cape Girardeau.

Not only are Faulkner and Twain connected to this geographical place, they are also connected with each other. Both are small-town boys who became great American writers and achieved international fame. Both converted local and regional material into universal themes. Both wrote about nature, race, religion, politics, and history. Both are noted for their humor as well as their tragedies. Faulkner considered the two of them to be literary kin. He said, "Mark Twain was the first truly American writer, and all of us since are his heirs, we descended from him." At another time he said, "[Sherwood Anderson] was the father of my generation of American writers.... [Theodore] Dreiser is his older brother, and Mark Twain is the father of them both." On Faulkner's literary family tree, then, Twain is

Faulkner's grandfather; and the essays in this collection demonstrate some of the reasons for the accuracy of Faulkner's observation.

The volume opens, as did the conference, with Robert H. Brinkmeyer Jr.'s essay, "South x West: Faulkner and Twain at the Crossroads." Brinkmeyer examines the lives and works of the two authors in the context of the contrasting values of the nineteenth-century Western frontier (freedom) and the twentieth-century Southern community (conformity). As Brinkmeyer demonstrates, these conflicting elements have been present in American culture since its beginning—and they continue to be present today. Thus Twain's Huckleberry Finn and Faulkner's Ike McCaslin (to use only two of Brinkmeyer's several examples) are representative Americans struggling to balance the paradoxical needs of individual freedom and social responsibility.

Predictably, the Twain work most featured in this volume is *Adventures of Huckleberry Finn*. In "Plundering the Old Southwest: Twain and Faulkner as Reivers," Leland Krauth demonstrates that just as Twain pilfered material from the Southwestern humorists for some of the episodes in *Huckleberry Finn*, so did Faulkner, in *The Reivers*, borrow heavily from Twain's masterpiece. Both writers, Krauth notes, utilize the figure of the innocent, poke fun at illiterate bumpkins, and dramatize the casual amorality of commoners. However, unlike Twain, Faulkner incorporates sexual content into his narrative.

Gretchen Martin further examines Twain's and Faulkner's indebtedness to the frontier humorists of the Old South. In "Twain, Faulkner, and the Humor of the Old South: Southern Narrative and the Technique of Disclosure," Martin considers ways that *Huckleberry Finn*, *The Sound and the Fury*, and *Absalom, Absalom!* employ the narrative technique of "disclosure." Using Twain's back-country characters and Faulkner's Mr. Compson, Martin demonstrates how the revelations of fictional narrators expose and develop epistemological, social, and psychological issues.

David M. Monteith, in "'That Doomed and Fatal Blood': *Adventures of Huckleberry Finn* and *The Unvanquished*," compares Huckleberry Finn's rejection of a repressive, hypocritical Southern society and his consequent escape to Bayard Sartoris's situation in *The Unvanquished*. Both characters, Monteith argues, are children who have inherited the burden of a Southern tradition rooted in racial oppression, and both must seek their salvation as diasporic white subjects in relation to a black companion—respectively, Jim and Ringo. According to Monteith, both Twain and Faulkner emerge from an oppressive Southern past to position the future as a problematic site of an essential process of retributive absolution.

In "Huck Goes to Harvard," Laurel E. Eason draws some intriguing parallels between Huck Finn's decision to "light out for the territory" and Quentin Compson's pilgrimage to Harvard, as depicted in *Absalom, Absalom!*. While acknowledging that the two novels differ radically in tone, Eason finds both works to be serious treatments of such topics as the American frontier, war, class structure, racial strife, dysfunctional families, and religion. Both Huck and Quentin get an education, Eason contends, about the South in particular and human nature in general.

Robert W. Hamblin's "Faulkner's Hucks and Jims" analyzes comments Faulkner made about *Huckleberry Finn* during a class session at the University of Virginia in 1958. In his remarks Faulkner contrasted Twain's famous character with J.D. Salinger's Holden Caulfield of *The Catcher in the Rye*. Hamblin interprets Faulkner's remarks as supportive of a belief in an individuality that must be defined and discovered in relation to moral and communal values. He finds that Faulkner parallels the relationship of Huck and Jim in the pairings of Ike McCaslin and Sam Fathers in "The Bear," Chick Mallison and Lucas Beauchamp in *Intruder in the Dust*, and Lucius Priest and Ned McCaslin/Uncle Parsham in *The Reivers*.

Parallels in Faulkner's novels to Twain's *Pudd'nhead Wilson* provide the focus of four essays. Jason Cowan's "The Mulatto Avenger in Twain and Faulkner: Miscegenation and Identity in the South" examines the issue of miscegenation in the portrayals of Tom Driscoll and Rosanna in Twain's novel and Lucas McCaslin and Sam Fathers in Faulkner's *Go Down, Moses*. Cowan considers the crisis in self- and societal identity caused by the South's historical privileging of white in the white/black binary.

Mixed racial identity is also the subject of Alisa M. Smith-Riel's "Can Affectation Lead to Freedom?: Faulkner's *Absalom, Absalom!* and Twain's *Pudd'nhead Wilson*." In her study of Twain's Roxy and Faulkner's Eulalia Bon, Smith-Riel concludes that, in Southern society prior to the Civil War, the answer to the question posed by her title is no, since in both cases the attempts of mulattos to subvert the power of whites through affectation lead to disastrous consequences.

Matthew Sutton's essay, "Step Right Up: Spectacle and Showmanship in *Pudd'nhead Wilson* and *The Hamlet*," focuses upon outrageous, carnivalesque aspects of the respective novels, utilizing the career and practices of legendary showman P. T. Barnum as a context for analysis. The actions of the extraordinary Capello twins in Dawson's Landing, as well as Flem Snopes's horse sale and the "salting" of the Old Frenchman Place, are viewed as uncanny events and cynical manipulations of the public trust in the best (that is, worst) tradition of Barnum.

In "Absorbed in Reading the 'Worst Heart of the World': Faulkner, Twain, and Their 'Failed Detectives,'" Fumiyo Hayashi examines the roles of characters who search for truth in situations of uncertainty and ambiguity. David Wilson of *Pudd'nhead Wilson* is linked to a number of Faulkner characters—among them Gavin Stevens of *Light in August*, Ike McCaslin in *Go Down, Moses*, V.K. Ratliff in the Snopes trilogy, and the several narrators of *Absalom, Absalom!*—as "amateur detectives" who seek explanations for mysterious and seemingly inexplicable actions and behaviors. Hayashi finds a prototype for all such characters in the narrator of Edgar Allan Poe's "The Man in the Crowd."

Françoise Buisson, in "From Unreadable Experience to Initiation: The River in Twain's *Life on the Mississippi* and Faulkner's 'Old Man,'" notes how the stylistic ebb and flow of the respective narratives, characterized as they are by disjunctions, digressions, hyperboles, and complicated sentence structures, serve as a metaphor of experience. The protagonist in each work—Twain's pilot and Faulkner's convict—becomes a quixotic adventurer in the humorous picaresque tradition, negotiating the metamorphoses and anamorphoses of the treacherous, unpredictable, and apparently unreadable river.

Two papers extend the discussion of Faulkner and Twain to include a third writer. M. Thomas Inge, in "To Kill a Prejudice: Racial Relations and the Lynch Mob in Twain, Faulkner, and Harper Lee," examines the treatment of race in *Adventures of Huckleberry Finn*, *Intruder in the Dust*, and *To Kill a Mockingbird*. Countering readers who see these novels as paternalistic, or even racist, Inge argues that, viewed in their historical contexts, all three books make hopeful contributions to improved race relations and are consequently works of compassion rather than prejudice.

Thomas Eaton's essay, "Weeping or Wanting: Post-Death Dislocation in Moral Constructs in Faulkner, Twain, and Zola," considers the treatment of the dead in Faulkner's *A Fable* and *As I Lay Dying*, Emile Zola's *Earth*, and Twain's "A Curious Dream." Employing Richard Alexander's notion that human morality is little more than reproductive necessity, Eaton argues that the burial scenes in each of the four focal works mirror humankind's wrestling with the moral compulsion of burying the dead with dignity and respect, and the biological necessity of moving forward in a world dispossessed of the dead.

The two concluding essays in the volume push the discussions of Faulkner and Twain beyond merely literary concerns to consider the two authors in the context of national and international political issues. Mary A. Knighton, in "Swinks and Snopeses: The Germ of the 'Global Provincial' in Twain and Faulkner," analyzes Twain's 1905 unfinished manuscript, "Three Thousand Years among the Microbes," and Faulkner's Snopes trilogy in the international context of their time and place. Noting both writers' keen awareness of the contradiction between the ideal of American equality and the consequences of ruthless, self-serving capitalism, Knighton discusses Twain's attitudes toward the Russo-Japanese war of 1904–1905 and Faulkner's relationship to communism, fascism, and the Cold War.

Charles A. Peek's essay, "Faulkner, Twain, and Just about Everybody Not Currently Working in Washington," explores the manner in which the public, iconic images of both Twain and Faulkner continue to ignore the complicated and often troubling realities of the actual men and their works. Citing the authors' respective treatments of war in Twain's "The War Prayer" and Faulkner's *Soldiers' Pay*, *Flags in the Dust*, and *A Fable*, Peek concludes that the works of both men are "voices against the deceitful use of words that perennially sacrifices the young and is busily doing it again."

Considered in their entirety, the essays in this book not only bear convincing testimony to the genius of Faulkner and Twain but also demonstrate their continuing appeal to readers and a striking relevance to contemporary situations and issues.

Robert W. Hamblin

Notes on the Conference

On October 19–21, 2006, Southeast Missouri State University's Center for Faulkner Studies hosted its first conference, entitled "Faulkner and Twain." Sponsored by both the Center for Faulkner Studies and the Missouri Humanities Council, the conference featured presentations by thirty-nine scholars representing six countries and thirteen American states. Presentation topics included Faulkner's and/or Twain's treatments of the river, the frontier, humor, race, class, gender, and history, as well as the teaching of both Faulkner and Twain in the classroom. The papers featured in this volume address both authors.

The conference opened at 6 PM, Thursday, October 19, with a buffet dinner. Provost Jane Stephens provided the welcome, and Robert W. Hamblin, the Director of the Center, introduced keynote speaker Robert Brinkmeyer, a leading scholar in twentieth-century Southern literature and culture. Immediately following the keynote address, entitled "South x West: Faulkner and Twain at the Crossroads," Dr. and Mrs. Hamblin hosted a reception at their home in honor of Dr. Brinkmeyer.

Panels and Presentations took place on Friday and Saturday, October 20–21, beginning at 8:30 AM on Friday and concluding at 12:00 PM on Saturday. Six sessions were offered, with two programs per session. In addition to the papers presented, Mary A. Knighton organized and moderated the panel "Faulkner and Twain in Japan," which included three other visiting Japanese scholars.

Books, manuscripts, and other memorabilia from the Louis Daniel Brodsky Collection of William Faulkner materials and the Charles L. Harrison collection of Mark Twain books were on exhibit throughout the conference in Kent Library. Library Dean Sarah Cron; Louis Daniel Brodsky, the Curator of the Brodsky Collection; and Lisa Speer, Special Collections Librarian, hosted a special showing of the Rare Book Room from 5:30 to 6:30 PM, Friday, October 20. During that time, Brodsky shared personal stories about the Collection, which is one of the principal Faulkner collections in the world.

At 7:00 PM, Friday, October 20, participants enjoyed "Mr. Twain, Meet Mr. Faulkner," a readers' theater presentation based on the writings of Twain and Faulkner. Scripted and directed by Roseanna Whitlow, Instructor of Communication Studies at Southeast Missouri State University, the dramatic presentation included appearances from Twain and Faulkner impersonators, Lester Goodin and Pat Abbott.

The conference then concluded with a historical tour on Saturday afternoon, October 21. Frank Nickell, Director of Southeast Missouri State University's Center for Regional History, conducted the bus tour of the Mississippi River riverfront and other historic sites in and around Cape Girardeau.

The conference planners are grateful to all the individuals, organizations, and businesses that supported our first Faulkner conference. We offer a special thanks to Southeast Missouri State University, the Office of the Provost, the College of Liberal Arts, the Department of English, and Kent Library, for hosting the event; and the Missouri Humanities Council, for its sponsorship.

South x West:
Faulkner and Twain at the Crossroads

Okay, first off: Why Twain and Faulkner?

For me the answer begins with Virginia Woolf. When I was a graduate student at the University of North Carolina, I was planning to study British modernism and specifically Virginia Woolf. I was much under the sway of my girlfriend; she loved Woolf, and we frequently read Woolf together. While I was writing my MA thesis on Woolf, I was also taking a seminar on her work. Perfect timing, right? Nope. The seminar was one of my worst educational experiences, and certainly my worst as a graduate student. My professor, who shall remain nameless, spent the whole semester agonizing over whether Woolf ever had an orgasm. (At the end of the semester, he finally decided, somehow, that she hadn't. Hence, she wrote great fiction.) The upshot of that semester: I finished my MA thesis and haven't read a word of Virginia Woolf since.

I was now adrift as a potential scholar. I was still with my girlfriend, but I could no longer read Virginia Woolf with her. I needed a new field. Two things happened: my girlfriend and I started reading Faulkner together, and I enrolled in a course in Southern literature with Louis Rubin. In this course, which eventually sent my life off in a new direction, Rubin talked a great deal about the connection between Faulkner and Twain.

The course began with Faulkner's *Absalom, Absalom!*, and Rubin focused on the love/hate relationship that Quentin Compson—and by extension, Faulkner—had for the South. Rubin found this love/hate relationship not only crucial for understanding Faulkner's art and imagination, but also for almost all writers of the Southern literary renaissance. Quentin Compson's agonized response, at the end of *Absalom, Absalom!*, to Shreve's question about why Quentin hated the South—"*I don't hate it. . . . I don't. I don't! I don't hate it! I don't hate it!*" (303)—echoed throughout the course. And, more importantly, at least for those of us now in this room, he noted that it was Mark Twain (and also, to a somewhat lesser extent, Edgar Allan Poe and Kate Chopin), who most looked forward to Faulkner and the Southern literary renaissance, since it was Twain, of all the Southern writers in the nineteenth century, who most shared this fundamental love/hate for the region. William Dean Howells might have seen Twain as

17

a "desouthernized Southerner," but not Rubin. Twain, to his eyes, was the forefather of twentieth-century Southern literature.

Whether or not one accepts Rubin's thesis, there is certainly a good bit of evidence to suggest that Twain looked forward to Faulkner. Close to twenty years before Faulkner was born and another thirty or so before he began work on his most significant fiction, Twain wrote what may be two of the best descriptions of Faulkner's imaginative vision and narrative style in several passages on the riverboat captain, Mr. Brown, from *Life on the Mississippi*:

> He could *not* forget any thing. It was simply impossible. The most trivial details remained as distinct and luminous in his head, after they had lain there for years, as the most memorable events. His was not simply a pilot's memory; its grasp was universal. If he were talking about a trifling letter he had received seven years before, he was pretty sure to deliver you the entire screed from memory. And then without observing that he was departing from the true line of his talk, he was more than likely to hurl in a long-drawn parenthetical biography of the writer of that letter; and you were lucky indeed if he did not take up that writer's relatives, one by one, and give you their biographies, too.
>
> * * * * * * *
>
> Moreover, he cannot stick to his subject. He picks up every little grain of memory he discerns in his way, and so is led aside. Mr. Brown would start out with the honest intention of telling you a vastly funny anecdote about a dog. He would be "so full of laugh" that he could hardly begin; then his memory would start with the dog's breed and personal appearance; drift into a history of his owner; of his owner's family, with descriptions of weddings and burials that had occurred in it, together with recitals of congratulatory verses and obituary poetry provoked by the same; then this memory would recollect that one of these events occurred during the celebrated "hard winter" of such and such a year, and a minute description of that winter would follow, along with the names of people who were frozen to death, and statistics showing the high figures which pork and hay went up to. Pork and hay would suggest corn and fodder; corn and fodder would suggest cows and horses; cows and horses would suggest

the circus and certain celebrated bare-back riders; the
transition from the circus to the menagerie was easy and
natural; from the elephant to equatorial Africa was but
a step; then of course the heathen savages would suggest
religion; and at the end of three or four hours' tedious jaw,
the watch would change, and Brown would go out of the
pilot-house muttering extracts from sermons he had heard
years before about the efficacy of prayer as a means of
grace. And the original first mention would be all you had
learned about that dog, after all this waiting and hunger-
ing. (308–309)

There's something, too, in Twain's description of the river pilot as "the
only unfettered and independent human being that lived in the earth"
(313), together with his descriptions of the pilots' sacred brotherhood,
that seems to look forward to the fierce independence of the modernist
writer—and thus Faulkner—together with the literary priesthood of the
high modernists.

While I'm having a bit of fun here, I've deliberately drawn from *Life
on the Mississippi* because it seems to me one of the most obvious texts
of Twain's that looks forward to Faulkner's Mississippi and art. For besides
the river pilot's goal of learning everything about the Mississippi River,
calling to mind Faulkner's encyclopedic knowledge of his Mississippi,
Yoknapatawpha, there's the more general sense of tragic decline that
pervades both writers as they survey, past and present, the land they love
so deeply. The lost idyll of the South haunts both writers, the beauty of an
idealized and nostalgic past always lurking invitingly, as in a palimpsest,
through the present. I don't think anyone has characterized this sort of
shadowed vision better than Twain, here describing his return to Hannibal
after many years away:

The only notion of the town that remained in my mind
was the memory of it as I had known it when I first
quitted it twenty-nine years ago. That picture of it was still
as clear and vivid to me as a photograph. I stepped ashore
with the feeling of one who returns out of a dead-and-
gone generation. I had a sort of realizing sense of what the
Bastille prisoners must have felt when they used to come
out and look upon Paris after years of captivity, and note
how curiously the familiar and the strange were mixed
together before them. I saw the new houses—saw them
plainly enough—but they did not affect the older picture

in my mind, for through their solid bricks and mortar I
saw the vanished houses, which had formerly stood there,
with perfect distinctness. (538–539)

At the same time that much of *Life on the Mississippi* seems to look
forward to Faulkner, Faulkner's essay "Mississippi" seems in many ways to
look back to Twain. "Mississippi" is a strange little essay, a memoir of sorts
that is a mishmash of truth and fiction, peopled not only with real people
but with characters from Faulkner's fiction (presented as if they were real
folk), just the sort of thing one can imagine Twain writing. In the essay,
Faulkner casts both a warm and a cold eye on his home state and its history, indicative of his two minds about both Mississippi and more generally
the South. Near the end of the essay, Faulkner alternates between passages
describing the things he loves and the things he hates about his home
country, and almost all of these descriptions dovetail closely with interests
and feelings held by Twain. Most of Faulkner's passages describing his
deep love for the South invoke memories of childhood escapades and
holiday cheer, together with the beauty of nature and the honorable code
of hunting—Faulkner's gloss, in other words, of *The Adventures of Tom
Sawyer*. Most of the passages describing Faulkner's hate for the South
focus on the South's intolerance, violence, and injustice, particularly in its
treatment of black people—Faulkner's gloss of *Adventures of Huckleberry
Finn*. The final sentence of the essay is perhaps the single best sentence
Faulkner ever wrote about his complicated and conflicted feelings about
the South—and also one of the best observations ever written about
Twain's similarly complicated and conflicted feelings. Speaking of the
South, Faulkner writes: "Loving all of it even while he had to hate some of
it because he knows now that you dont love because: you love despite; not
for the virtues, but despite the faults" ("Mississippi" 42–43).

I realize that I am speaking very generally here, drawing conclusions
that I'm sure to many of you appear entirely obvious. But what I'm trying
to do is to establish a broad rationale for this conference, a reason for us to
be meeting and talking. What I'm really arguing is that indeed there are
profitable ways to study Twain and Faulkner together, both on the broad
level that I've been speaking about and in the more specific ways in which
the two writers will be examined in the conference sessions.

That said, I'd like to take a stab at my own specific discussion of Twain
and Faulkner, looking at what I see as a crossing of the ways in both of
their works—not one of crossings that I've already mentioned, that is,
between modernity and traditionalism, or between love and hate—but a
crossing between two regional paradigms, the South and the West, that I
see working in their work, specifically in Twain's *The Adventures of Tom*

Sawyer and *Adventures of Huckleberry Finn* and Faulkner's *Go Down, Moses*. What I want to argue is that these three works are perhaps best read as border novels, fraught with tensions between and confluences of matters often associated with these two American regions, whose cultural myths—the imaginative constructions shaping each region's dominant culture—stand in stark contrast with one another. Indeed, it's this uneasy coming together of Southern and Western mythologies that perhaps best defines these three works, establishing a startlingly rich and at times conflicted view of their fictional worlds.

While I'm perfectly aware I'm simplifying here, I nonetheless want to sketch out briefly, before I look specifically at the works under discussion, the two cultural myths I see at work in the texts. The Southern cultural myth, as has been discussed by countless observers, is founded on a strong sense of localism, with place the foundation for establishing identity and purpose, a dynamic summed up in the words of Wendell Berry that "if you don't know where you are, you don't know who you are" (qtd. in Stegner 199). Being grounded means being rooted in one's locale and its culture; being grounded valorizes stability, continuity, tradition, family, community. Not foregrounded in the Southern myth are mobility and time, both of which, in the Southern scheme of things, represent disruptive forces of instability and discontinuity that threaten to undo the order of traditional culture. In commenting on the Southern resistance to time and progress (progress characteristically conceived as change for change's sake, or, put another way, endless motion forward with no real purpose and toward no specific destination), Lucinda MacKethan writes that in the traditional South "time and progress belong to the world outside, or so the myth goes; on the plantations or in the small, sleepy southern towns that are the popular images of the South, time is held back by the places themselves" (181). A Southerner's nightmare, by this thinking, might be Gertrude Stein's characterization of America: "Conceive a space that is filled with moving" (qtd. in Stegner 72).

Quite different is the mythology of the West that involves ongoing movement forward into new frontiers and territories. (Let me add here that I realize that both the Southern and Western mythologies have in recent times been interrogated, revised, debunked, and/or discarded—this rethinking has been largely all for the good; but that said, regardless of their fictionality, the Southern and Western myths have clearly had a shaping influence on both the regions and the nation.) Underlying the Western mythology—which has been one of the primary shaping mythologies of America, a nation which has largely defined itself in motion from East to West—is the impulse to leave the confines and burdens of society and history behind, moving into new frontiers and territories (with outer space, we know from Star Trek, now "the final frontier"). This westward impulse foregrounds space rather than place, the future rather than the past, individualism rather than community, and in all this stands diametrically opposed to the mythology of the South. As I have put it elsewhere, in terms of cultural mythology, America might be understood as a wagon train pushing ever westward, while the South is the walled fort that the wagon train leaves behind.

Classic American literature of the nineteenth century—or at least what was once called classic American literature—often focuses on an individual white male moving west, conquering new frontiers, a path that leads him, in Richard Slotkin's evocative phrase, to regeneration through violence—that is, the emasculated male, undone by the wiles of women and the deadening routines of domestic and city life, is made whole again through ultimate, violent tests of his manhood. This is Slotkin:

> The American must cross the border into "Indian country" and experience a "regression" to a more primitive and natural condition of life so that the false values of the "metropolis" can be purged and a new, purified social contract enacted. Although the Indian and the Wilderness are the settler's enemy, they also provide him with the new consciousness through which he will transform the world. The heroes of the myth-historical quest must therefore be "men (or women) who know Indians"—characters whose experiences, sympathies, and even allegiances fall on both sides of the Frontier. (14)

As Slotkin suggests, the Western hero through his adventures becomes knowledgeable in the ways of Indians—ways that draw from the laws of nature rather than those of organized society—so that he somehow merges on a profound level the two opposing perspectives. In its most obvious manifestation, the white hero is accompanied and schooled by an Indian, as in Cooper's Leatherstocking novels, where Natty Bumppo plows through the wilderness with his Indian companion Chingachgook. Southern literature, in contrast, at least that written by white males, focuses not on the pioneer hero (to leave one's community, in the Southern scheme of things, is less heroic than idiotic, a dangerous cutting oneself off from the nurturing bonds of community) but on the hero who can somehow integrate himself into the community while at the same time remaining displaced enough to maintain his individuality. Frequently this necessary displacement occurs in the hero's confrontation with the white South's legacy of racial oppression, often brought about by the hero's companionship with a black person. In contrasting the Western and the Southern novel, Leslie Fiedler writes that "the heart of the Western is . . . the encounter with the Indian," while the heart of the Southern is the encounter with the black person—or as Fiedler says, in his typically blunt fashion, "without the Negro . . . there is no true Southern" (21, 19).

I want to use these two simple paradigms of regional myths to suggest how Twain's *The Adventures of Tom Sawyer* and *Adventures of Huckleberry Finn*, along with Faulkner's *Go Down, Moses*, blend these two traditions, crossing them in ways that complicate the regional patterns and thus thicken the underlying dynamics at work in the novels. I want to begin with Faulkner's *Go Down, Moses* because I believe this blending is a bit easier to recognize; from what we learn about Faulkner's novel, I think we will be in a better position to interrogate the similar interplays and confluences of traditions in Twain's novels.

In terms of Ike McCaslin's struggles with his family's past and his role in the family and the community, *Go Down, Moses* is a profoundly Southern—and Western—text. At the center of the novel is Ike's effort to expiate his family—and more generally, the South—from the curse he sees them suffering from because of slavery in general and his grandfather's incestuous coupling with his black daughter in particular. Ike hopes that his Christ-like renunciation of his inheritance and patrimony will free himself and his family from the cascading and imperiling effects of his ancestors' earlier crimes. Thus to Ike's eyes, he stands as a beacon of hope for his family and the South, his strict idealism offering a way for white Southerners to make good in their wrongful enslavement and disgraceful mistreatment of blacks. To people in the community, including his family, however, Ike's actions appear incomprehensible if not foolhardy; by their Southern eyes, Ike seems merely to be walking away from his responsibilities to his family and his community, both of which need his leadership. At one point in the novel, standing before Lucas, Ike feels the withering judgment of the community. Lucas knows, Ike thinks, *"[t]hat I reneged, cried calf-rope, sold my birthright, betrayed my blood, for what he too calls not peace but obliteration, and a little food"* (105).

Ike's community finds his actions so incomprehensible because, in effect, Ike has not stayed home but has fled west—that is, Ike has imaginatively lit out for a life in the woods instead of staying home to assume his rightful place as leader of his family. That Ike's repudiation of his inheritance represents this westering impulse is underscored by the fact that Ike's idealism is based on his understanding—learned from Sam Fathers, a mixed-blood Indian—of the beauty and order of the natural world. Ike, in other words, aspires to be the Western hero, the man who knows Indians, the man who bridges the worlds of nature and society. When

Sam marks Ike with the blood of his first deer, Ike knows that he is now forever marked "not as a mere hunter, but with something Sam had had in his turn of his vanished and forgotten people" (175). Rather than seeing himself tied in blood and sinfulness to his grandfather, Ike, following Sam, now sees himself one in blood and identity with the natural world. "Oleh, Chief. Grandather," Sam says (177), saluting the tremendous buck that he and Ike see near the end of "The Old People," and it is from that buck, representing the wilderness in all its power and mystery, from which Ike, in his wilderness identity, now sees himself imaginatively descending. "There was something running in Sam Fathers' veins which ran in the veins of the buck too," Ike thinks in "Delta Autumn" (334), and that something—rather than the sins of his grandfather—he believes runs in his veins as well.

As Western hero, seemingly regenerated through the violence of the hunt and through his connection with the natural world, Ike seems poised to return to his society as its leader. But he doesn't return. Instead, driven by his westering impulse, Ike plunges deeper into both—into the Mississippi woods and the west of his imagination. Significantly, as Ike makes deeper and deeper forays into the wilderness during his hunting trips, he realizes that to enter fully the depths of the natural world, he must discard all trappings of his life within society—his gun, his compass, and his watch; only in this complete relinquishment can he proceed into "the green and soaring gloom of the markless wilderness" (199). As an old man, Ike imagines himself standing outside history and living in a timeless and unchanging world:

> He seemed to see the two of them—himself and the wilderness—as coevals, his own span as a hunter, a woodsman, not contemporary with his first breath but transmitted to him, assumed by him gladly, humbly, with joy and pride, from that old Major de Spain and that old Sam Fathers who had taught him to hunt, the two spans running out together, not toward oblivion, nothingness, but into a dimension free of both time and space where once more the untreed land warped and wrung to mathematical squares of rank cotton for the frantic old-world people to turn into shells to shoot at one another, would find ample room for both—the names, the faces of the old men he had known and loved and for a little while outlived, moving again among the shades of tall unaxed trees and sightless brakes where the wild strong immortal game ran forever before the tireless belling immortal

> hounds, falling and rising phoenix-like to the soundless
> guns. (337–338)

In living most deeply in this imaginatively conceived timeless dimension, Ike in a sense reverses the flow of time, growing younger as he grows older, moving from adult experience to childlike innocence; or as Faulkner puts it, Ike was "born into his father's old age and himself born old and became steadily younger and younger until, past seventy himself and at least that many years nearer eighty than he ever admitted any more, he had acquired something of a young boy's high and selfless innocence" (103).

Ike may think he bridges the world of the wilderness and the world of his community—he ends up teaching children how to hunt—but he really doesn't because no one in the community takes him seriously and because time moves inexorably forward no matter what Ike imagines. "'Where have you been all the time you were dead?'" Roth asks Ike in "Delta Autumn" (329), expressing the community's view that Ike's retreat into the wilderness has in effect left him dead to the world of society and history. And while Ike turns his back on history and progress, the wilderness itself is shrinking before the inexorable creep of society, with the logging trains stabbing deeper and deeper into the woods, signaling the wilderness's doom. Once hearing the sound of panthers, the hunters now hear

> the long hooting of locomotives: trains of incredible
> length and drawn by a single engine, since there was no
> gradient anywhere and no elevation save those raised by
> forgotten aboriginal hands as refuges from the yearly
> water and used by their Indian successors to sepulchre
> their fathers' bones, and all that remained of that old time
> were the Indian names on the little towns and usually
> pertaining to water—Aluschaskuna, Tillatoba, Homoch-
> itto, Yazoo. (325)

As the wilderness world shrinks, so too does Ike's, his idealism progressively collapsing his existence entirely into his imaginative dream world. As a misplaced Western hero floundering in a Southern community struggling with the onslaughts of time and history, as the man who knows Indians, Ike will soon be as forgotten as the Mississippi Indians themselves.

Ike in the end has learned well from the teachings of his father figure of the West, the Indian Sam Fathers—but perhaps too well for his own good. What he hasn't learned is what those of the South, both black and white, try to teach him: that people are never entirely free from responsibility to others, that people live best when they live connected in time, place, and community—and in love. While Ike can recognize the sexual abuse of his grandfather, he can't see that that abuse shadows his own repudiation of his rightful place in the community; he can't see, that is, that his repudiation shatters bonds of love and affection, weakening his family and destroying his marriage. Nor can he see that in upbraiding Roth's black mistress (and a distant kinswoman) that he also ironically repeats the racial violence, though not of course in the same degree, of his grandfather—the very violence that set him on his Western journey in the first place.

Ike in his isolation stands at the opposite extreme from Rider, the protagonist of "Pantaloon in Black," who is utterly consumed with passion for his wife, even after her death. Critics have often wondered why Faulkner included "Pantaloon in Black," a story not concerned with the McCaslin family, in *Go Down, Moses*, but I think it's pretty clear: Rider is the Southern counterpart to Sam Fathers. If Sam Fathers represents the extremes of Western individualism, Rider represents the extremes of the Southern communalism, with Rider's unswerving commitment to his dead wife and their marriage plunging him into a psychological wilderness that isolates him from the larger community that rallies to support him. "'Hit look lack Ah just cant quit thinking. Look lack Ah just cant quit,'" Rider says (154), in words that also could speak of Ike's obsessions with the eternal wilderness. For very different reasons, Ike and Rider tear themselves from their nurturing communities, and their plights point to one of the central ideas of the novel: that at their extremes, both the Western and the Southern paradigms lead to self-destruction. Somewhere in between these two extremes, somewhere in the crossing of the South and the West, Faulkner suggests, with *Go Down, Moses*, the means for living responsible, caring, and honorable lives are located—perhaps seen in the chastened Lucas Beauchamp at the end of "The Fire and the Hearth," who finally sees the destructive ends of his ludicrous—and thoroughly Western—pursuit of treasure; or perhaps in Gavin Stevens, who for all his bumblings in the title story, is at least doing his best to help both the black and the white communities.

Mark Twain's *The Adventures of Tom Sawyer* and *Adventures of Huckleberry Finn* likewise cross the Southern with the Western paradigm, in the process suggesting the constructive and destructive elements of each, though this crossing works in different ways in the two novels. The simpler, less problematic intersection occurs in *Tom Sawyer*, where the town of St. Petersburg and the life there point to the confluence of South and West. In terms of location, St. Petersburg sits at the frontier between the South and West, incorporating elements of each region. In its domestic and social order, symbolized by the rule of the townswomen, the judge, and the preacher, the town is markedly Southern; but in its proximity to the wilderness and its dangers (both in terms of violence and of outside forces entering into the town), the town is decidedly Western. It's entirely significant in this regard that Tom and his friends identify themselves as "western boys" and that one of Tom's dreams is to head out for the "Far West" (Twain, *Tom Sawyer* 29, 60). St. Petersburg, that is, stands at the beginning of the West and at the end of the South.

The South and the West, together with their confluence, are represented by the three main boys of the novel: Sid, Tom, and Huck. As representative of the South, Sid, prim and proper, diligently follows all the domestic and social rules of St. Petersburg and takes joy in unmasking other boys, particularly Tom, who don't; he is, as Twain writes, "a quiet boy and had no adventurous, troublesome ways" (11). Huck, on the other hand, as representative of the West, is pretty much a loner, drifting in and out of town, living by his own rules and owning up to no one but himself. To the mothers of the town, "he was idle, and lawless, and vulgar and bad"—precisely what they do their best to keep their own boys from becoming. (And I'm reminded here of a wonderful line from Eudora Welty's *Golden Apples*, describing the town of Morgana's efforts to keep Snowdie MacLean from wandering too far from the role prescribed for women: "We shut the West out of Snowdie's eyes of course" [14]).

To the boys, however, Huck represents freedom, particularly freedom from the world of their mothers, freedom that is the stuff of their dreams:

> Huckleberry came and went, at his own free will. He slept
> on doorsteps in fine weather and in empty hogsheads in
> wet; he did not have to go to school or to church, or call
> any being master or obey anybody; he could go fishing or
> swimming when or where he chose, and stay as long as
> it suited him; nobody forbade him to fight; he could sit
> up as late as he pleased; he was always the first boy that
> went barefoot in the spring and the last to resume leather
> in the fall; he never had to wash, nor put on clean clothes;
> he could swear wonderfully. In a word, everything that
> goes to make life precious, that boy had. So thought every
> harassed, hampered, respectable boy of St. Petersburg. (45)

Situated between Sid and Huck is Tom, a boy of both worlds who lives under the town's domestic and social rules (though pushing them to their limits) while at the same time imaginatively possessing the free spirit of the West. Firmly anchored in town life, Tom nonetheless seeks out "desolate places that were in harmony with his spirit," places "far from the accustomed haunts of boys" (26). As with so many heroes of the West, Tom constantly pursues the new, unburdened by time and history. His response after being chastised for playing hooky is characteristic of his uncanny ability to move forward, unburdened by the past:

> Within two minutes, or even less, he had forgotten all
> his troubles. Not because his troubles were one whit less
> heavy and bitter to him than a man's are to a man, but
> because a new and powerful interest bore them down
> and drove them out of his mind for the time—just as
> men's misfortunes are forgotten in the excitement of new
> enterprises. (12)

Tom actually never does literally wander very far from town; he does his farthest ramblings imaginatively. An avid reader, Tom reads books, as Montserrat Ginés points out, "with an obsessive zeal, seeking to embellish his existence, clamoring for a life instilled with the substance, vigor, and heroic intensity of fiction" (27). And he is quite successful at this effort, making everyday life the stuff of romance, often by looking West to the world of Indians. At one point, Tom imagines joining up with Indians with whom he would

> hunt buffaloes and go on the war-path in the mountain
> ranges and the trackless great plains of the Far West,
> and away in the future come back a great chief, bristling
> with feathers, hideous with paint, and prance into
> Sunday-school, some drowsy summer morning, with a
> blood-curdling war-whoop, and sear the eye-balls of all
> his companions with unappeasable envy. (60)

Tom thus may be "the boy who knows Indians," but the Indians he knows—other than Injun Joe, who in his actions is less the Native American, alien "other" than he is simply a bad man—are merely those of boys' dreams, having little to do with the real West (a point Twain later underscores in his unfinished story, "Huck Finn and Tom Sawyer Among the Indians"). Tom in the end looks imaginatively West but remains rooted in the South: he is, finally, a homeboy, loyal to the town and its ways. Tom's reply to Huck's question about what he will do with the treasure they hope to find shows Tom dutifully falling in line with the town's expectations of him and other youth: "'I'm going to buy a new drum, and a sure-'nough sword, and a red neck-tie and a bull pup, and get married.'" Regarding Tom's plans to marry, Huck replies: "'Tom, you—why you ain't in your right mind'" (152).

In terms of regional crossings, what's most significant about *Tom Sawyer* is that the center holds so well, that elements of the West are so easily integrated into Southern life and that, as a hero, Tom combines the best of both worlds. Quite different, and much more problematic, is the regional crossing in *Adventures of Huckleberry Finn*. By shifting the focus to Huck, Twain writes a much more Western novel, with the driving force of the novel centrifugal, pushing outward from the stability of St. Petersburg, rather than inward, as in the case with the centripetal dynamics of *Tom Sawyer*. As in *Tom Sawyer*, Huck represents the restless and lawless West; he is an outsider who cherishes freedom and movement rather than stability and stasis—in his case, that dread "sivilizing" at the hands of Miss Watson. Huck's response to those civilizing efforts: "All I wanted was to go somewheres; all I wanted was a change, I warn't particular" (*Huckleberry Finn* 626). That somewheres of course ends up being down the Mississippi River. Although Jim and Huck travel literally South, their trip is best understood, in terms of regional dynamics, as a journey West into the wilderness, with their arrival at the Phelps' farm at the end of the novel representing their return to society, the Phelps' place a version writ small of the world of St. Petersburg. This turning of the axis with regards to traveling the Mississippi River—going South as figuratively going West—Twain had already suggested in *Life on the Mississippi*, where he portrays the journey down the river as a move from civilization into the frontier. Twain describes the region of the Upper River as marvelously cultured and civilized, where people live

> who think for themselves, and who are competent to do it, because they are educated and enlightened; they read, they keep abreast of the best and newest thought, they fortify every weak place in their land with a school, a college, a library, and a newspaper; and they live under law. Solicitude for the future of a race like this is not in order. (565)

Such solicitude, however, Twain goes on to suggest, increases as one journeys down the river, with the trappings of civilization falling away as the miles increase. A similar movement, from society into the wilderness, underlies *Adventures of Huckleberry Finn*, where, by the time Huck and Jim reach Arkansas, they've entered a frontier of the meanest and most despicable sort, a place fit for hogs where people live like hogs.

From this directional perspective, Huck emerges as the Western hero fleeing civilization accompanied by his dark partner who will school him in the ways of the wilderness—not unlike Cooper's Leatherstocking and Chingachgook or, indeed, Ike McCaslin and Sam Fathers. In fact, in his role as guide, in terms of the Western paradigm, Jim acts more as a Native American than as a Black man, a point that Leslie Fiedler makes when he writes that with Jim, Twain "turned his Negro protagonist into a Noble Savage, i.e., an Indian in blackface" (19). Behind Fielder's statement lies his taxonomy of American mythology. This is Fiedler: "A myth in which the non-White partner for whom the European American yearns is Black rather than Red, we tend to interpret as a parable of an attempt to extend our sexuality, to recover our lost *libido*; while one in which the White man longs for an Indian, we are likely to read as signifying a desire to breach the limits of reason, to extend our consciousness" (178). Whether one agrees with Fiedler's American mythology, in his tutelage of Huck, Jim does resemble Sam Fathers (who is mixed blood, part black and part Indian, which is one way we might think of Jim), his wisdom leading Huck to pursue a higher truth—a truth based on love and friendship—that ultimately alienates him from his society.

What Huck learns from his trip West, South down the Mississippi River with Jim, becomes clear during the episode at the Phelps' farm. Here, once and for all, Huck sees what he had suspected all along: that Tom's wild embellishments of reality, and the shenanigans that arise from them, "had all the marks of a Sunday school" (638); that is, despite their seeming rebelliousness, Tom's tales and pranks don't challenge the status quo as much as they prepare the town's boys for their roles within the status quo's order. Even more disturbing, Huck comes to see that Tom's play-acting in setting up Jim's escape differs little, except in legitimacy, from the con-games of the Duke and the Dauphin, and is really nothing more than pure selfishness; and that selfishness, furthermore, stands highlighted in all its ugliness when viewed alongside Jim's unselfishness when he remains to nurse Tom's wounds, an act that Jim performs despite knowing full well that it all but guarantees his capture and return to slavery.

It's no surprise then that Huck in the end decides that he must "light out for the Territory ahead of the rest" (912). Just back from the wilderness of the Mississippi River, where he had lived largely free from society's constraints and had been schooled by Jim in a more honest and caring way of life, he now decides to head literally West, hoping to re-find that way of life. He's fleeing not merely the civilizing hand of Aunt Sally, who wants to adopt him, but also the civilizing hand of Tom, the bad boy who is really the good boy. But what, finally, are we to make of Huck's flight—the flight of the moral hero away from his society? I think Ike McCaslin's fate gives us one way to think about it, a way that both admires Huck's nobility as he pursues a higher good and recognizes—and regrets—Huck's final irresponsibility to society. It's far from upbeat to realize that all that Huck has learned about the incivility of civilization will go to naught in terms of instituting positive change, at least by Huck's hand. Rather than working himself back into society so that he can make it better, Huck, as did Ike, steps outside society to find his peace; and as much as we admire Huck's repudiation (as well as Ike's), his departure West leaves the incivility of Southern society, slavery and everything else, unchallenged.

The ending of *Adventures of Huckleberry Finn* thus undoes—or repudiates—the happy combination of Southern and Western paradigms that *The Adventures of Tom Sawyer* had established. Tom and St. Petersburg no longer balance the best of both paradigms but instead represent the South in all its stultifying and mystifying power; indeed, in *Huckleberry Finn* such balance now seems impossible, or at least impossible for Twain to imagine except in fleeting moments. For Huck, the one figure who could create that balance, in the end casts his lot entirely with the West, just as Tom casts his entirely with the South. This turning in two directions is less a crossing than a split—a split, as evidenced by Faulkner's *Go Down, Moses*, written some sixty years after *Adventures of Huckleberry Finn*, that would go on to haunt the Southern imagination for generations to come.

Works Cited

Faulkner, William. *Absalom, Absalom!* 1936. New York: Vintage, 1990.

———. *Go Down, Moses*. 1942. New York: Vintage, 1990.

———. "Mississippi." In *Essays, Speeches and Public Letters*, edited by James B. Meriwether. New York: Random House, 1965. 11–43.

Fiedler, Leslie A. *The Return of the Vanishing American*. New York: Stein and Day, 1968.

Ginés, Montserrat. *The Southern Inheritors of Don Quixote*. Baton Rouge: Louisiana State UP, 2000.

MacKethan, Lucinda Hardwick. *The Dream of Arcady: Place and Time in Southern Literature*. Baton Rouge: Louisiana State UP, 1980.

Slotkin, Richard. *Gunfighter Nation: The Myth of the Frontier in Twentieth-Century America*. New York: Atheneum, 1992.

Stegner, Wallace. *Where the Bluebird Sings to the Lemonade Springs: Living and Writing in the West*. New York: Random House, 1992.

Twain, Mark. *Adventures of Huckleberry Finn*. 1884. In *Mississippi Writings*. New York: Library of America, 1982. 617–912.

———. *The Adventures of Tom Sawyer.* 1876. In *Mississippi Writings.* New York: Library of America, 1982. 1–215.

———. *Life on the Mississippi.* 1883. In *Mississippi Writings.* New York: Library of America, 1982. 217–616.

Welty, Eudora. *The Golden Apples.* New York: Harcourt, Brace, 1949.

Plundering the Old Southwest:
Twain and Faulkner as Reivers

Speaking of his generation of modernists, William Faulkner once asserted in a now well-known remark that "Mark Twain" was the "grandfather" of them all. (Sherwood Anderson was, in Faulkner's literary genealogy, the father [Gwynn and Blotner 281].) The ties between Twain and Faulkner are as intriguing as they are multiple. Perhaps because they are so many, the connections between these two of our greatest writers have not been fully surveyed. There is, however, one line on the map that is too prominent to miss: both Twain and Faulkner knew, enjoyed, used, and transformed the tradition of Southwestern humor. They approached that body of writing as reivers, stealing freely from it, enjoying their plunder, and ultimately recasting it all in significant ways.

Twain raided first, and when Faulkner came to pilfer from the tradition, Twain himself was a part of it, indeed the chief part from which Faulkner would plunder.

In 1867, as the Traveling Correspondent for the *Alta California*, Mark Twain posted a short review, really just a brief notice, of George Washington Harris's *Sut Lovingood's Yarns*. Harris was by then a strong force in the outpouring of Southwestern journalistic humor that began, more or less (there were English and Colonial origins), in 1835 with Augustus Baldwin Longstreet's *Georgia Scenes* and flooded and ebbed thereafter until about 1870. Twain admired Harris's book, celebrating its humor and perceptively observing that while it would be well received in "the West," the "Eastern people" would find it "coarse and possibly taboo" (Twain, *Travels* 221). His evaluation discloses both his delight in Southwestern humor and his sense of its dangers—threats to authors because of audience. When he penned his review of Harris, Twain was, though he didn't quite know it, on his way east to travel abroad and to write *The Innocents Abroad*, his first best seller and a small fortune maker. But while he was engaging foreign lands, his imagination remained enthralled by his homeland and its raucous, slipshod, and yet compelling forms of humor.

Twain was steeped in the tradition of Southwestern humor, and he plundered it for stock situations, character types, risible incongruities, and narrative structures. He owned the works of Augustus Baldwin Longstreet, Joseph M. Field, William Tappan Thompson, George Washington Harris,

Johnson Jones Hooper, and Joseph G. Baldwin. By any accounting, this is a sumptuous gathering from the Old Southwest. But to know a territory—real or literary—is not the same as to inhabit it. How did Twain homestead within the tradition? What did he make for himself out of Southwestern humor?

The answer is, as many things are with Twain, complicated, but finally illuminating. In his definitive study of Southwestern humor, *Fetching the Old Southwest*, James H. Justus notes that the so-called amateurs of this genre "triggered" Twain's "career" (151). Certainly in his early years as a vagabond writer, Twain appropriated materials from the Old Southwest rather straightforwardly. His youthful sketch, signed "S.L.C.," "The Dandy Frightening the Squatter," published in the Boston-based *Carpet-Bag* in 1852, pits a fancy dude from the East against a Mississippi riverbank squatter. In a way typical of Southwestern humor, Twain makes the dude a man of pretentious words and bravado, the squatter a man of honesty and violent action. The piece is notable only because it signals the nascent Mark Twain's interest in the comic forms of the Old Southwest. Thirteen years later, however, the then-named Mark Twain recast such stock materials into new—and memorable—form. "Jim Smiley and His Jumping Frog" (1865) both builds on and transcends the conventions it employs. It has the frame device often said to be the hallmark of Southwestern humor (see Blair and Lynn): a nameless but refined gentleman opens and closes the sketch. And within the frame, a seeming backwoods bumpkin, Simon Wheeler, holds forth to tell the antics of Jim Smiley, a gambling fool, finally bested by a mysterious stranger who fills Smiley's frog with buckshot, while Smiley, ever hot for the contest, sogs through a swamp to catch a frog for the stranger to race. The tale deploys the conventional contrast of regional types, Eastern vs. Western; it familiarly evokes a rural place, Angel's Camp; it exploits the typical conflict of languages, genteel vs. vernacular; it displays a menagerie of animals—the fifteen-minute nag, the bull-pup, rat-terriers, chicken cocks, and tom-cats, as well as the celebrated jumping frog; and it revels in the con man, who was both a reality in the Old Southwest and a favorite character for its humorists. What lifts Twain's tale beyond its origins, though, is the sheer brilliance of his dialect.

Thereafter, Twain inserted elements of Southwestern humor—often transmuted—into one work after another. *The Innocents Abroad* places the common in conflict with the elite and often makes use of backwoods metaphors (a Parisian barbering is like being "scalped"); *Roughing It* is full of frontier tall tales and cagey con men; *The Gilded Age* offers an unforgettable version of the tall-talker in the ever optimistic, always scheming Colonel Sellers; *Tom Sawyer* depends on the stereotypes of the old spinster and the villainous Indian; *Huckleberry Finn*, to which I will return, has been said to use many motifs of the Southwestern tradition, including its frame; *A Connecticut Yankee in King Arthur's Court* seems to some to be a version of the Southwestern sketch in its framing; and even "The Mysterious Stranger" bears the trace-mark of the tradition as No. 44 plays the Jew's harp and performs a minstrel show. The list could go on, but in short, no matter what he wrote (or where he lived), Twain drew, time and again, in large or small measure, on his literary homeland: the Old Southwest.

That backward turning is most important—and most significant—in his one indisputable masterpiece, *Adventures of Huckleberry Finn*. Critics have repeatedly noted that the novel is permeated by motifs from Southwestern humor, but seldom have they explored Twain's departures from and transformations of this familiar material. One pauses, to say again, that the stuff—a usefully vague term—of the Old Southwest was somehow never a stale but always a renewing part of Twain's creative process. But how did he use it?

Scholars have identified six elements of *Huck Finn* that are unmistakably indebted to Southwestern humor: the tall-talkers, the camp meeting, the circus, the Royal Nonesuch, the consummate con men, the Duke and the King, and of course the vernacular narrator, Huck Finn himself. In one of the most searching commentaries on Twain and Southwestern humor, Pascal Covici Jr. once pointed out that, unlike his predecessors, Twain was preoccupied with "revealing a discrepancy between seeming and reality" (Covici 15). But what he does beyond that is to transform the "reality" of traditional situation and character even as he exposes their "seeming."

Twain's way of reshaping the materials of Southwestern humor is revealed quite clearly in his rendering of the traditional camp meeting. Camp meetings were of course both realities of frontier life and standard episodes in the humor that fastened onto it. Johnson Jones Hooper's *Some Adventures of Captain Simon Suggs* features a notable camp meeting, which Twain almost certainly knew. Hooper's meeting is staged as a thrill-filled melodrama, replete with overt fleecing and sexual excitement. The meeting is, first to last, bogus, as the religious longings that should inform the event are replaced by theatrical, monetary, and especially sexual urges. "Men and women," he writes, "rolled about on the ground, or lay sobbing or shouting in promiscuous heaps." He emphasizes the sexual energies animating the crowd's frenzy:

> "Keep the thing warm!" roared a sensual seeming man, of stout mould and florid countenance, who was exhorting among a bevy of young women, upon whom he was lavishing caresses. "Keep the thing warm, breethring!—come

to the Lord, honey!" he added, as he vigorously hugged
one of the damsels he sought to save.

"Gl-o-ree!" yelled a huge . . . woman, as in a fit of the
jerks, she threw herself convulsively from her feet, and fell
'like a thousand of brick,' across a diminutive old man in a
little round hat, who was squeaking consolation to one of
the mourners.

"Good Lord, have mercy!" ejaculated the little man.
(Hooper 120–21)

Hooper's language, rife with puns, is both daring and amusing. It is typical
of the so-called strong masculine vein of Southwestern humor that enjoyed
the sexual.

In his version of such a camp meeting, Twain preserves the sense of
underlying monetary, sensational, and theatrical impulses, but he all but
eliminates the sexual. Huck offers this description:

The women had on sun-bonnets; and some had linsey-
woolsey frocks, some gingham ones, and a few of the
young ones had on calico. Some of the young men was
barefooted, and some of the children didn't have on any
clothes but just a tow-linen shirt. Some of the old women
was knitting, and some of the young folks was courting on
the sly. (Twain, *Huck Finn* 171)

Huck's account is far from Hooper's. He reports no sexual antics and uses
no language of bawdy innuendo. His one suggestion of sexuality is so mild
as to posit an essential innocence: "some of the young folks was courting
on the sly." "Courting" is a long way—verbally as well as actually—from
men and women rolling in "promiscuous heaps," shouting, "Keep the
thing warm!" throwing themselves on each other, and ejaculating, "Good
Lord, have mercy!" Twain does approach the lewdness of the conventional
humorist when he has Huck describe the King's money-raising:

So the king went all through the crowd with his hat,
swabbing his eyes, and blessing the people and praising
them and thanking them for being so good to the poor
pirates away off there; and every little while the prettiest
kind of girls, with the tears running down their cheeks,
would up and ask him would he let them kiss him, for
to remember him by; and he always done it; and some

of them he hugged and kissed as many as five or six
times. . . (173)

The King is clearly getting a bit of a sexual rush, but Huck's narration
mutes the lecherous, inviting us to laugh instead at the girls' misplaced
sentimentality.

Twain expurgates the bawdy aspects of the traditional Southwestern
camp meeting. He effects similar changes in his tall-talkers, the circus, the
Royal Nonesuch, and the con men. The Royal Nonesuch is his version of
Gyascutus, a favorite exhibition of indecency in Southwestern humor, but
Twain does not describe the performance in any graphic detail. In short,
he purges the sexual and sensual and lascivious elements of the tradition.
In analyzing Twain's ties to George Washington Harris (who has a camp
meeting almost as orgiastic as Hooper's), one critic has argued that they
share a sense of "man's predisposition to dehumanize himself" (Cohen 21).
But more often than not Twain refuses to let his characters debase themselves by being the carnal, somewhat bestial, creatures of their tradition.

Even more important than Twain's bowdlerizing of traditional episodes
in Southwestern humor is his selection of material from that body of writing. The stock materials have often been defined, and in the introduction
to their excellent collection of this humor, Hennig Cohen and William B.
Dillingham provide a comprehensive set of categories:

1) The hunt
2) Fights, mock fights, and animal fights
3) Courtings, weddings, and honeymoons
4) Frolics and dances
5) Games, horse races, and other contests
6) Militia drills
7) Elections and electioneering
8) The legislature and the courtroom
9) Sermons, camp meetings, and religious experiences
10) The visitor in a humble home
11) The country boy in the city
12) The Riverboat
13) Adventures of the rogue
14) Pranks and tricks of the practical joker
15) Gambling
16) Trades and swindles
17) Cures, sickness and bodily discomfort, medical treatment
18) Drunks and drinking
19) Dandies, foreigners, and city slickers

20) Oddities and local eccentrics

(Cohen and Dillingham xvii)

While no work of Southwestern humor contains all of these, many come much closer than *Huckleberry Finn*. What is most notable, however, is not the number of these conventional topics absent in Twain's novel but the particular kinds that are absent. First, he omits all those subjects—like courtings, frolics, dances, weddings, and honeymoons—that naturally involve adult sexuality. And second, he omits, or skims over, those activities—like hunting, fighting, gambling, gaming, horse racing, heavy drinking, and military maneuvering—that are the customary pastimes of manly backwoods living. (When such antics do appear, in such figures as the tall-talkers in the raftsmen's passage, the Grangerfords and the Sheperdsons, and Colonel Sherburn, they are clearly mocked by Twain.) In short, Twain purges from the tradition its exuberant celebration of exciting sexuality and rough-and-tumble masculinity.

Twain also transforms the tradition's treatment of the other— specifically, the woman and the African-American. As James Justus points out, the Southwestern humorists drew large stereotypical portraits of both the black slave and the backwoods woman (190–229); they shied away from any full engagement of the divisive slavery issue and skirted any serious reevaluation of the status of the Southern woman. Reveling in—and censoring—their rowdies, they left women and African Americans as shadowy figures living on the margins of their manly worlds.

To the extent that women did emerge in this humor, they were often violations of the ideal of Southern femininity, even as they fell into stereotype. The women of the tradition are, by and large, either unappealing, starchy homebodies, subject to scorn and even assault, or alluring, buxom wenches, pursued in imagination or fact as objects of sexual desire. Some of these women, indeed the most notable ones, are in their way liberated to be sexual and free to live for their own ends (Justus 220–229); they do not conform to the Cult of True Womanhood with its emphasis on domesticity, piety, purity, and submissiveness (see Welter). They traduce the ideals of the proper woman and the Southern Belle. Twain sustains a part of this tradition and turns the other on its head. He does create conventional old maids—the Widow Douglas and Miss Watson, for instance (see Walker)—but, again, he purges the tradition of its exuberant sexuality by turning all other women in his novel into pure angels, sexless creatures, or pre-pubescent ones. Huck gets a crush on Mary Jane Wilks, but she is as pure and sweet and fluffy as the foam on the edge of the Mississippi. And Huck's infatuation is a far cry from, say, the longings of Sut Lovingood, who lusts after women and believes that "'Men wer made a-purpus jis' tu eat, drink, an' fur stayin awake in the yearly part ove the nites; an' wimen wer made tu cook the vittils, mix the sperits, an' help the men du the stayin awake'" (Harris 77). Huck's affection for Mary Jane, his puppy love for the girl he exclaims over as "handsome!" is expressed in comic innocence: "she had more sand in her than any girl I ever see" (*Huck Finn* 161). True to the tradition, Twain marginalizes women, but departing from it, he makes every one of his fictional women asexual, pure, and good.

His transformation of the African slave is even more striking. While, as Ed Piacentino has argued, some Southwestern humorists inched toward a representation of the black slave (or freedman) as human (52–71), most did not, preferring to type their black figures as ignorant, bestial, and untrustworthy—benighted, immoral predators. Most made, in Scott Romine's haunting terms, their "darkness" "visible" as "pollution" (72–83). Twain's divergence could not be more striking, for of course his runaway slave, Jim, epitomizes the very virtues Southern apologists for the "peculiar institution"—and their kindred Southwestern humorists—extolled as white: courage, kindness, empathy, and self-sacrifice. Perhaps in no other aspect of his appropriation did Twain so sever his ties to the tradition that inspired him.

The most volcanic change Twain generated lies in his narrator, the almost too familiar Huck. In the typical Southwestern tale, once the narrative passes from the genteel listener, to the low-life rapscallion, the language shifts from refined to coarse as the tale records rowdiness. But Twain dissolves the traditional divisions between gentleman and vulgarian in three ways: first, by eliminating the gentleman from his narrative; second, by bestowing on Huck many of the attributes of the gentleman himself; and third, by transforming Huck's language from the crude dialect characteristic of the Southwestern rowdy who tells his own story into a more supple vernacular. Though it is seldom noted, Twain endows Huck with traits more typical of the gentleman than the rough. Where the usual Southwestern figure is unfeeling, amoral, and often violent, Huck is just the opposite: he feels deeply about everything—and for everyone; though confused about what is right and what is wrong, he is fundamentally moral, especially of course about Jim; and he is never violent.

As he replaces the traditionally aggressive, violent male, with passive, loving Huck, Twain all but signals his reconception. He has a number of characters describe Huck in comically misguided ways. The Widow Douglas thinks he is a "poor lost lamb"; Miss Watson considers him simply a "fool"; and Pap sees his son as "a good deal of a big-bug" (*Huck Finn* 1, 13, 23). However, it is only Jim, the most sensitive and right feeling character in the novel, who articulates what Twain seems to have felt about his ragtag hero. Full of gratitude for what he takes to be Huck's help and loyalty, Jim calls Huck not only "de ole true Huck" but also a "white genlman" (125). Huck is a curious fusion of the backwoods bumpkin and the refined gentleman, for in him the ignorant and free-spirited comport with the right-feeling and duty-bound. He is as far, in terms of character, from the traditional Southwestern figure as Hartford is from Memphis.

Twain's most pervasive departure from the Southwestern tradition is his transformation of Huck's language. As narrator of his own adventures, Huck preserves a notable linguistic decorum—a propriety that would have puzzled the likes of a Southwestern protagonist like Sut Lovingood. Huck reports that Pap's talk "was all the hottest kind of language" (34), but in his own telling, he never uses anything even close to crudity, vulgarity, or profanity. Twain's brilliant creation of Huck's vernacular is often cited as a sign of his sympathy for the common person over the refined, of his allegiance to the simple folk rather than the genteel. But his linguistic prestidigitation may actually signal the reverse: instead of committing himself to the common per se, he elevates the common beyond itself. Huck simply talks better than his precursors, and of course his talk bespeaks his character.

In significant ways, then, Twain profoundly transforms the tradition he plundered, purging it of the bawdy and sexual, humanizing the black slave, turning his protagonist into a man (or young man) of feeling, and transforming the coarse dialect into a more versatile and more nearly universal speech. All this is a part of what Faulkner gathered in when he himself was a reiver of the Old Southwest.

Faulkner, like Twain before him, knew the Old Southwest not only as a literary tradition but also, albeit somewhat belatedly, as a lived reality. Faulkner was even more deeply embedded in the Old Southwest than Twain. As one critic has put it, he "picked up a great deal of . . . material" by "watching the daily life and listening to the tales of the region" (Collins 260). In a very real way, Faulkner lived in the midst of what the Southwestern humorists wrote about, and it is no surprise that his works are permeated—far more than Twain's—by the elements of that tradition.

To even begin to think of the motifs of Southwestern humor in Faulkner's fiction is to face endlessness. From *Flags in the Dust* to *The Reivers*, Faulkner's work is saturated with them, as wild and full as the flood in *The Wild Palms*. If one returns to the taxonomy of the materials of Southwestern humor provided by Cohen and Dillingham (see above), one sees at once that Faulkner's oeuvre is a virtual compendium of them. Some rise above others, as prominent as the log surging downriver in *As I Lay Dying*. To cite just a few, "Spotted Horses," often extracted from *The Hamlet*, is clearly a Southwestern tale of a horse-trading con man; Jason in *The Sound and the Fury* shares "a basic similarity of spirit" with Sut Lovingood (Ross 237); Eula Varner is as buxom and voluptuous as any woman in the

Southwestern canon; "The Bear"—the "indomitable and invincible" one out of "the old wild life" (*Go Down, Moses* 193)—is a brilliant variation of Thorpe's "The Big Bear of Arkansas," the "unhuntable bear," that just "died when his time come" (Thorpe 279); and the entire Snopes trilogy recreates the characters and actions typical of the tradition. More broadly, Faulkner seems to have assimilated the Southwestern humorists' "entire sense of felt life" (Ross 236). Like Twain before him, Faulkner admired Sut Lovingood:

> And then I like Sut Lovingood from a book written
> by George Harris about 1840 or 50 in the Tennessee
> mountains. He had no illusions about himself, did the best
> he could; at certain times he was a coward and knew it
> and wasn't ashamed; he never blamed his misfortunes on
> anyone and never cursed God for them. (Meriwether and
> Millgate 251)

But Faulkner's chief progenitor was not George Washington Harris but Mark Twain whose works were by Faulkner's time the culmination of the Southwestern tradition. Faulkner rated *Huckleberry Finn* one of the "greatest" books in American literature (along with *Moby-Dick*), though he found its method somewhat "clumsy" (Gwynn and Blotner 15, 145). Twain was, as Faulkner put it, one of the "predecessors," one of the "masters" from whom he learned his "craft" (Gwynn and Blotner 243). He admired the "moil and seethe of simple humanity" in his work, and felt that Huck would escape the dilemma confronting not just fictional characters, representative of their time, but also their creators: the threat of "being desouled as the stallion or boar or bull is gelded" (Gwynn and Blotner 243, 245).

Of all the works in which Twain's influence on Faulkner manifests itself, none stands out as starkly as *The Reivers*. *The Reivers* is of course Faulkner's valedictory novel in which he raids his own body of work to create through allusion one last richly textured installment in his saga of the South. But he also plunders Twain's *Huckleberry Finn*. He called his novel "a kind of Huck Finn" and pointed to some connections of plot and character (*Selected Letters* 123–124). Indeed, at the simplest level, Faulkner reconfigures central elements of Twain's precursory text: Huck becomes Lucius, Jim becomes Ned, and the raft journey downriver becomes an excursion from Jefferson to Memphis in a stolen automobile. But the ties and transformations run much deeper.

While Twain bowdlerized the tradition of Southwestern humor by expurgating its frolicsome depiction of adult sexuality, Faulkner restores that part of the tradition. He initiates his Huck-like protagonist into the very world of bawdiness from which Twain excludes Huck. Ironically, however, Faulkner's Lucius retains his innocence even as he loses it. Faulkner's plot, or at least its main narrative strand, moves Lucius and Boon Hogganbeck from their staid and proper home-world to a cathouse in Memphis, where the object of Boon's desire, and eventually his true love, Corrie, works. Lucius thus enters unwittingly into a center of sexual commerce unlike anything in Huck's world. The contrast could hardly be more striking: When Huck encounters the House of Death on the river with Jim, he sees only the tawdry remnants of probable sexual activity—some women's "under-clothes," old whiskey bottles, and pornography scrawled on the wall, writing and pictures that Huck innocently or morally (or both) calls "ignorantist" (*Huck Finn* 61). Huck sees, without understanding, signs of sexuality; Lucius tries not to see them, yet is forced to.

Lucius does not really comprehend the realm he has entered. When he arrives at the bordello and Boon tries to explain to him that he is about to learn some things "'he never even thought about before'" and further warns him that he should do whatever Reba—the whorehouse madam—tells him to, the eleven-year-old Lucius replies with distinctly Huck Finn-like innocence: "'I never knew any ladies anywhere that wasn't trying to make somebody take a bath'" (*The Reivers* 104, 103). The language that envelopes him as he and Boon (and eventually Ned) have dinner in the establishment eludes him. He does not understand "He just nature-minded," let alone "whore-hopping" (134, 108). Lucius's fall into an awareness of adult sexuality does not actually occur until Otis, Corrie's degenerate relative, not only explains intercourse, what he calls "pugnuckling," to him but also gleefully tells Lucius how he used to charge men to peep at Corrie's acts of intercourse through a secret hole he had cut in the wall of the bedroom. Lucius's response defines the innocence of mind he has just lost: he fights Otis on behalf of the fallen Corrie. But there is no eradicating the consciousness Lucius has been given.

Faulkner's restoration of the sexuality common to the Southwestern tradition but expurgated by Twain is emphatic in plot, situation, and character, but it is never graphic. (In one sense he honors his precursor's circumspection even as he violates it.) Ironically, as Lucius learns the darker facts of life, as he loses the child's natural innocence, he restores Corrie's. She is so touched by his defense of her lost honor, she quits her profession (and of course eventually marries Boon). Faulkner thus creates a counterpoint that is not only comic but also moral: Lucius loses his innocence; Corrie (who reverts to her true name, Everbe) repossesses hers. And Lucius is the agent of her redemption. Trying to define Faulkner's own "ultimate values," Cleanth Brooks once argued that the chief ones were probably "pity and love" (275). Lucius certainly feels both pity and love for Corrie, and Faulkner ensures that those qualities have the power to transform her.

Faulkner's restoration of the sexual in Southwestern humor is surrounded—and to a degree muted by—his other plot lines: the theft of the car, the horse race, and the final return home. Within these events, Faulkner first follows and then reforms Twain's text in significant ways.

Though cast in different terms, Faulkner's treatment of the "manly" is closely akin to Twain's. Like Twain, he makes fun of the rough male, on the one hand, and restores the ideal of the gentleman, on the other. He begins *The Reivers* with comic wildness, as Boon steals a gun and goes on a shooting rampage, vowing to kill Ludus, who Boon feels has insulted him either by calling him a "narrow-asted son of a bitch" or a "norrer-headed" one (*The Reivers* 15). What makes it all comic is the fact that everyone in Jefferson knows that Boon cannot hit a barn with a gun, let alone a barn door, less still a man. He only creases a girl's backside and breaks a store window. Like his Southwestern predecessors, Boon, who is part Indian, part white, and all wild-man, is only at home in the wilderness, where he once hunted (unsuccessfully) and served as a guide for General Compson. After his rampage, this latter-day ring-tailed roarer is arrested and then released on bail. He is curtailed by civilization, and this alone signals a tempering of the Old Southwest.

The gun Boon steals in his futile attempt to kill Ludus is kept illicitly by John Powell, one of Boon's co-workers, and Powell considers it "the living symbol of his manhood" (*The Reivers* 7). Faulkner deliberately evokes the guns—and the violence—common to the tradition he plunders, but like Twain—one thinks of his ironic treatment of Colonel Sherburn—he mocks the roughs who resort to such puerile props for their manhood. In an ironic twist, he makes Butch, the local sheriff of Parsham, yet another violent backwoods rough. Butch first tries to bully the reformed Corrie into bed and then bribes her into it (he agrees to release Boon if she has sex with him). He is a pistol-toting ruffian who intimidates everyone he can, a sheriff who ignores the very law he should uphold. Like John Powell, though, Butch derives his sense of manliness from his firearm. In a kind of poetic justice, Boon eventually, as Ned, prodded by Uncle Parsham, explains to Lucius, "'Whupped that Law. That Butch. He nigh ruint him . . . whupped him, pistol and all'" (255).

As normative counterpoint to the violent men he mocks, Faulkner offers this tribute to a true man:

> "And Mr Poleymus may be little, and he may be old; but
> he's a man, mon. They told me how last year his wife had
> one of them strokes and cant even move her hand now,

and all the chillen are married and gone, so he has to wash
her and feed her and lift her in and outen the bed day
and night both, besides cooking and keeping house too
unlessen some neighbor woman comes in to help." (*The
Reivers* 257)

Faulkner celebrates here a gentle, loving, and care-taking manhood the
likes of which cannot be found in Southwestern humor—except in Twain's
Jim. To show that such gentle manliness is co-equal in black and white,
Faulkner has both the white Constable Poleymus and the black Uncle
Parsham not only treat Lucius with kindness but even offer to pay his way
home. Both Twain and Faulkner create patriarchies, but the controlling
males in *Huck Finn* are all given to violence (even the judge who is duped
by Pap threatens to reform him with a shotgun), while those in *The Reivers*
are men of law and good manners. Twain makes Huck the true gentle-man
in his novel, and Faulkner follows his lead by making Lucius a gentleman
in the making. Faulkner laughs a little at his would-be gentleman who,
driven by what he calls "Non-virtue" (*The Reivers* 54), has a riotous excursion with too many glimpses into the sordid, and he gently mocks him by
having Lucius repeatedly make "his manners" by doing a curtsey-like bow
when he is in company (100), but Faulkner is finally quite serious about
the importance of being a gentleman. Lucius's final lesson, taught to him
by Grandfather, sounds as if it comes from a courtesy manual: "'A gentleman can live through anything. He faces anything. A gentleman accepts
the responsibility of his actions and bears the burden of their consequences,
even when he did not himself instigate them but only acquiesced to them,
didn't say No though he knew he should'" (302).

While Faulkner treats his versions of the stock Southwestern rowdy
very much as Twain does his, and while he, like Twain, affirms the
importance of the gentleman, Faulkner's depiction of women is unlike
Twain's. Obviously in creating several hardworking whores, not to mention
a take-charge call-house madam, Faulkner emphasizes a female sexuality
absent in Twain's women. But Faulkner's reformation of Twain's material
goes even farther in yet another direction. Where Twain creates two
spinsters—one Miss Watson, an old maid; the other, the Widow Douglas,
a now-single widow—another widow in Aunt Polly, and a childless
married woman in Aunt Sally, Faulkner generates a bevy of fertile married
women, mothers and grandmothers (and aunts), black as well as white.
And Faulkner's women have a presence—a power—in his novel unlike the
shadowy, ineffectual ones in Twain's. Faulkner's narrator articulates in general terms the sense of women that defines Faulkner's realization of them
in this novel: "Because they are wonderful. They can bear anything because

they are wise enough to know that all you have to do with grief and trouble is just go on through them and come out on the other side" (*The Reivers* 111). Faulkner's women do more than endure, however; from the whores in Memphis to the mothers in Jefferson, they act—or choose not to act—as free agents. Significantly, they exert themselves within a moral universe, not unlike Twain's, on one side of its morality or another, but the difference is as important as it is obvious: Faulkner's women are not the mere types Twain deploys; his women have a character and efficacy foreign to Twain's.

In his fine study, *Faulkner: The House Divided*, Eric J. Sundquist points out that Faulkner became a great novelist when he took up the issue of "race" in all its historical and sociological complexity (5). While *The Reivers* puts black and white together (and sometimes pits them against each other), the novel is not directly concerned with race. What it does, however, is to rewrite Twain's Jim in the figure of Ned. Twain deals more directly and effectively with the African American than his predecessors in Southwestern humor, but his Jim remains something of a stereotype, provoking considerable critical controversy, since at times he seems too simple, a fictional version of the minstrel darky. Faulkner's Ned sometimes plays that role, acts as if he is Sambo, but it is only a mask donned to mislead others. Unlike Jim, Ned is acutely intelligent, wily, and guileful. He manipulates others for his own purposes, which are both compassionate—he wants to extricate his cousin Bobo Beauchamp from his entanglement with a con man—and self-serving: he wants to enjoy himself in Memphis and make some money on the horse race. Ned does what Ralph Ellison's sage old grandfather tells the Invisible Man to do: "'overcome 'em with yeses, undermine 'em with grins, agree 'em to death and destruction'" (*Invisible Man* 20–21). Sometimes Ned turns defiant, however, as he does when he tells Constable Poleymus, "'There's somewhere the Law stops and just people starts,'" and in the end, Ned drops his mask: "He was not Uncle Remus now"—to which the narrator Lucius adds, "But then, he never was when it was just me and members of his own race around" (*The Reivers* 243, 182). Faulkner's creation of Ned is his most searching revisioning of Twain, and Ned stands as the single most important black figure in all of Southwestern humor.

Southwestern humor exploited the difference between the gentleman and the vulgarian. In his seminal essay, "'The Barber Kept on Shaving': The Two Perspectives of American Humor," Louis D. Rubin Jr. defines the central source of American humor overall as the clash between the genteel and the vulgar. For Rubin the genteel is theoretical, learned, and cultivated; the vulgar is pragmatic, commonsensical, and realistic. Each makes the other look ridiculous (385–407). In terms of these alignments, Twain clearly sides with the vulgar (at least in *Huck Finn*), while Faulkner inclines toward the genteel. The difference is registered in narrative mode. Twain turns his tale over to Huck, who tells his own story in his vernacular language. Faulkner, on the other hand, narrates his fiction through the older—wiser—now fully formed gentleman, Lucius, who tells, as Faulkner's subtitle indicates, "A Reminiscence." Yet Lucius's gentlemanly telling often incorporates vernacular language, suggesting that the class division inherent in the genteel/vulgar split has somehow been bridged. The difference in narrative mode anticipates the striking divergence in the endings of the two novels.

Both *Huck Finn* and *The Reivers* end happily enough, of course, and both avoid the harsh irony often found at the close of a typical Southwestern tale. Indeed, at least one critic has compared Twain's novel to Faulkner's and found that Huck "encounters reality, while Lucius Priest remains in a fantasy world" (Volpe 348). On the contrary, Faulkner's ending is real enough, and Twain's is contrived to be joyful, as Jim is free, Pap is dead, and Huck is surrounded by loving folk tantamount to a surrogate family. Notably, however, there are no patriarchs in Twain's ending. (Uncle Silas Phelps, the only adult male in sight, is too addlepated to count as a patriarch.) Twain has purged Huck's world of its most destructive element. In the face of Aunt Sally's willingness to take him in and civilize him, Huck makes his famous avowal: "I can't stand it. I been there before" (*Huck Finn* 362). As many critics have pointed out, Huck himself dislikes only the petty constraints of civilization, not its hypocrisy, duplicity, and immorality, none of which he really grasps. But Twain lets the complaint sound beyond Huck's grievances to indict the corrupt civilization he has so carefully created.

Plundering his precursor, the apex of the Southwestern tradition, Faulkner effects one last reformation of Twain's material. For he structures the ending of his tale as a return to a beneficent civilization presided over by wise and kindly patriarchs (see Taylor for a critique of this). Blacks and whites are living in harmony; young and old are reconciled; the vulgar are cared for by the genteel; and the wild and reckless are domesticated. No one is about to light out for any territory because no one wants to run away from this benign homeland. If Twain softens and humanizes the Southwestern tradition while Faulkner reintroduces some of its bawdiness, in the end Faulkner turns the tradition even more firmly, more sharply, than Twain does back toward the conventional. And of course neither Twain nor Faulkner lets his hero become "desouled," to use the term Faulkner did when thinking of his literary grandfather, and this alone makes them anomalies within their tradition.

Note

Some of the ideas about Twain presented here were first worked out in different terms in my essay, "Mark Twain: The Victorian of Southwestern Humor," *American Literature* 54 (1982): 368–384.

Works Cited

Blair, Walter. *Native American Humor*. New York: American Book, 1937.

Brooks, Cleanth. "Faulkner's Ultimate Values." In *Faulkner and the Southern Renaissance*, edited by Doreen Fowler and Ann J. Abadie. Jackson: UP of Mississippi, 1982.

Cohen, Hennig. "Mark Twain's Sut Lovingood." In *The Lovingood Papers*, edited by Ben Harris McClary. Knoxville: U of Tennessee P, 1964. 19-24.

Cohen, Hennig, and William B. Dillingham. Introduction to *Humor of the Old Southwest*. 2nd ed. Athens: U of Georgia P, 1975. xiii–xxviii.

Collins, Carvel. "Faulkner and Certain Earlier Southern Fiction." In *The Frontier Humorists: Critical Views*, edited by M. Thomas Inge. Hamden, CT: Archon, 1975. 259–265.

Covici, Pascal Jr. *Mark Twain's Humor: The Image of a World*. Dallas: Southern Methodist UP, 1962.

Ellison, Ralph. *Invisible Man*. New York: Signet, 1952.

Gwynn, Frederick L., and Joseph L. Blotner, eds. *Faulkner in the University: Class Conferences at the University of Virginia, 1957–1958*. 1959. New York: Vintage, 1995.

Faulkner, William. *Go Down, Moses*. 1942. New York: Random House, 1955.

———. *Selected Letters of William Faulkner*. Edited by Joseph Blotner. 1977. New York: Vintage, 1978.

———. *The Reivers: A Reminiscence*. New York: Vintage, 1962.

Harris, George Washington. *Sut Lovingood's Yarns*, edited by M. Thomas Inge. New Haven: College and University P, 1966.

Hooper, Johnson Jones. *Some Adventures of Captain Simon Suggs*. Philadelphia: Carey and Hart, 1845.

Justus, James H. *Fetching the Old Southwest: Humorous Writing from Longstreet to Twain*. Columbia: U of Missouri P, 2004.

Lynn, Kenneth S. *Mark Twain and Southwestern Humor*. Boston: Little, Brown, 1959.

Meriwether, James B., and Michael Millgate, eds. *Lion in the Garden: Interviews with William Faulkner, 1926–1962*. New York: Random House, 1968.

Piacentino, Ed. "Contesting the Boundaries of Race and Gender in Old Southwestern Humor." In *The Humor of the Old South*, edited by Thomas Inge and Edward J. Piacentino. Lexington: UP of Kentucky, 2001. 52–71.

Romaine, Scott. "Darkness Visible: Race and Pollution in Southwestern Humor." In *The Humor of the Old South*, edited by Thomas Inge and Edward J. Piacentino. Lexington: UP of Kentucky, 2001. 72–83.

Ross, Stephen M. "Jason Compson and Sut Lovingood: Southwestern Humor as Stream of Consciousness." In *The Humor of the Old South*, edited by Thomas Inge and Edward J. Piacentino. Lexington: UP of Kentucky, 2001. 234–246.

Rubin, Louis D. Jr. "'Barber Kept on Shaving': The Two Perspectives of American Humor." In *The Comic Imagination in American Literature*, edited by Louis D. Rubin Jr. New Brunswick: Rutgers UP, 1983. 385–405.

Sundquist, Eric J. *Faulkner: The House Divided*. 1983. The Johns Hopkins UP, 1985.

Taylor, Walter. "Faulkner's *Reivers*: How to Change the Joke without Slipping the Yoke." In *Faulkner and Race: Faulkner and Yoknapatawpha*, edited by Doreen Fowler and Ann J. Abadie. Jackson: UP of Mississippi, 1987. 111–129.

Thorpe, Thomas Bangs. "The Big Bear of Arkansas." In *Humor of the Old Southwest*. 2nd ed. Edited by Hennig Cohen and William B. Dillingham. Athens: U of Georgia P, 1975. 267–279.

Twain, Mark. *Adventures of Huckleberry Finn*. 1884. Berkeley: U of California P, 2001.

———. *Mark Twain's Travels with Mr. Brown*. Edited by Franklin Walkner and G. Ezra Dane. New York: Knopf, 1940.

Volpe, Edmond L. *A Reader's Guide to William Faulkner*. New York: Farrar, 1964.

Walker, Nancy. "Reformers and Young Maidens: Women and Virtue in *Adventures of Huckleberry Finn*." In *One Hundred Years of Huckleberry Finn: The Boy, His Book, and American Culture*, edited by Robert Sattelmeyer and J. Donald Crowley. Columbia: U of Missouri P, 1985. 171–185.

Welter, Barbara. *Dimity Convictions: The American Woman in the Nineteenth Century*. Athens: Ohio UP, 1976.

Twain, Faulkner, and the Humor of the Old South: Southern Narrative and the Technique of Disclosure

The humorists of the Old South, also known as Southwestern humorists or frontier humorists, had a significant impact on two of the most celebrated writers of the southern literary canon, Mark Twain and William Faulkner. While several studies have traced the influence of the humorists in the works of these authors, in this essay I demonstrate, specifically, how the narrative technique of "disclosure" broadened the narratological scope of Twain's *Adventures of Huckleberry Finn* and Faulkner's *The Sound and the Fury* and *Absalom, Absalom!* Published in newspapers and collections from the 1830s through the Civil War, Southwest humorists featured the life experiences of backwoods and frontier communities from the perspective of, typically, an upper-class genteel narrator. This narrative structure has been characterized as a *cordon sanitaire*, situating the narrator (and audience) above and apart from the dialect-speaking backcountry characters. However, because backcountry characters are depicted candidly recounting tales of foolish behavior, fear, and defeat, information known only to themselves, they are not clowning for the narrative lens but are practicing narrative "disclosure," thus inviting others to laugh with them rather than at them. Both Twain and Faulkner employ and develop this narrative technique. While Twain broadens the content provided through "disclosure" to expose epistemological assumptions, Faulkner extends the technique to reveal psychological veracity.

There are three distinct narrative agents employed throughout the genre, which I will refer to as the primary narrator, the narratee, and the unnamed narrator, although as Gerald Prince points out, one character can occupy a variety of narrative roles. The primary narrator is a character with a distinct personal identity, gender, social position, and name, and who functions within the dramatic events of the story. The narratee has a specific identity as well, but operates primarily as the character to whom the events are conveyed by the main character and has little or no active dramatic function other than as an audience. The narratee is important because this role provides a forum for the main character. Gerald Prince explains that "the portrait of the narratee emerges above all from the narrative addressed to him" (313).

These narrative agents often share what Gérard Genette terms "external focalization" and contain embedded narratives (228), usually initiated by the main character meeting up with a narratee and engaging in conversation which leads to the main tale. The primary narrative is the initial encounter, and the embedded narrative is chronologically secondary but serves as the main story. These dialogues provide a vehicle for the dramatic events of the story, develop characterization, and illustrate interclass relationships.

Embedded narratives also facilitate the technique of "disclosure," which reveals cultural norms by what these characters explain or imply is socially appropriate or inappropriate behavior. The embedded narrative structure facilitates this technique because characters are often depicted retelling moments of defeat, fear, and foolish behavior to the narratee, either in conversation or epistolary form. In recounting these "dilemmas," featured characters are shown to be willing, sometimes eager, to provide disclosure.

Alexander G. McNutt's characters, Jim and Chunkey, recount stories in which they show no reluctance to describe scenes in which they appear foolish, frightened, or absurd. They are uneducated, uncouth, and ill-mannered (by genteel standards), but they are brave, honest, and highly independent. Thus, their backcountry sense of honor is not only unaffected by their tales, but it is the conflation of backcountry notions of liberty and honesty that facilitates the freedom necessary to provide disclosure. For example, Jim illustrates no reticence in describing his fear when he becomes pinned underwater beneath old cyprus logs, vines, and driftwood. He tells the Captain, "'Moses! Warn't I in a tight place *that* time? Well, I reckon I were. I'd been willin' to fite the biggest *he* [bear] on the creek, and gin him the fust bite, to have been out'" (124). He narrowly escapes drowning and recounts his terrifying experience to the Captain in full and candid detail.

Chunkey, too, portrays no hesitation in acknowledging his frightening predicament when Jim pays him back for leaving him in the river (although there is no evidence to suggest that he was aware of Jim's perilous dilemma). His alarm develops gradually through a series of difficulties, which begin when he realizes that "'it war the first time in my life that I'd bin lost, and that *did* pester me mightily'" (135). His anxiety develops into fear when he realizes that, in addition to being lost, two panthers are stalking him, and when he finds that he has only one bullet and half a shot of powder, his fear mounts to terror. He carefully loads his only shot and confesses, "'I raised my arm, trimblin' like a leaf . . . The har had been standin' on my head for more nor an hour, and the sweat were gist *rollin'* off me'" (136). He takes aim but recalls, "'I were all in a trimble! I know'd *that* woulddent do, and *ris*" (137). Chunkey gathers his courage, fires his only shot, and then engages in a physical fight with one of the panthers, noting, "'she fightin' for her *supper*, I fightin' for my *life*" (137). His thorough description of emotions regarding the incident lends credibility to his story; had he not described his fear, the tale would most likely have appeared incomplete, and had he denied his fear, the scene would have been unbelievable. His relief and pride at having survived the battle, particularly having "whipped a panter in a fair fight," inspires him to "*cock a doodle dood* a spell, for joy!" (138). Chunkey's narrative illustrates that life on the frontier requires physical strength, courage, and knowledge of the environment for survival, but does not demand the projection of, as Bertram Wyatt-Brown puts it, fearless stoicism, like the chivalric tradition (59). Thus, characters are free to describe these moments in full and candid detail—behavior which in no way compromises their sense of masculinity.

Thomas Bangs Thorpe's "Stoke Stout, of Louisiana" exemplifies another character unselfconsciously describing fear. Narrative authority is further empowered in this sketch because Stoke not only provides full disclosure, but shares his distressing experience in a letter addressed to the "Kernul." Stoke recounts the frightening and aggravating predicament he found himself in one day when cornered by Old Mister Stiggin's bull. In recalling the moment that he realizes he is in danger, he writes: "I hearde sumin sai, 'Phfo-o-o!' loud nor I can rit it, an' specktin what it wer, I sez to miself, 'I'ze back owt,' an' I jist peept az I sott, an' thar wur Old Mister Stiggin's bull, thot old yaller feller yu kno, what haz the karracktur ov the ternest down, an' most dangersommest bull in the raynge" (151). Stoke explains that he is forced to hide out in a water hole and wait patiently for an opportunity to escape. He thinks the bull may be getting sleepy and wonders if he should try to slip away, but admits candidly: "I wur afeered to try an' sea" (152). Fortunately, the bull simply trots off, and Stoke is freed, and as he notes, "kood brethe a little" in relief (152). He provides a detailed depiction of the situation and his emotional responses, but the account in no way signifies embarrassment or shame.

Likewise, John Robb provides several characters who candidly admit fear. In "Nettle Bottom Ball," Jim Sikes openly recounts the fear he has of Betsy Jones's father. He tells a group of men that merely remembering "'old Tom Jones' *yell*, when he swar he'd "chaw me up," gives my meat a slight sprinklin' of ager whenever I think on it'" (176). Dan Elkhorn also admits his fear candidly when he is pinned in the river by a bear. He notes, "'The varmint war a waitin' for me, and whinin' as ef he had been ill-treated, and thar I wur perched up on a sawyer, bobin' up and down in the water'" (183). He admits, "'I got a little scary'" (183). Similarly, the primary narrator in "Smoking a Grizzly" tells the story of a "scrape" when a Grizzly is after him to a group of men. The old man notes, "'[I] hadn't a weepun about me . . . You had better believe boys, that my skin got moist suddint—thar waren't no dry diggins under my red shirt, long afore that grizzly got down the hill'" (191). He uses "lucifer" matches to start a fire, and the smoke scares the bear. He recalls, "'The bar crept up to the lucifers and took a smell, and if the musckels of my jaws hadn't been so tight with fear, I'd hev bursted into a reg'lar snort of laughin', at seein' how he turned up his nose and sniffled'" (192). The tale is not confided to a personal friend, but to a group of strangers, indicating that the man's description of fear is in no way relevant to shame. Further, he is able to appreciate the comedy of the situation after he is out of danger, and his act of retelling these events invites the audience to share the humor.

In addition to disclosing accounts of fear, characters also reveal moments of foolishness. Both genteel and backcountry customs created an environment that fostered an almost obsessive regard for personal honor, but the appearance-oriented Cavalier tradition rendered ridicule of any sort a direct attack. Being made to look foolish challenged the image of sober dignity and often required a formal response. However, the obsessive defense of appearances is not relevant to one's sense of honor on the frontier. Like the candid depictions of fear, characters often freely describe scenes in which they appear foolish. John Robb's character Hoss Allen, for instance, recalls an event in which he appears absurd, and furthermore, it is a tale that "he is very fond of relating" (164). He recalls for a group of men a situation that was especially irritating and uncomfortable. While traveling in his best clothes one day, Hoss arrives at a river, decides to strip off his clothing, tie the bundle to his horse's head, and swim across. His horse reaches the bank first, and Hoss complains to his auditors: "'While I was gittin' up the bank, the d——d thing got away, and started off with my clothes on his head! And the more I run, and hollered, and 'whoa'd,' the more I couldn't catch the cussed vermit! 'Way he'd go, and I arter—hot as h——ll, too, all the way, and yaller flies about'" (165). Hoss claims that the horse knew what he was doing and insists that every time he got close to the horse, as he tells it: "'That d——d beast just nat'rally waited till I got out, and looked at me all over, and I could act'ily see him laffin! And I was nasty enough to make a hoss laugh, any how!'" (165). As readers, we know a horse can neither laugh nor manipulate events as Hoss claims he does, illustrating that Hoss's use of exaggeration provides a thorough sense of his mounting frustration.

Hoss continues literally and figuratively to "expose" himself. In addition to being totally naked, he is also tormented by enormous flies, becomes covered head to toe in mud, and is forced to chase the horse around in the blazing sun in pursuit of his clothing. He claims that his appearance was so ridiculous, the "dam horse" laughed so hard that the bundle fell off his head into the water and drifted down the river. On seeing this, Hoss candidly reports, "I just nat'rally, lay down on the bank, and cussed all creation'" (165). Under no compulsion to control his temper, Hoss indulges in a cathartic temper tantrum. Furthermore, he does not evince any embarrassment when he realizes that his naked tantrum is witnessed by a boy on a skiff, who happens to be in the process of trying on the clothing he has just fished out of the river. Indeed, Hoss notes with appreciation: "'The feller sees how it was, and pulls a-shore, and helps me'" (166). He ends the sketch by reminding the boys that when they need a good laugh, "'just think of Hoss Allen!'" (166). Hoss not only shows no reticence in describing this ridiculous situation, he clearly enjoys recounting it. His candid report illustrates that he is under no obligation to omit unflattering details and indeed utilizes exaggeration to emphasize his physical and emotional suffering.

The common practice of disclosure demonstrates that the characters' accounts of fearful, embarrassing, and ridiculous moments derive from a tradition of frank honesty and appreciation for natural human folly rather than a function of comedic performance. These backcountry characters can and do laugh at themselves, and significantly, do so without shame.

Mark Twain also employs the technique of disclosure to demonstrate fear, pain, and humorous folly, but develops the information shared to include narratives that reveal shame, as well as showing far greater significance in distinctions of morality. Huckleberry functions as the primary narrator but often as narratee as well. Throughout the text, there are a variety of sources of information, functioning as narrative vehicles, available to Huckleberry. Pap represents and offers a type of naturalistic morality in which his advice is geared toward physical survival, particularly what he feels are the rights due a white man, while the Widow Douglas represents religious and social morality, in other words the institutionalized morality of Christian-oriented propriety, but what their codes share in common is a foundation based on racial hierarchy. The Widow Douglas demonstrates her sense of moral responsibility regarding race by the routine of bringing the slaves in for evening prayers (34); whereas Pap evidences his attitude toward race relative to his code by the outrage he expresses when he feels his social rights have been violated by "'a free nigger there, from Ohio.... They said he was a p'fessor in a college.... They said he could *vote*.... [W]hen they told me there was a State in this country where they'd let that nigger vote, I drawed out. I says I'll never vote agin'" (52–53). Thus, the codes of morality between Widow Douglas and Pap are vastly different but share an important foundation of racial orientation.

Twain also utilizes the technique of embedded narratives often in the form of analepses regarding what Widow Douglas and Pap have told Huckleberry, which Huck draws on to assist him in decision making. The primary narrative is of course the trip down the river, but the embedded narratives create a unique format within the primary text by embedding what Toni Morrison calls the "Africanist presence at its center" ("Amazing, Troubling Book" 308). This presence carries with it a moral force that deviates intensely from both social and natural morality. The crucial decision within the primary narrative is of course whether Huck will send the note. In contemplating the decision, Huck draws from Pap's morality in terms of self-protection and the Widow's in terms of social and legal mores, but he ultimately draws from the morality offered by Jim through the practice of disclosure. For example, Jim confesses a moment he is ashamed of regarding the treatment of his daughter, recalling, "'the time I treat my little 'Lizabeth so ornery," realizing after striking her that, as Jim tells Huck: "'she was plumb deef an dumb, Huck, plumb deef en dumb—en I'd been a-treat'n her so!" (155). In disclosing this information, Jim demonstrates to Huck a type of morality very different from either Widow Douglas's or Pap's morality. Toni Morrison deems this dialogue "real talk—comic, pointed, sad," and notes that it is "talk so free of lies it produces an aura of restfulness and peace unavailable anywhere else in the novel" ("Amazing, Troubling Book" 388). The stories Jim shares with Huck about his wife and children lead Huck to conclude, despite what he had been led to believe, that "he cared just as much for his people as white folks does for their'n. It don't seem natural, but I reckon it's so" (154). Jim's accounts of his family contrast with what Huck has been taught to accept as "natural," which begins the process of shifting Huck's epistemological sensibilities.

In tearing up the note, it is clear that Huck rejects the naturalist morality of Pap because his decision has nothing to do with self-protection—indeed he is well aware of the dangers of his action—nor the institutional morality of the Widow, which is clear because he believes this act will send him to Hell. Huck accepts Jim's notion of morality which functions by weighing his needs against the potential of harm to others. Thus, when Tom arrives, Huck is shocked that Tom is also willing to breach social morality. Numerous scholars characterize this moment as a loss of moral fortitude and, in terms of structure, a technical failure. However, this moment functions to remind readers of the severe social and legal consequences of aiding a runaway slave. Huckleberry notes that Tom "was a boy that was respectable, and well brung up; and had a character to lose; and folks at home that had characters . . . to stoop to this business, and make himself a shame, and his family a shame, before everybody" (216). Huck has changed epistemologically; the rest of the world has not, nor have the consequences if they are caught, which Twain keeps in sight throughout the last twelve chapters. Yet these final chapters have become a lightning-rod for critical discord, particularly what has been regarded as Jim's passivity concerning his escape. Jane Smiley asserts that neither Huckleberry "nor Twain has come up with a plan that would have saved Jim in the end. Tom Sawyer does that" (62-63). This assessment, however, suggests that Jim makes no decisions for himself nor takes any action for his own self-protection, but this is just not the case. Indeed, Jim asserts his independence throughout the text (initially, when he runs rather than submit to being sold and takes up with Huck as a protective strategy), and his flight alone has a significant impact on both Huck and his owner. While we are not provided the information until the end, Tom reveals that Jim is indeed free because "[Miss Watson] was ashamed she ever was going to sell him down the river, and *said* so; and she set him free in her will" (260). Thus, his actions serve his interests when he feels it is morally reasonable.

Smiley goes on to assert that "considerable ink has flowed over the years in an attempt to integrate the Tom Sawyer chapter with the rest of the book, but it has flowed in vain" (63). This assessment, however, ignores Jim's active presence. For Jim, Tom's sources of textual authority seem as illogical and irrational as the legal texts that authorize his enslavement, texts that he is barred from examining by the laws that forbid his education. Thus, when conditions develop beyond his level of toleration, he threatens to do what he already has done, which is to leave. Jim cautions Tom: "I's willin' to tackle mos' anything 'at ain't onreasonable, but ef you en Huck fetches a rattlesnake in heah for me to tame, I's gwyne to *leave*, dat's *shore*" (239). Tom is then forced to submit to Jim's demands. Thus, despite the antics of a young boy with a strong penchant for the quixotic, Twain maintains the moral impulse throughout the novel, particularly when Jim reveals himself to help the doctor care for Tom. This decision is as significant as Huck's decision to go to Hell. Indeed, Twain reminds readers, rather forcefully, of the danger this exposes Jim to because he is indeed recaptured, and his captors want "to hang Jim, for an example to all the other niggers around there, so they wouldn't be trying to run away like Jim done," but they are reminded that "he ain't our nigger, and his owner would turn up and make us pay for him, sure" (256). The statement carries a rather sinister insinuation for Twain's postbellum readership, implying that the financial concern that kept the group in check was the only reason Jim was not put to use as a "warning." What saves Jim's integrity, moreover, is his rejection of naturalistic and social morality by refusing to save himself at the expense of a boy in need of medical attention, and it is Jim's integrity and moral code that saves Huckleberry's humanity, which is accessed by Jim's ability to provide disclosure and Huckleberry's willingness to listen.

Several studies have acknowledged the influence of the humorists on the South's most celebrated writer, William Faulkner. Thomas W. Cooley Jr. argues that "since readers first discovered that Faulkner could be funny, almost everyone who has commented on Faulkner's humor links him to the comic tradition of the old Southwest" (268). In "Faulkner Draws the Long Bow," Cooley examines Faulkner's use of the "tall tale," while Malcom Cowley and Robert Penn Warren examine Faulkner's humor and use of vernacular. Yet, Faulkner also developed aesthetic and narrative techniques from the humorists as well, specifically his use of disclosure by situating Quentin Compson in the role of narratee in his most profound works, *Absalom, Absalom!* and *The Sound and the Fury*. Faulkner also drew from and developed the embedded narrative method to a monumental scale; essentially, the majority of his short stories and novels function as embedded narratives of the Yoknapatawpha narrative, which is embedded within the primary narrative of the South. Furthermore, the novel *Absalom, Absalom!* is embedded within the narrative events of *The Sound and the Fury*.

The narrative events of *Absalom, Absalom!* begin in late September 1909, less than a month after Quentin Compson has claimed incest to his father, and end in January 1910, less than six months before his suicide in June 1910. Furthermore, Quentin functions as a central yet paradoxically marginal character in *Absalom, Absalom!*, one who is present during every narrative "telling" in the novel, but whose role is predominantly that of passive listener, rather than active teller or featured character. And it is Quentin's "relation to narrative" that, as John T. Matthews points out, "confines him both to the margins of life and the margins of the story" (72). Matthews further characterizes Quentin's role in *Absalom, Absalom!* as a "largely silent witness" (72). As narratee to the stories of others, his predominantly silent role is necessary to the narrative succession of events, but it is a role he often reluctantly assumes, and he evidences mounting distress as the stories he hears are told and retold, indicating a deterioration of what is already shaky psychological ground. As the narrative events of *Absalom, Absalom!* unfold, we become witness to the psychological effects this telling and retelling has on him. Ultimately, it is Quentin's inability to escape his role as narratee and the distressing nature of the information he receives that lead to the psychological impasse that compels his suicide.

The embedded structure of *Absalom, Absalom!* provides a key interpretive tool to Quentin's psychological malaise relative to the events and issues he experiences in *The Sound and the Fury*, particularly revealed through the parallel roles between himself and Henry Sutpen. Throughout *Absalom, Absalom!*, Henry functions as an active counterpart to Quentin's passivity, further enforcing his sense of failure due to his inability, or often lack of opportunity, to act. The novel is organized into nine chapters, beginning with Rosa Coldfield talking to Quentin in a hot, airless room in her home, which establishes his role as narratee, "listening, having to listen, to one of the ghosts . . . telling him about old ghost-times" (4). The interruption of the verb phrase, "having to listen," suggests that Quentin has no choice but to accept Miss Rosa's request to function as an audience for a story that he "already knew. It was a part of his twenty years' heritage of breathing the same air and hearing his father talk about the man" (7).

What Quentin hears is significant because, as Gérard Genette points out, the role of the narratee "could lead one to think that the receiver's role here is purely passive, that he is limited to receiving a message he must take or leave and to 'consuming' after the event a work that was completed far from him and without him" (259). Genette further observes that the narrative event "obviously cannot change the fact that a narrative, like every discourse, is necessarily addressed to someone and always contains below the surface an appeal to the receiver" (260). It is this "below the surface" appeal that resonates throughout *Absalom, Absalom!*, particularly situated as it is within the narrative events of *The Sound and the Fury*. This appeal surfaces when Quentin Compson asks his father why Rosa Coldfield chose him to listen. His father replies, "'Years ago we in the South made our women into ladies. Then the War came and made the ladies into ghosts. So what else can we do, being gentlemen, but listen to them being ghosts?'" (*Absalom, Absalom!* 7). Thus, his cultural obligation as dutiful son and southern gentleman offers no other option but to yield, as narratee, to the embedded narratives of his father and Miss Rosa. Furthermore, Quentin's role as listener is also strongly evidenced throughout his section in *The Sound and the Fury* by the frequency of the tag clause "father said" occurring dozens of times.

As Genette observes, narrative discourse often contains an appeal encoded in narrative language, but an appeal also suggests the possibility of resistance. The timing of Miss Rosa's request is important because it occurs only a few weeks after Quentin's claim that he and Caddy "have committed incest" (Faulkner, *The Sound and the Fury* 94). Thus, Quentin's resistance to Miss Rosa's story is not merely that of a young man who would rather not spend the day listening to her, but the content of Miss Rosa's narrative is particularly troubling due to the information she provides about Sutpen, which is then elaborated upon by Quentin's father, most notably the issue of incest. Mr. Compson's account regarding Judith, Henry, and Bon seems especially reckless due to Quentin's clear distress over the issue of his sister's sexuality and his claim to his father that he and Caddy "did a terrible crime" (94). However, Gary Storhoff reminds readers that "the Compson family is organized around the alcoholism of Mr. Compson, who stanches the family's emotional bleeding with his ever-constant 'hushing,' his self-deceptive embrace of stoicism, and his refusal to acknowledge the emotions of his children" (470). Mr. Compson's alcoholism provides a reasonable explanation for his carelessness in discussing these events with his troubled son, and further, indicates additional evidence regarding the depths of Quentin's emotional crisis because, as Storhoff notes, the alcoholism of a father "set up terrific emotional incongruities" that are further compounded by Mr. Compson's "ever constant 'hushing'" (471).

Mr. Compson's "hushing" is particularly problematic for Quentin in his attempt to take an active role by positioning his father in the role of narratee. Quentin implores his father to listen to him, stating: "'if youll just wait Ill tell you how it was it was a crime we did a terrible crime it cannot be hid you think it can but wait . . . Ill tell you how it was" (*The Sound and the Fury* 94). Quentin believes that his "confession" will isolate Caddy and him "amid the pointing and the horror walled by the clean flame" (74), believing that "if we could have just done something so dreadful that they would have fled hell except us. *I have committed incest I said Father it was I it was not Dalton Ames*" (51). Mr. Compson's response simultaneously overturns the narrative structure by rejecting Quentin's narrative assertion and repositioning Quentin in the role of narratee by stating, "'You cannot bear to think that someday it will no longer hurt you like this now were getting at it,'" and adds that Quentin will not understand, as his father claims: "'until you come to believe that even she was not quite worth despair'" (177–178). Quentin replies, "'I will never do that'" (178). Quentin's assertion demonstrates his resistance to a shift in his epistemology. Furthermore, his father's response reinforces Quentin's belief system as he advises:

> i think youd better go on up to cambridge right away
> you might go up into maine for a month you can afford
> it if you are careful it might be a good thing watching
> pennies has healed more scars than jesus . . . then you will
> remember that for you to go to harvard has been your
> mothers dream since you were born and no compson has
> ever disappointed a lady. (*The Sound and the Fury* 178)

Quentin, however, does not take this advice because less than a month later, he is summoned to listen to an account of Thomas Sutpen by the enraged and unforgiving Rosa Coldfield, a task he can not evade because "no compson has ever disappointed a lady."

Mr. Compson's advice and the language he employs reinforces Quentin's rigid belief system. Further, the language he uses demonstrates a specific linguistic style, which Bernhard Radloff deems "the particular, historical language of Quentin's tradition" (262). The distinction is important because as George Levine explains, "words inevitably carry not only the burden of description (and perception) but the burden of value. A change in language implies a change both in perceptions and values" (342). Thus, when Mr. Compson tells Quentin that Miss Rosa "will need someone to go with her—a man, a gentleman," he demonstrates a linguistic system built on the foundation of an antebellum code of honor that theoretically reflects social and cultural ideals, which Minrose Gwin characterizes as "the grand narrative of white patriarchy" (11). Significantly, the "grand narrative" of the South is not the historical South, but the narrative myth created, as Lucinda MacKethan explains out of an image of arcadia, or put another way, "an agrarian paradise" (9). W. J. Cash notes that what "the Old South of the legend in its classical form was like is more or less familiar to everyone.... Its social pattern was manorial, its civilization that of the Cavalier, its ruling class an aristocracy coextensive with the planter group" (ix). Familiarity with the legend pervades common assumptions of the South; Thadious Davis, for example, points out that "Shreve's knowledge is a result of his melodramatic vision of the South, Quentin's of his long personal and historical experience of the South" (95). Yet "the knowledge" of each reflects to a large degree "the legend."

As so many scholars have observed, the legend grew out of the need of the South to justify chattel slavery and the plantation system. Southern antebellum social theorists and writers, as Scott Romine notes in *The Narrative Forms of Southern Community*, "theorized nothing less than a Dixie version of the City on the Hill ... predicated on a rigid social hierarchy perceived to be both necessary and beneficial" (65). Embedded within this primary narrative is Faulkner's Yoknapatawpha narrative, further embedded by the account of Quentin Compson's response to his sister's sexuality, but as Faulkner notes in the appendix, who loved not his sister's body but "some concept of Compson honor precariously and (he knew well) only temporarily supported by the minute fragile membrane of her maidenhead" (207), or in other words, again from the appendix, "the principle that honor must be defended whether it was or not because defended it was whether or not" (204).

Until the summer of 1909, Quentin has simply lived within the tradition of his inheritance, but his sister's behavior casts his previously unquestioned principles into chaos. Myra Jehlen argues that in *The Sound and the Fury* Faulkner "demythologized the young aristocrat" and points out:

Where Bayard Sartoris was for the most part only another version of the legendary cavalier, Quentin Compson is a more modern character trying merely to make moral sense out of the doom which has overtaken his family. If he attaches undue symbolic value to his sister's virginity, it is less for the sake of cavalier values than out of a need for a point of moral reference. (321)

Prior to Caddy's sexual awakening, Quentin maintains a clear point of moral reference, which is similar to Henry Sutpen's before his trip to New Orleans. According to Mr. Compson, Henry's code of honor resides in his "fierce provincial's pride in his sister's virginity" (76). And, as Mr. Compson explains Henry's story to his son, he notes that Henry:

> was a young man grown up and living in a milieu where the other sex is separated into three sharp divisions, separated (two of them) by a chasm which could be crossed but one time and in but one direction—ladies, women, females—the virgins whom gentlemen someday married, the courtesans to whom they went while on sabbaticals to the cities, the slave girls and women upon whom that first caste rested and to whom in certain cases it doubtless owed the very fact of its virginity. (87)

Yet, like Henry, Quentin is also "the country boy with his simple and erstwhile untroubled code in which females were ladies or whores or slaves" (91). Caddy's behavior, however, certainly complicates Quentin's previously untroubled code, creating conflict and confusion. Caddy is clearly not a slave, and her sexual experience violates the defining principle of a "lady," thus leaving Quentin, with his limited options, only one way to view his sister, which he demonstrates when he calls her "whore whore" just before his confrontation with Dalton Ames (*The Sound and the Fury* 101).

Similarities between their sisters become further problematic for Quentin as he listens to Miss Rosa's account of the confrontation between Henry and Judith after Henry shoots Bon. The narrator notes, "He (Quentin) couldn't pass that" (140). Quentin could not get past "that door, the running feet on the stairs . . . the two of them, brother and sister . . . speaking to one another in short brief staccato sentences like slaps":

> *Now you cant marry him.*
> *Why cant I marry him?*
> *Because he's dead.*

Dead?
Yes. I killed him. (139)

Throughout the novel, Quentin is distinctively affected by this particular event. The date of Miss Rosa's narrative is significant relative to the narrative events in *The Sound and the Fury* because only weeks earlier, Quentin and Caddy also speak to each other "in short brief staccato sentences like slaps" (*Absalom, Absalom!* 140). Quentin asks Caddy, "'Why wont you bring him to the house, Caddy? Why must you do like nigger women do in the pasture the ditches the dark woods hot hidden furious in the dark woods?'" (59). Quentin further presses Caddy, "'What did you let him for?'" She replies, "'I didn't let him I made him . . . What you think of that?'" (84). Unlike Henry, who is given the opportunity to "do the office of the outraged father's pistol-hand when fornication threatened" (*Absalom, Absalom!* 146), Caddy's actions undermine Quentin's ability to respond to a threat. Quentin is thus reduced to respond to the fact of fornication rather than the menace of fornication, but he fails in this endeavor as well. When he confronts Dalton Ames and warns him to leave town, Ames responds, "'listen no good taking it so hard its not your fault kid it would have been some other fellow'" (101). Dalton Ames produces a gun and offers it to Quentin, but rather than follow through with his threat to kill Ames, he faints, as he puts it, "like a girl" (103). This failure is juxtaposed to Henry's ability to act. As Henry and Bon approach the house in which Judith sews her wedding gown, Henry warns Bon: "'Don't you pass the shadow of this post, this branch, Charles'" (106). Bon replies, "'I am going to pass it, Henry'" (106). The result of this action culminates in, as Faulkner writes, "the two of them slashing at one another with twelve or fourteen words" (142).

For Quentin, reviewing the events with Shreve is an especially painful process and demonstrates clear signs of emotional strain that grow increasingly definitive as the narrative events progress. Hearing Shreve recapitulate these events becomes particularly distressing because as Romine observes, when "representative narrators attend to the outside world, they often encounter disorder and discord where they expected stability and consent" (18). This disorder and discord is evident in the first section set at Harvard when Shreve asks Quentin to "tell about the South" (142). As Faulkner notes, this question was not "Shreve's first time, nobody's first time in Cambridge since September: *Tell about the South*" (142). Thus, not only is Quentin asked to tell about the South by Shreve, but the implication suggests that Quentin has been compelled to "tell about the South" by many others, and Shreve's constant interruptions, recapitulations, and narrative reviews create disorder and discord rather than stability and consent.

The first scene set in the dorm room at Harvard also indicates the closed-ended frame of Miss Rosa's telling and the introduction of Shreve as narrator, again positioning Quentin in the role of narratee. Not bound to listen by the obligations of a dutiful son or southern gentlemen, Quentin's role as narratee to Shreve's talking signifies his psychological commitment to the narrative events. Yet after Shreve begins talking, Quentin demonstrates growing distress at "having to hear it again," but cannot seem to extricate himself from his role as listener. Shreve's role as active teller is important because it simultaneously positions Quentin again in a passive role and indicates that Quentin has already told Shreve a large amount of the information they then discuss. As Shreve summarizes the narrative, Quentin thinks "Yes, *I have had to listen* too long" (157, emphasis added).

The move to Harvard also signifies a distinction in language. Shreve does not use the language of honor to tell the story, which is demonstrated by his repeated references to Miss Rosa as "the old gal" (142). Quentin's distress at what he perceives as a breach of honor, particularly relative to southern femininity, is evident by his interruptions and attempts to correct Shreve with the appropriate title "Miss Rosa." As the story progresses, however, Quentin resigns from the effort of amending Shreve and allows the references to Miss Rosa to go uncorrected, indicating a sign of his mounting fatigue. Bernhard Radloff characterizes Shreve's interest as a game he plays in order to "solve the 'puzzle' of why Henry killed Bon" (264). Radloff argues that Shreve enters "into the spirit of Quentin's world as a playful self-surrender to a game: he gives himself up to a game in which he plays with the rhetoric of the tradition" (262). Quentin "in turn, is put into play by the rhetoric of his heritage from the moment of his birth" (264). As Radloff suggests, Shreve willingly enters into a game, yet is able to extricate himself because, as he puts it in *The Sound and the Fury*: "'God, I'm glad I'm not a gentleman'" (65). Quentin, however, is put into play by his heritage rather than engaging in play, but rather than allow the narrative to simply run its course by telling Shreve the story and ending, Quentin is compelled to continue the game of repeating and reviewing events that are particularly painful. The question regarding why Henry shot Bon is the motivating force for Shreve, but is not for Quentin because he believes he already knows the answer to this question. Hershel Parker contends that Quentin realizes "the secret" on the evening that he accompanies Miss Rosa to the Sutpen mansion, and argues that it is when he looks at Jim Bond, he realizes "that to have a Sutpen face Bond must have gotten it through Charles Bon, who therefore must have been Sutpen's son" (325). Cleanth Brooks, however, writes, "I believe that he learned the secret from Henry's own lips," but as Brooks points out, it is not possible to know definitively (388). However, it is important to keep in mind that Quentin *believes* that Henry and Bon are brothers and that what instigates the shooting is not common blood but Bon's black blood. Yet Quentin does not simply share this information with Shreve and end the story but distributes information that guides Shreve toward this revelation, perhaps hoping that by reviewing and analyzing these events, an outsider might discover resolution that has evaded Quentin.

Quentin's role as narratee is particularly problematic because the stories he hears force him to confront long-held historical assumptions. Lucinda MacKethan explains that the idyllic vision of the Old South is, as her title *The Dream of Arcady* suggests, a dream constructed by writers

> who have nurtured in their portrayals of their region some aspect of that ancient pastoral district famed for its rural peace and simplicity. It must be stressed immediately that their Arcadian designs have often come from unquestioning faith or private preference rather than any reasoned exploration or objective perception of the ideal itself as it relates to their images of the South. (3)

Sooner or later, MacKethan explains, those invested in this dream are "subjected to the inescapable moment of awakening" (5). For Quentin, his role as narratee instigates a process of analysis that begins shaking him "awake," forcing a confrontation with implications that suggests an image of the South that closely resembles his grandfather's account of Haiti as "a theatre for violence and injustice and bloodshed and all the satanic lusts of human greed and cruelty, for the last despairing fury of all the pariah-interdict and all the doomed" (*Absalom, Absalom!* 250). According to John T. Matthews in "Recalling the West Indies: From Yoknapatawpha to Haiti and Back," the resemblance is due to a similar model of "white imperial power" (242). Matthews explains that "the plantation South derives its design from new-world models, owes a founding debt to West Indian slave-based agriculture, extracted labor and profit from African-Caribbean slave trade, and practiced forms of racial and sexual control" (239). In conjunction with what Quentin learns from his father and Miss Rosa, his discussions with Shreve reveal stubborn attempts to recover his continuously receding ideal, which is inextricably bound to his sense of self. As many scholars have noted, Quentin's crisis is his discovery of loss associated with his sister's sexuality, but Quentin's loss is further compounded by a sense of the loss of loss. His father tells him that virginity, like honor, is just a word made by men; thus, Quentin has lost the ability to accept without "exploration or objective perception" (MacKethan 3). Quentin can manage loss, psychologically, particularly of something beautiful, "Et ego in Arcadia" (*The Sound and the Fury* 28). He has been reared within a paradigm of loss, evidenced for example by the pinned-up shirtsleeve of his grandfather, or as Shreve offers, the bullets in the dining-room table, and the cultural coping mechanisms of surviving the loss, particularly the cathartic retelling of the beauty of what was lost. The loss of beauty will always be mourned, will always be a loss. Furthermore, the loss of beauty is compounded by gaining an ugly and brutal reality. Quentin's dilemma is fixed between a romantic ideal and the real, but rather than examine the real, he continuously attempts to recover, or at least find compensation for the ideal, and the embedded narratives of his father and Miss Rosa create a staggering psychological conflict with the primary narrative, ultimately exposing the image of arcadia as a simulacrum of southern history that deviates intensely (and for Quentin, horrifically) from the narrative accounts of his father and Miss Rosa.

What Quentin Compson learns as narratee is that the stories he hears by Miss Rosa and his father do not fit into the primary narrative, no matter how many times he and Shreve rework them. Moreover, as the narrative progresses, Quentin's narrative authority is subjugated by Shreve, who then repositions Quentin in the role of narratee. Unaware of Quentin's personal crisis regarding Caddy, Shreve muses carelessly:

> "Jesus, think of the load he had to carry . . . raised in
> provincial North Mississippi faced with incest, incest of
> all things that might have been reserved for him, that all
> his heredity and training had to rebel against on principle,
> and in a situation where he knew that neither the incest
> nor training was going to help him solve it." (271–272)

Shreve's audience, however, is Quentin, who like Henry Sutpen, was also raised in provincial North Mississippi, faced with incest, and in a situation where he knew that neither the incest nor the training would help him any more than it did Henry. As Quentin listens, his attention fluctuates between hearing and succumbing to narrative despair. He muses: "Am I going to have to hear it all again . . . I am going to have to hear it all over again I am already hearing it all over again I am listening to it all over again I shall have to never listen to anything else but this again forever" (222). Later that evening, lying in bed, Quentin thinks: "Nevermore of peace. Nevermore of peace. Nevermore. Nevermore. Nevermore" (298). Ultimately, Quentin's inability to escape his role as narratee leads to the psychological impasse that ends in his suicide because he cannot evade the information insinuating that the death of Bon "for a little matter like a spot of negro blood" (*Absalom, Absalom!* 247), nor the thousands in gray driven by the notion of honor, or even the bullets in the dining-room table, signify not the loss of an ideal but simply violence, revealing ultimately, as Quentin muses on the day of his suicide, "a sinful waste [as] Dilsey would say" (*The Sound and the Fury* 57).

Faulkner's narrative method of embedded events situates Quentin predominantly in the role of narratee; he is, however, not just a passive listener but indeed actively committed to narrative resistance and with good reason. For Quentin, the loss of beauty is more psychologically manageable than the possibility that "the South," which Shreve is so interested in hearing about, might not reflect, as his grandfather suggests, "a spot of earth which might have been created and set aside by Heaven itself," but rather, again according to his grandfather, "a theatre for violence and injustice and bloodshed" (*Absalom, Absalom!* 250). His role as narratee, however, forces him to listen too long to too much, compelling him to seek relief in "silence darkness sleep the water peaceful and swift not goodbye" (*The Sound and the Fury* 109).

Despite regional, educational, and social differences among the authors of antebellum Southwestern humor, thematic and stylistic similarities throughout the genre were no mere accident or coincidence. What united these writers was not loyalty to a particular school of thought or artistic belief, or, as many scholars have noted, a political agenda, but rather the weighty influence of mutual admiration, which became a generative aesthetic force and gave life to a style of writing that the established literary journals too often dismissed as vulgar. Drawing from one another, contributors unintentionally created a cohesive literary movement, which proved a rich resource for later writers, such as Mark Twain, William Faulkner, and numerous others.

Note

Portions of this essay have been previously published. For permission to include these sections here, grateful acknowledgment is made to Peter Lang Publishing and to *Southern Studies: An Interdiciplinary Journal of the South*.

Works Cited

Brooks, Cleanth. "The Narrative Structure of *Absalom, Absalom!*" *Georgia Review* 20 (1975): 366–394.

Cash, W. J. *The Mind of the South*. New York: Knopf, 1941.

Cooley, Thomas W. Jr. "Faulkner Draws the Long Bow." *Twentieth Century Literature: A Scholarly and Critical Journal* 16.4 (1970): 268–277.

Cowley, Malcolm. Introduction to *The Portable Faulkner*. Edited by Malcom Cowley. New York: Penguin, 1946. vii-xxxiii.

Davis, Thadious. "The Signifying Abstraction: Reading 'the Negro' in *Absalom, Absalom!*" In *William Faulkner's* Absalom, Absalom!*: A Casebook*, edited by Fred Hobson. New York: Oxford UP, 2003. 69–106.

Faulkner, William. *Absalom, Absalom!* 1936. New York: Vintage, 1986.

———. *The Sound and the Fury*. 1929. Edited by David Minter. Norton Critical Edition. New York: W.W. Norton, 1994.

———. "Appendix: The Compsons." In *The Portable Faulkner*, edited by Malcolm Cowley. New York: Penguin, 1946. 704-722.

Genette, Gérard. *Narrative Discourse: An Essay in Method*. Trans. Jane E. Lewin. Ithaca: Cornell UP, 1980.

Gwin, Minrose. "The Silencing of Rosa Coldfield." In *William Faulkner's* Absalom, Absalom!*: A Casebook*, edited by Fred Hobson. New York: Oxford UP, 2003. 151–188.

Jehlen, Myra. "Faulkner's Fiction and Southern Society." In *The Sound and the Fury*. 2nd ed. Edited by David Minter. Norton Critical Edition. New York: W. W. Norton, 1994. 317-323.

Levine, George. "Realism Reconsidered." In *Essentials of the Theory of Fiction*, edited by Michael J. Hoffman and Patrick D. Murphey. Durham: Duke UP, 1996. 234–245.

MacKethan, Lucinda Hardwick. *The Dream of Arcady: Place and Time in Southern Literature*. Baton Rouge: Louisiana State UP, 1980.

Matthews, John T. "Faulkner's Narrative Frames." In *Faulkner and the Craft of Fiction: Faulkner and Yoknapatawpha*, edited by Doreen Fowler and Ann J. Abadie. Jackson: UP of Mississippi, 1989. 71–91.

———. "Recalling the West Indies: From Yoknapatawpha to Haiti and Back." *American Literary History* 16.2 (2004): 238–262.

McNutt, Alexander G. "Chunkey's Fight with the Panthers." In *The Big Bear of Arkansas and Other Tales*, edited by William T. Porter. Philadelphia: Carey and Hart, 1845. 128-139.

Morrison, Toni. *Playing in the Dark: Whiteness and the Literary Imagination*. Cambridge: Harvard UP, 1992.

———. "This Amazing, Troubling Book." In *Adventures of Huckleberry Finn*. 3rd ed. Edited by Thomas Cooley. Norton Critical Edition. New York: Norton, 1999. 385-392.

Parker, Hershel. "What Quentin Saw 'Out There.'" *Mississippi Quarterly* 27 (1974): 323–326.

Prince, Gerald. "Introduction to the Study of the Narratee." In *Essentials of the Theory of Fiction*. Edited by Michael J. Hoffman and Patrick D. Murphy. Durham: Duke UP, 1996. 213-233.

Radloff, Bernhard. "Dialogue and Insight: The Priority of Heritage in *Absalom, Absalom!*" *Mississippi Quarterly* 42 (1989): 261–272.

Robb, John S. *Streaks of a Squatter Life, and Far-West Scenes*. Edited by John Francis McDermott. Gainesville: Scholars' Facsimiles and Reprints, 1962.

Romine, Scott. *The Narrative Forms of Southern Community*. Baton Rouge: Louisiana State UP, 1999.

Smiley, Jane. "Say It Ain't So, Huck: Second Thoughts on Mark Twain's 'Masterpiece.'" *Harper's Magazine* 292 (1996): 61–67.

Storhoff, Gary. "Faulkner's Family Crucible: Quentin's Dilemma." *Mississippi Quarterly* 51 (1998): 465–482.

Thorpe, Thomas Bangs. "Stoke Stout, of Louisiana." In *The Big Bear of Arkansas and Other Tales*, edited by William T. Porter. Philadelphia: Carey and Hart, 1845. 13-31.

Twain, Mark. *Adventures of Huckleberry Finn*. 1884. Edited by Gerald Graff and James Phelan. Boston: Bedford/St. Martin's, 2004.

Wyatt-Brown, Bertram. *Southern Honor: Ethics and Behavior in the Old South*. New York: Oxford UP, 1982.

"That Doomed and Fatal Blood":
Adventures of Huckleberry Finn and *The Unvanquished*

In his introduction to Albert Memmi's study *The Colonizer and the Colonized*, Jean-Paul Sartre maintains, "A relentless reciprocity binds the colonizer to the colonized" (xxvii) and "If colonization destroys the colonized, it also rots the colonizer" (xvii). What Sartre suggests here is a reciprocity that is closely associated with implications of oppression read as retributive; that is, in debasing and dehumanizing one people, the imperial center necessarily debases and dehumanizes itself while simultaneously positioning itself in the eyes of the world as deserving reprisal. This process of retributive oppression has been frequently applied to postcolonial texts, yet its significance has also been traced into the landscape of American literature read through slavery. My paper will investigate this reciprocity formulated through the imaginative engagement or entanglement of the child with the history and the culture of the South. Through the eyes of the child figure of Mark Twain's *Adventures of Huckleberry Finn* and William Faulkner's *The Unvanquished,* we find a South portrayed as a polluted site of societal inspiration. The issue of slavery in the South is presented to us in these texts as a flawed genesis which sends concentric ripples of guilt throughout Southern history. It becomes the burden of the child protagonist, Huck Finn and Bayard Sartoris respectively, to engage, through a dual process, his inheritance of the South: first, he must realize and accept the responsibility of guilt, and second, he must challenge his inheritance through legitimation crises as a means of absolution leading to resolution.

The narrative form of these texts as constructed through and by the perceptions and observations of the child is an essential quality for this thematic formulation. Jane Smiley, in her essay "Say it Ain't So, Huck," observes, "[Twain] found himself writing not a boy's novel, like Tom Sawyer, but a man's novel, about real moral dilemmas and growth" (356). Though Twain's text certainly does concern itself with "real moral dilemmas and growth," one must be cautious of the reduction of the function and content of the "children's" story implicit in this comment to simplicity or frivolousness. Since the inception of the fairy story, the child's narrative has always concerned itself with key social factors and the difficult questions of integration and transition into the adult world. (For a more theoretically sound rendition of this argument, see Bruno Bettelheim's *The Struggle for Meaning* or Jack Zipes's *Spells of Enchantment*.) For Twain and Faulkner, the child is essential to an understanding of the difficult dilemma of the South for two reasons: one, the child is the living and logical site of inherited guilt, and two, the child, in a Romantic turn, is the most likely to succeed in, first, challenging and, next, exacting change in and for his society's future. As such, the child figure becomes the metonymic representative of the necessary process of retribution and absolution for the dubious beginnings of his society's history.

Yet each author approaches this task through different thematic means. I shall first investigate Twain's use of *contrapasso*, the Dantean formulation of countersuffering where on a cosmological level the punishment of the subject will always correspond directly to his or her crime. I will then look at Faulkner's text as it develops the life-long trauma of inheritance and the movement towards legitimation crisis symbolized by Bayard Sartoris and his progression away from a culture of violence towards a new beginning.

Harold Beaver's influential text "Run, Nigger, Run" looks at the ways that *Adventures of Huckleberry Finn* is a fugitive-slave narrative and posits Jim's experience and ability to manipulate Huck as central to the work. However, when considering some of the significant thematic tendencies of the slave narratives of the nineteenth century (as written by Frederick Douglass, Harriet Jacobs, and Mary Prince, not to mention fictional works like William Wells Brown's *Clotel* or Harriet Beecher Stowe's *Uncle Tom's Cabin*), there emerge remarkable similarities between the experiences of the fugitive slave and not Jim, but of Huck himself. For example, in Chapters 10 and 11 Huck dresses up as a girl. The theme of crossing sexual boundaries as a means of further disguising an attempt to pass not only as white but to pass one's sex as well was an important thematic device at once useful in a pragmatic way, that is, to fortify the camouflage, but also as social commentary challenging the arbitrary nature of sexual and racial significations. For Huck, cross-dressing is a means of disguise for the use of garnering information, but also it is a means of remaining invisible to his society. The details of Huck's attempts to pass as a young girl—how to walk properly, how to speak—echo the painstaking and dangerously critical effort of the passing mulatto female in slave narratives. The difficulty of "acting" or "passing" as a different sex is not unlike, and for some is concomitant with, the effort to pass as a different race; it is, for the fugitive slave and for Huck, the fiction of identity as a means of maintaining "true" individual invisibility.

Further similarities include the deceptive use of spelling in Chapter 17 where Huck, in order to recall his fictional identity, uses the pride of young Buck Grangerford as a means of gaining information, challenging Buck that he cannot spell Huck's forgotten fabricated name. This recalls the efforts of authors like Frederick Douglass who uses the young schoolboys of Baltimore by challenging their ability to write, and thus "stealing his education." Of course, Huck does not steal the ability to write, it is freely offered him; however, what this episode does intimate is the same essential deception needed to succeed in the world of the fugitive—it speaks to a necessary mentality of masquerade and counter-manipulation.

A final thematic example leads into my next point. In almost every slave narrative, there occurs a scene of voyeurism through which the degradations and crimes against one's own oppressed people, as well as the weaknesses and essential moral corruption of the dominant class, are witnessed. Recall Harriet Jacob's gaze as she languishes in her tiny cloistered attic, or Frederick Douglass's frequent mention of the burden of bearing witness as he looks through peepholes or watches overseers from a hidden vantage. These fugitive slaves see while remaining unseen, and their panopticonic gaze exacerbates the paranoia of the oppressing society. However, it is *what* is seen that interests us in Huck's case. As T.S. Eliot argues, "Huck we do not look at—we see the world through his eyes" (349); and what do we see? The satirization of the unreconstructed South, its degradations and absurdities, has been exhaustively investigated in Finn's narrative. Yet for Huck, the burden of witnessing goes beyond satire. Huck must gaze upon the worst of his own Southern white community: conspiring killers, tragic and meaningless feuds, the indolence of the men of Arkansas, and later their lynch-mob mentality staunchly criticized as cowardice by Sherbourne, and worst of all, Huck, in a moment of literal voyeurism from behind a coffin, must watch the Duke and the Dauphin plotting the financial and emotional exploitation of an entire family. Just as Frederick Douglass will live with the image of his degraded and beaten aunt branded upon his memory, or as Harriet Jacobs will forever pay both physically and mentally for her internment in that cramped attic, so too will Huck be forced to watch the society he is meant to inherit in its multifarious incarnations of degradation.

And as he watches the worst of the white South, Huck must struggle to accept what he sees as the best of the South embodied in the black subject, Jim. The most telling and deliberate difference between character types can be established between Jim, Miss Watson, and, as Toni Morrison writes, "[Pap's] kind of people" (Cooley 387). Miss Watson is, in postcolonial terms, the empty educator, teaching a flawed version of religion and an antiquated and questionable version of civilization. Pap as metonymic of the poor white South is the type of character Huck meets most often in his voyage down the river. The Edenic myth of subsistence found in texts like *I'll Take My Stand* or *Let Us Now Praise Famous Men* is exposed through the sometimes terrifying moments of Huck's existence in Pap's cabin in the woods. I haven't the time to catalogue all that Miss Watson and Old Finn embody in their representative formulations; what interests here is the danger that these character types hold for Huck. Both when with Miss Watson and when with Old Finn, Huck's social mentality wavers and he begins to accept their ways of life. These incidents, occurring before Huck's experiences down the river, illustrate the two most likely avenues of inspiration for the formation of a social identity, either the hegemonic "proper" civilization of Tom Sawyer or Aunt Sally or the nostalgic, lazy, backwoodsmen of Cash's *The Mind of the South*. Through his observations down the river, Huck is forced to realize that both of these avenues are essentially corrupt, flawed foundations of a culture that he is in dangerous proximity of accepting and replicating.

Thus, Huck's legitimation crisis is in reality a sort of forced attrition. Huck must literally experience through both sympathy and empathy, through both the heart and the head, the life of the oppressed slave. The similarities between Huck's experience and the slave narratives of the time intimate Twain's project of imposing upon his figure of the child a series of retributive oppressions as a means of forcing Huck to arrive at a critical epiphanic societal realization regarding the two worlds of Miss Watson and his Pap. Twain even goes so far as to make Huck the proclaimed servant of the King in Chapter 24. Through these experiences of oppression, Huck comes to understand that the worlds of both Miss Watson and Pap represent an impossible option. The result is the long line of criticism on Huck's homelessness; for his liminal state between two worlds, between the worlds that distinguish "stealing" and "borrowing" argued in Chapter 12, makes his position in what Twain represents as the American South untenable. Huck, as the subject of oppression, realizes that the future of the South must lie somewhere else, and the most probable site of inspiration will be Jim.

Huck's sense of homelessness at home is where I would like to begin my investigation of Faulkner's Bayard Sartoris, for Bayard's narrative is a long translation of his legitimation crisis which is a necessary repudiation of his home. By contextually placing Bayard at the time of Northern occupation during the Civil War, Faulkner isolates a historical moment of entanglement where the patriotic belief in the South is most deliberately maintained as a necessary device of survival; that is, Faulkner's Bayard will have to challenge his society when it is at the paranoid height of patriotic and hegemonic strength. Faulkner develops Bayard's dilemma of homelessness at the outset of the novel, where a young Bayard and Ringo hover over an imagery yet "living" map of the South. This begins the thematic development of polluted land in the text. Even as the boys endeavor to reconstruct the battlefields of the war, they are thwarted in their attempt by two factors: the triumph of Loosh and the resistance of the land. Bayard notes, "The ground drank water faster than we could fetch it from the well" (*The Unvanquished* 3–4). As they strive to use the land, to impose upon it the imagined victory of the South through violent means in a war that is, though certainly not wholly, but largely motivated by the defense of slavery, they are forced to recognize the land's inexhaustible consumption of water as symbolic of the futility of their cause. This is not a new sentiment regarding the Civil War in the South, the sense of an inevitable loss set against the heroic power of the South to resist despite the odds. However, in Faulkner's texts, we find a clear distinction between what we might call the philosophy of "They Endured" put forth in *The Sound and the Fury* (427)and the philosophy of John Sartoris' "Indomitable Unregret" in *The Unvanquished* (159).

Bayard begins the narrative with this indomitable unregret. He and Ringo fire upon the occupying army; when forced to leave his home in the chapter "Retreat," he takes some of the land with him, thinking that he takes a piece of home when in fact what he is taking is the token of his resistance to change. Because the land for Bayard will become an inherited burden, he will discover later in the text that he must leave the land behind, let it lie fallow, let the corruption of the land through internecine war and racialized crime dissipate and then, when the soil has agreed to become revitalized, replenished, find a new crop to plant. However, Bayard must, like Huck, first witness the corruption of the Old South; he must play a role in the old order, must be forced to taste of it, before he comes to realize that societal changes must be made. That is, Bayard must move away from Indomitable Unregret into accepting Endurance.

The way that Bayard will make this transition is through an experience of the culture of violence that he must inherit. His father, John Sartoris, will not only fight in the war, but he will continue his fight even after the war, during Reconstruction. His killing of the Burdens, his monomaniac obsession to rebuild the South *as it was before the war*, even if through— and likely necessarily by—violent means, represents his Indomitable Unregret. It is an Unregret worse even, we will find in *The Unvanquished*, than Sutpen's monomania, because Sartoris's effort implicates and involves the entire South, or at least all of Jefferson as a small community in the South which will symbolize microcosmically the entire South, while Sutpen only wishes to degrade and corrupt himself.

Consider, for example, the symbol of the train in *The Unvanquished*; it runs through the text as Twain's river runs through *Adventures of Huckleberry Finn*. However, the progress implicit in the symbol of the train—progress of technology, progress of literal movement quickened and efficient—is subverted in Faulkner's text. The first experience of the railroad is to see it wrapped in bizarre bows left by General Sherman. The Northern army has halted the progress of the South, has by occupation made the South's progress impossible. Yet more disturbing is the reconstruction of the railroad after the war, spearheaded by John Sartoris. His political manipulation and violent antagonism towards Redmond results inevitably in Sartoris's death—Sartoris's reconstruction suggests the repetition of a faulty beginning. After the war, the Indomitable Unregret of a John Sartoris is the stubborn reiteration of Southern corruption. John Sartoris has not learned from the conflict, has not repudiated the tenets of a flawed past, but has instead deliberately perpetuated them. This reconstruction of the Old South by the Old South threatens a cyclical tragedy implicating the potential and possibility of the New South. This is not endurance, the forbearance to accept the burden or even the blame of the past, but rather this is Unregret, the refusal to acknowledge dubious beginnings, a failure to recognize the futility of the war, or the inhuman violence of slavery and fratricide, that has forced the land to forsake the South and its cause.

Bayard will take part in the culture of violence when he hunts Grumby, *The Unvanquished*'s version of one of Pap's people. Urged on by Uncle Buck, Bayard will exact revenge from the man who has killed his grandmother. However, when it comes time to repeat this inherited hegemonic value in revenge of his murdered father, there has been a significant change in Bayard. His discussion with Drusilla in "An Odor of Verbena" shows that Bayard has repudiated violence as a means of positive reconstruction. Bayard challenges Drusilla's idealistic perception of his father's actions, asking, "'How can they get any good from what he wants to do for them if they are—after he has—'" and Drusilla finishes for him, "'Killed some of them?'" (256). In challenging his father's method of reconstruction, Bayard intimates the burden that his experiences signify from his young life. Bayard's involvement in the war and hunting Grumby were early expressions of his unthinking acceptance of an imposed hegemonic role in society. Compare this with Huck's acceptance of the culture of the Widow and later the culture of his Pap, and we find an important thematic consistency in both works—the child will begin the narrative firmly entrenched in the complex relationship of coercion and consent implicit in hegemony, and the narrative thrust will be the movement of the child into legitimation. Thus, Bayard, like Huck, is the child figure who, through the process of bearing witness, grows to understand the impurity implicit in these assumed values. By allowing Redmond to fire at him, but refusing to fire back, Bayard has repudiated the culture of violence. He has also acknowledged the symbolic implications of the sullied land as betokened by the dust from *Intruder in the Dust*; Bayard, like Charles Mallison Jr., has seen what the land—the dry land that consumes the water of Bayard's living map or which is a witness and a malign force for Chick Mallison— signifies. The land's refusal against and of the history of the South must find its antidote in the figure of the seeing, witnessing child who has the courage to move away from Indomitable Unregret, and move towards the ability to simply Endure; as Gavin Stevens says "Regret [the past injustices, but] dont be ashamed" (*Intruder in the Dust* 206). As in Huck's narrative, the ability to Endure, this new site of inspiration for the child, comes from the black subject, a telling consistency between the texts.

Bayard's epiphany is not sudden; it is a calculated process of thought suggesting that he has engaged his society with his eyes open. Yet Bayard's pivotal introspective moment is when he muses,

> despite my raising and background (or maybe because of them) I had for some time known what I was becoming and had feared the test of it; I remember how I thought while her hands still rested on my shoulders: *At least this will be my chance to find out if I am what I think I am or if I just hope; if I am going to do what I have taught myself is right or if I am just going to wish I were.* (247–248)

This shows Faulkner at his old tricks again; challenging us as readers to carefully decipher whether what Bayard believes is right and wishes he were, what he hopes he will do, is in fact what he does. Bayard's mainte- nance that his actions are made despite or because of his upbringing gives us assurance that Bayard has resolved to halt the cycle of corruption in the South. He has by his own admission taught himself to challenge the assumptions of revenge. His own experience with the culture of violence, his existence in it, becomes the site of his vicarious oppression because the culture of violence and its attendant oppressions speak to the violent oppression that is the root of Southern history. Bayard inherits the name of Sartoris, but the people of his community realize that he has refused, repudiated that inheritance when Drusilla and George Wyatt both admon- ish him, asking, "'Who are you? Is your name Sartoris?'" (284). To endure the history of the name, while also the slings and arrows of his community, thrusts Bayard outside society yet trapped within it. Like Huck, he chooses homelessness as the necessary antidote to a Southern history that he has, at a young age, experienced as a decayed source of troublingly empty inspiration.

Avtar Brah, in her essay "Diaspora, Border and Transnational Identi- ties," maintains that a legitimation crisis is the diasporic reaction to one's awakened cultural assumptions. Both Huck and Bayard, through the process of legitimation, make themselves homeless at home, diasporic not in a geographical sense, but in a historical and societal sense because they choose not Unregret, but Endurance. Both narratives provide us with the imaginary unmediated vision of the child as each learns, to his astonishment, the problems of the society that he has been born into and which he has taken for granted. These texts are tragic because they show us the awful demands put upon the child of the South, the difficult and painful process of repudiation. They are also tragic in their presentation of the South itself; for it is undeniable that the child is singular in these texts; his vision is unique in an imagined South which has refused to see and accept the crimes of the past, to take inheritance not as honor or estate or even inspiration, but as the inevitable inescapable burden of a "doomed and fatal blood" (*Go Down, Moses* 293).

Works Cited

Agee, James, and Walter Evans. *Let Us Now Praise Famous Men.* 1941. Boston: Houghton, 1960.

Brah, Avtar. *Cartographies of Diaspora.* London: Routledge, 1996.

Cooley, Thomas, ed. *Adventures of Huckleberry Finn.* A Norton Critical Edition. New York: Norton, 1999.

Eliot, T.S. Introduction to *Adventures of Huckleberry Finn*, edited by Thomas Cooley. A Norton Critical Edition. New York: Norton, 1999. 348–354.

Faulkner, William. *Go Down, Moses.* 1942. New York: Vintage, 1973.

———. *Intruder in the Dust.* 1948. New York: Vintage, 1972.

———. *The Sound and the Fury.* 1929. New York: Vintage, 1946.

———. *The Unvanquished.* 1938. New York: Vintage, 1966.

Ransom, John Crowe. "Reconstructed But Unregenerate." In *I'll Take My Stand.* 1930. New York: Harper, 1951.

Sartre, Jean-Paul. Introduction. *The Colonizer and the Colonizer.* By Albert Memmi. Boston: Beacon P, 1967.

Smiley, Jane. "Say it Ain't So, Huck: Second Thoughts on Mark Twain's 'Masterpiece.'" In *Adventures of Huckleberry Finn*, edited by Thomas Cooley. A Norton Critical Edition. New York: Norton, 1999. 354–361.

Twain, Mark. *Adventures of Huckleberry Finn.* 1884. In *Adventures of Huckleberry Finn*, edited by Thomas Cooley. A Norton Critical Edition. New York: Norton, 1999. 1–296.

Huck Goes to Harvard

Mark Twain's *Adventures of Huckleberry Finn* (1884) and William Faulkner's *Absalom, Absalom!* (1936) constitute two major novels about acquiring an American education. According to these works, one subject that an American education teaches is racism. Another is, on a more positive note, or should be, how hard it is to know anything at all. Each of the novels mentioned at the outset contains central characters that learn these truths through two pedagogical modes: (1) both conversation with others and internal dialogue about how race works in their "world," how one survives in a racially conscious environment, and (2) how hard it is to be sure even of "facts." Two who learn these lessons with the reader are Twain's Huck and Faulkner's Sutpen, white males who could at the outset certainly be called "white trash," two Americans at the bottom of the social ladder who must learn about race and form opinions based on that learning, then act upon those opinions and facts. Even the temperamentally taciturn Sutpen tries to explain to Quentin's father how he learned about race and place, totally new concepts for him at that time, which information the reader learns ambiguously filtered through Quentin's late winter-night conversations at Harvard with his Canadian roommate Shreve, many years after the occurrences under discussion take place. Huck's revelations, on the other hand, seem clear, overt, as we listen in on his inner monologues and his conversations with Jim, although Huck, too, finds thinking inconclusive on major moral issues.

Russell Baker's review of Stephen Miller's *Conversation: A History of a Declining Art* in the *New York Review of Books* for May 11, 2006, praises Huck and Jim's ruminations on the raft as representative of the art of conversation (4–6). Ultimately, it seems to me, this art evolves from their near-Socratic posing of questions and searching for their answers. To engage in such searches certainly constitutes, or should, a Harvard degree, and to preserve the voices of the speakers seems to me to embrace the best of American education: joining the ideal to the practical. Indeed, Lionel Trilling, in an introduction to one edition of *Huckleberry Finn*, compares the prose of Twain and Faulkner, both of which, he observes, "reinforce[s] the colloquial tradition with the literary tradition" (xvi).

From Chapter 1 on, we find ourselves in Huck's mind, where we are already invited in line one to read a book, to learn something: "You don't know about me without you have read a book by the name of *The Adventures of Tom Sawyer*" (1). In chapter after chapter, Huck encourages the reader to share his thinking. And then there are Huck's dialogues, most importantly with the black slave Jim, in which life lessons are pondered. One passage might illustrate a possible answer to the question: "What is a friend?" When Huck in Chapter 15, entitled "Fooling Poor Old Jim," makes Jim doubt his sense of reality, whether he's been dreaming or awake, Huck asks Jim what all the details of the dream/reality "stand for," in this case "leaves and rubbish on the raft and the smashed oar" (80), which Huck has used to prove to Jim that he (Huck) had not left the raft in the fog, when indeed he had. Jim ponders the evidence and then declares:

> "What do dey stan' for? I's gwyne to tell you. When I got all wore out wid work, en wid de callin' for you, en went to sleep, my heart wuz mos' broke bekase you wuz los', en I didn' k'yer no' mo' what become er me en de raf'. En when I wake up en find you back ag'in, all safe en soun', de tears come, en I could 'a' got down on my knees en kiss yo' foot, I's so thankful. En all you wuz thinkin' 'bout wuz how you could make a fool uv ole Jim wid a lie. Dat truck dah is *trash*; en trash is what people is dat puts dirt on de head er dey fren's en makes 'em ashamed." (80)

Huck learns true shame (the abstract and ideal) in this dialogue and he acts on it (the practical): "It was fifteen minutes before I could work myself up to go and humble myself to a nigger; but I done it, and I warn't ever sorry for it afterward, neither. I didn't do him no more mean tricks and I wouldn't done that one if I'd 'a' knowed it would make him feel that way" (80). Clearly, empathy is a part of the lesson also, even in a racially charged situation where a different norm was supposed to apply.

Faulkner's readers are also drawn to learning, although we have to wait a while for this element to be clear. Indeed, it is the reader, at least until Chapter 6, and really throughout, who doubts knowing. Appetites are whetted when early on Miss Rosa acknowledges Quentin's next step in life: "'Because you are going away to attend the college at Harvard they tell me'" (5). With that acknowledgement, she issues him a challenge:

> "So maybe you will enter the literary profession as so many Southern gentlemen and gentlewomen too are doing now and maybe someday you will remember this and write about it. You will be married then I expect and perhaps your wife will want a new gown or a new chair

for the house and you can write this and submit it to the
magazines. Perhaps you will even remember kindly then
the old woman who made you spend a whole afternoon
sitting indoors and listening while she talked about people
and events you were fortunate enough to escape yourself
when you wanted to be out among young friends of your
own age." (5)

The questions for the dialogue in Faulkner's context thus seem to be:
"What is the South?" "What happened?" "What does it all mean?"
"Where were the mistakes?" "Do you hate it there?" Faulkner's first five
chapters seem to provide plenty of plot material from variant viewpoints
meandering around these questions, out of which gradually some possible
answers become somewhat clear. Any definite answers to the five questions
ultimately remain muddy. The reader must wait until Chapter 6, to find
Quentin at Harvard with his roommate Shreve. An "open text book" lies
on the table, and on it "the white oblong envelope" and the letter with
"his father's sloped fine hand" (141) announcing the death of Miss Rosa
Coldfield, which knowledge had prompted much of the prior and following speculation between Quentin and Shreve. The educational question
of whether man knows anything or can know anything, especially about
someone else's motives and intents, seems clearly posed in the dubious.

Why might the readers of the two works focus on the characters of
Huck and Sutpen to compare the learning process and outcomes? These
two "white trash" figures have similar beginnings, that time in life when the
learning process begins, the time adults often look back to as the keystone
by which the rest of life is revealed. For both Huck and Sutpen, that early
view included an absence of a mother figure, alcoholic fathers (both called
"pap"), their origins unknown, dysfunctional families (Sutpen is never sure
of his age), minimal or no schooling and reading (although, Huck is aware
of and besieged by Tom Sawyer's reading, and Sutpen trusts the advice
of his schoolteacher of only three months to travel to the West Indies: he
then later sends his own son to college). So the early "Harvards" of the
two characters really constituted the "school of hard knocks." In explaining
himself to Mr. Coldfield, Sutpen acknowledges,

> "Perhaps a man builds for his future in more ways than
> one, builds not only toward the body which will be his
> tomorrow or next year, but toward actions and the sub-
> sequent irrevocable courses of resultant action which his
> weak senses and intellect cannot foresee but which ten or

twenty or thirty years from now he will take, will have to take in order to survive the act." (196)

In each case, such a practicality was a good choice; the ability to formulate questions and search for answers grew well in that rather mortarless school. For Huck, the main question seems to be: "How can I reconcile what I know from living with what I am now being told by authority figures like my father, the Widow Douglas, her sister Miss Watson, the Duke and Dauphin, the Grangerfords, and even Tom Sawyer?" As he is maturing at the time of the telling of the novel, that "living" involved Jim's life and experience and treatment of Huck, so that the questions of knowing and race are clearly integrated. A few examples from the above list will illustrate. Early in the novel, the Widow Douglas tries to instruct Huck in the need for prayer, not just for the obvious but for "spiritual gifts" (10). As Huck ponders this advice in the woods he comes to the conclusion that "I couldn't see no advantage about it—except for the other people; so at last I reckoned I wouldn't worry about it anymore but just let it go" (10). On another occasion, he waffles. When starving on the river, he comes upon a big loaf of bread. Hungry, Huck eats first, and then thinks ". . . [N]ow I reckon the widow or the parson or somebody prayed that this bread would find me, and here it has gone and done it. So there ain't no doubt but there is something in that thing . . . when a body like the widow or parson prays, but it don't work for me, and I reckon it don't work for only just the right kind"(35). Finally, just before he utters the most famous moral decision in American literature, Huck decides to try to pray whether or not to turn Jim in as a runaway slave:

> "So I kneeled down. But the words wouldn't come. Why wouldn't they? It warn't no use to try and hide it from Him. Nor from *me*, neither. I knowed very well why they wouldn't come. It was because my heart warn't right; it was because I warn't square; it was because I was playing double. I was letting *on* to give up sin, but away inside of me I was holding on to the biggest one of all. I was trying to make my mouth *say* I would do the right thing and the clean thing, and go and write to that nigger's owner and tell where he was, but deep down in me I knowed it was a lie, and He knowed it. You can't pray a lie—I found that out." (199)

Thus the "fact" that prayer is helpful, a "wisdom" inculcated from "teachers," proves untrue—thus, one lesson learned.

In the humorous plot line, reality also sets in. Tom convinces Huck that they should free Jim as it would be done in the adventure novels that Tom has read. This component of the novel contains a litany of Tom's garbled understanding of those novels and Huck's common sense. One instance will make the point. Tom emphasizes that they must save Jim the "right way." He reminds Huck:

> "I've read all the books that gives any information about these things. They always dig out with a case-knife—and not through dirt, mind you; generly it's through solid rock. And it takes them weeks and weeks and weeks and forever and ever. Why, look at one of them prisoners in the bottom dungeon of the Castle Deef, in the harbor of Marseilles, that dug himself out that way; how long was *he* at it, you reckon?
>
> "I don't know."
>
> "Well, guess."
>
> "I don't know. A month and a half."
>
> "Thirty-seven year—and he come out in China. That's the kind. I wish the bottom of *this* fortress was solid rock."
>
> "*Jim* don't know nobody in China."
>
> "What's *that* got to do with it? Neither did that other fellow. But you're always *a-wandering* off on a side issue. Why can't you stick to the main point?"
>
> "All right—*I* don't care where he comes out, so he *comes* out; and Jim don't either, I reckon. But there's one thing, anyway—Jim's too old to be dug out with a case-knife. He won't last."
>
> "Yes he will *last*, too. You don't reckon it's going to take thirty-seven years to dig through a *dirt* foundation, do you?" (228)

Fortunately, Tom has to compromise his extravagant plans, and "letting on" becomes the *modus vivendi*. Huck's common sense becomes pedagogy.

Huck proves to be an early environmentalist as well. His knowledge of the river saves him from being caught by society, allowing him and Jim to head for freedom (with a slight fog-induced error, however, that sends them "down the river" instead of up—another instance in the narrative of the difficulty of knowing). Mark Twain imbues Huck with the knowledge the writer gleaned from his work as a steamboat captain. He knows, for example, to check a seemingly empty canoe for occupants (28). Out on the water, he can tell the time:

> I was pretty tired, and the first thing I knowed I was asleep. When I woke up I didn't know where I was for a minute. I set up and looked around, a little scared. Then I remembered. The river looked miles and miles across. The moon was so bright I could 'a' counted the drift-logs that went a-slipping along, black and still, hundreds of yards out from shore. Everything was dead and quiet; it looked late, and *smelt* late. (32)

He knows to hide in the driftwood to avoid detection (32). He knows how to hide a canoe (33). He is careful about the weight on the raft: "It warn't good judgment to put *everything* on the raft" (59). He knows how to build a wigwam on the raft (60). Society, in the form of the Widow Douglas and company, may tell Huck the virtues of shoes, clean sheets, and daily washing, but Huck's true nature as the first boy scout always wins out. Again, the practical application of common sense becomes Huck's teacher.

Certainly Huck's father is a dubious authority figure as teacher, since he tries to influence his son away from society. Knowing Huck, Pap might have been more successful, had it not been for his trying to keep Huck a prisoner, steal his money, beat him, and generally make Huck's life miserable. But he appears to influence a moral debate Huck has with himself. When he steals chickens to eat as he and Jim travel (hunger's being a practical problem), Huck remembers his father's advice: "Pap always said, take a chicken when you get a chance, because if you don't want him yourself you can easy find somebody that does, and a good deed ain't ever forgot. I never see Pap when he didn't want the chicken himself, but that is what he used to say, anyway" (61). This philosophical stance requires much conversation between Huck and Jim. Huck tells Jim that the widow had called Pap's logic

> a soft name for stealing, and no decent body would do it. Jim said he reckoned the widow was partly right and Pap was partly right; so the best way would be for us to pick out two or three things from the list and say we wouldn't borrow them any more—then he reckoned it wouldn't be no harm to borrow the others. (61)

In all these cases and many others, Huck appears as a pragmatist with a heart, an ethical relativist; one must do what one needs, and that most importantly means being a friend to his best friend Jim, regardless of the consequences. One could then say Huck's real life lessons remain in conflict with hypocritical societal norms. His is the education of learned experience. Applying then this fact to Huck's experience of the South, the violence and racism he experiences there he rejects, even as he continues to try to sort out the authoritarian advice from his own experience. "Do as I say, not as I do" seems the operative position of his "teachers," and Huck is wise to them.

For Faulkner's Sutpen, early beginnings also play a role, but he must cruelly unlearn this past. When Sutpen tries to describe to Quentin's grandfather his life (as Quentin explains it to Shreve, as Quentin's father had explained it to him), he analyzes the circumstances:

> "His [Sutpen's] trouble was innocence. All of a sudden he discovered, not what he wanted to but what he just had to do, had to do it whether he wanted to or not, because if he did not do it he knew that he could never live with himself for the rest of his life, never live with what all the men and women that had died to make him had left inside of him for him to pass on, with all the dead ones waiting and watching to see if he was going to do it right, fix things right so that he would be able to look in the face not only the old dead ones but all the living ones that would come after him when he would be one of the dead. And that at the very moment when he discovered what it was, he found out that this was the last thing in the world he was equipped to do because he not only had not known that he would have to do this, he did not even know that it existed to be wanted, to need to be done, until he was almost fourteen years old." (178–179)

His early life in the Virginia mountains had not exposed him to money, work, class, and race. He had been an absolute ignorant:

> "So he didn't even know there was a country all divided and fixed and neat with a people living on it all divided and fixed and neat because of what color their skins happened to be and what they happened to own, and where a certain few men not only had the power of life and death and barter and sale over others, but they had living human men to perform endless repetitive personal offices such as pouring the very whiskey from the jug and putting the

glass into his hand or pulling off his boots for him to go to bed that all men have had to do for themselves since time began and would have to do until they died and which no man ever has or ever will like to do but which no man that he knew ever had anymore thought of evading than he had thought of evading the effort of chewing and swallowing and breathing." (179–180)

He had naively assumed an equality among all men, but when he came out of the hills, "'He had learned the difference not only between white men and black ones, but he was learning that there was a difference between white men and white men, not to be measured by lifting anvils or gouging eyes or how much whiskey you could drink then get up and walk out of the room'" (183). The pivotal pedagogical moment comes when, running an errand for his father, knocking on the door of the mansion owned by his father's employer, he is greeted by a black slave who "'even before he had had time to say what he came for,'" told him "'never to come to that front door again but to go around to the back'" (188). In Huck fashion, Sutpen retreats to think about the matter, here in Platonic terms: "He said he crawled back into the cave and sat with his back against the uptorn roots, and thought'" (188). His thought process is uncomplicated; he does not go gunning for retribution, but he simply admits his innocence and now sees how the world is. The issue is not a moral one for Sutpen as it is for Huck; it is a matter of adapting to a new circumstance:

> "'... because he knew that something would have to be done about it; he would have to do something about it in order to live with himself for the rest of his life and he could not decide what it was because of the innocence which he had just discovered he had, which (the innocence, not the man, not the tradition) he would have to compete with'" (189).

Indeed General Compson told his son, Quentin's father, that Sutpen's "'very calmness was indication that he had long since given up any hope of ever understanding it [how things are]'" (212). But he does try to explain to General Compson and himself, how things came to be. In the best epistemological fashion, he asks the question, "'Where did I make a mistake?'" (212), with regard to his "design" (mastery over slaves, possession of land, wife, children, production of a grandson). But then he really seems to know the answer already, namely, that he had found out too late that he had married a woman in the West Indies with Negro blood and had had a son by her. Upon learning this now unacceptable fact, Sutpen divorces his wife while providing well for her and the child. Thinking the episode is behind him, he proceeds then to execute his plan in Mississippi, until he learns that this first mixed-race son is his "design son's" best friend at the University of Mississippi, with his own "design" to marry his "design daughter" (who would be his half sister). Thus his engagement in miscegenation thwarts Sutpen's "design." And his "mistake" is tied to racism. Again, it is the school of experience that teaches Sutpen. The South, where he has placed his lot, is ruled by a law forbidding miscegenation. At this point, "South" for Sutpen begins to mean "doom." The plot complications ensue from this "crime" of Sutpen: "the design son" Henry kills the first son Charles Bon, which deed sends Sutpen's wife Ellen to her bed and death, dooms "the design daughter" Judith to spinsterhood (the Civil War also intrudes here), and leaves Sutpen a broken wreck after the war, but still intent on resurrecting his design out of the rubble of his home and land. A series of ill-chosen moves brings about his subsequent murder. Sutpen thus tries to follow the ideal (his "design") even when real life is showing him its impossibility. The bulk of the novel involves multiple narrators (Faulkner, Quentin, the latter's father Mr. Compson, his father General Compson, Rosa Coldfield, a letter to Judith from Charles Bon, one from Quentin to Mr. Compson, and Quentin's Harvard roommate Shreve McCannon) trying to get the story straight, through remembered conversations, speculations, letters. Just as Sutpen never quite "gets" it, neither do the speculators. Finally, loss of life in war and in individuals and insurmountable racial codes constitute Sutpen's learning about the South, imperfect and ambiguous as that learning proves to be.

In retrospect, we know Huck at an age where certainty seems more secure. At that age, learning can be fact; it can be isolated wisdoms and insights. In contrast, we deal with Sutpen's entire life, over the course of which, certainty seems increasingly less secure. Wash Jones's refrain to Sutpen (even as he later murders his employer): "Well Kernel, they kilt us but they ain't whupped us yit, air they?'" (150) doesn't ultimately ring true. The South and Sutpen are "kilt." Miss Rosa had already acknowledged that truth when she observed that the "'Northern people have already seen to it that there is little left in the South for a young man'" (5). In contrast, Huck's world is "righted" at the end; he has created and acted upon his own morality, Jim is freed and can be reunited with his family, and Huck can "light out" for new adventures. South for Huck is not the oppressor it remains for the Sutpen legacy. Indeed, Sutpen's last relative, his great-grandson Jim Bond (Bon), another miscegenous "issue," disappears and/or dies in the fire that destroys the mansion on Sutpen's Hundred. The Sutpen line—both legal and illegal—dies; Sutpen is murdered; his house burns; his South dies, that South that he had tried to live without ever really understanding. (It is useful here to remember that Wash Jones kills Sutpen with a scythe, which Shreve dubs the "'symbolic laurel of Caesar's triumph—that rusty scythe loaned by the demon himself to Jones more than two years ago to cut the weeds away from the shanty doorway to smooth the path for rutting'" (145). (This "Caesar" had gone down in defeat.) Huck understands all too well, and decides for another Hell, which the reader never has to witness his experiencing. Thus the two Jims also illustrate the difference in the two works—freed Jim exults; after Tom Sawyer gives Jim forty dollars for being a good prisoner, Jim declares:

> "*Dah*, now, Huck, what I tell you?—what I tell you up
> dah on Jackson Islan'? I *tole* you I got a hairy breas', en
> what's de sign un it; en I *tole* you I ben rich wunst, en
> gwineter be rich *ag'in*; en it's come true; en heah she *is*!
> *Dah*, now! doan' talk to *me*—signs is *signs*, mine I tell you;
> en I knowed jis' 's well 'at I'uz gwineter be rich ag'in as I's
> a-stannin' heah dis minute!" (273)

And we already know the fate of Jim Bond, the last Sutpen, the "howling idiot":

> He, Quentin, could see it, could see the deputy holding
> her while the driver backed the ambulance to safety and
> returned, the three faces all a little wild now since they
> must have believed her;—the three of them staring,
> glaring at the doomed house: and then for a moment
> maybe Clytie appeared in that window from which she
> must have been watching the gates constantly day and
> night for three months—the tragic gnome's face beneath
> the clean headrag, against a red background of fire, seen
> for a moment between two swirls of smoke, looking down
> at them, perhaps not even now with triumph and no more
> despair than it had ever worn, possibly even serene above
> the melting clapboards before the smoke swirled across it
> again—and he, Jim Bond, the scion, the last of his race,
> seeing it [the burning house] too now and howling with
> human reason. . . . (300)

Knowledge for the last Sutpen remains ambiguous at best. In sum, certitude and ambiguity equal two types of recognitions gleaned from learning.

Finally, the reader must be aware that the contrasting tones of the two novels complement the two elements of education that the characters experience. In Twain's *Huckleberry Finn* the sober issues of not only race but of theft, violence, and dysfunctional families are approached with ironic humor, based on Twain's paradoxical view of human nature (a cursory perusal of *Letters from the Earth* will make this point abundantly evident). And although Faulkner certainly wrote with humor elsewhere ("Spotted Horses," *As I Lay Dying*, for example) and although there is certainly irony in *Absalom, Absalom!*, the pervading tone is one of lament for loss. The biblical title suggests father-son travail over at least three generations of Sutpens, with three generations of Compson males trying to understand what they are trying to explain. Quentin expresses the difficulty: "'Yes, of course I understand it,'" shortly followed by, "'I don't know'" (289). And all conclusions of the characters are grim. Perhaps it takes the one character, neither a Southerner nor a Yankee but an outsider, a Canadian, to be aghast: "'Now I want you [Quentin] to tell me just one thing more. Why do you hate the South?'" (303). Quentin's cold denial doesn't ring true (and indeed we learn in *The Sound and the Fury* that Quentin commits suicide some months after this disavowal). Not the stuff of humor. Perhaps the difference is again attributable to the fact that there is no follow up of Huck and Tom and Jim. Had Twain written a sequel, its tone might have changed (compare the cynicism of *Pudd'nhead Wilson*), and Huck and Tom might wind up drafted into the Confederate Army (or Northern Army, Missouri being the split state it was), and Jim might well have had trouble buying back his wife and children and starting out as a freed man. We will never know. Our Huck thus could wind up knowing a few facts: race is an issue, a friend comes first, the practical is the easiest way to do something. And he remains living in a continuous literary present. Sutpen, on the other hand, lives to question his life, to see where the flaw in his "design" was, to see his wager with the South be lost, his miscegenous "mistake" cursing his sons to the last "howling idiot," even though at his murder he is still trying to complete his "design." These varied insights into life, these American educations, Huck and Sutpen obtain (and the reader follows) through dialogues and through internal ruminations of the characters, whether presented rather clearly and overtly by Twain, or in the conditional and subjective by Faulkner and his multiple narrators.

What are the implications of these forms of education for the contemporary American? We know about race. Whether we are politically correct, or far right, or left, right in the middle, or white, black, or multiracial in our own skins, we know the issue isn't solved in our society. When Shreve foresees that the "'Jim Bonds are going to conquer the western hemisphere'" (302), that charged statement flies in the face of what Diana I. Williams refers to as "hybrid vigor," regarding Jean Toomer's belief in the benefits of racial mixing (196). But another element of Shreve's prediction does seem to be coming true. Consider Richard Rodriguez's new work *Brown: The Last Discovery of America*, which acknowledges the ever-increasing diversity of the U.S.; and even more positively, we know people are falling in love across color lines. Perhaps that is positive insight.

As far as knowing and what can be known is concerned, the epistemological issue still exists. Consider the sure (fundamentalists of all stripes) versus the scientists (who must often question their experiments), in contrast to the humanists (who have accepted man's sloppy imperfections as the plight of the human condition), struggling on, always seeking to know but ever-hesitant to seize upon a certain truth. Huck's certitude we enjoy (he gets to stay at the arrested age of early youth), while Sutpen's messy death we accept as more the norm for one who completes a life "full of days." In our time, sadly, an American dialogue does not always happen. Let us learn from these characters the necessity for not only internal but also external conversation. And let us learn from them that fact and ambiguity can co-exist even with practicality.

Works Cited

Baker, Russell. Review of *Conversation: A History of a Declining Art*, by Stephen Miller. *The New York Review of Books*, 11 May 2006: 4–6.

Faulkner, William. *Absalom Absalom!* 1936. New York: Vintage, 1990.

Rodriguez, Richard. *Brown: The Last Discovery of America*. New York: Viking, 2002.

Trilling, Lionel. Introduction to *Adventures of Huckleberry Finn*, by Mark Twain. San Francisco: Rinehart, 1948.

Twain, Mark. *Adventures of Huckleberry Finn*. 1884. San Francisco: Rinehart, 1948.

Williams, Diana I. "Building the New Race: Jean Toomer's Eugenic Aesthetic." In *Jean Toomer and the Harlem Renaissance*, edited by Geneviève Fabre and Michel Feith. New Brunswick, NJ: Rutgers UP, 2001. 188–201.

Faulkner's Hucks and Jims

"All modern American literature comes from one book by Mark Twain called *Huckleberry Finn*," Ernest Hemingway claimed (*Green Hills* 22). William Faulkner disagreed with many things that Hemingway said or wrote, but on this point the two men wholeheartedly agreed. "Mark Twain," Faulkner said, "was the first truly American writer, and all of us since are his heirs, we descended from him" (Meriwether and Millgate 137). On another occasion he observed, "[Sherwood Anderson] was the father of my generation of American writers and the tradition of American writing which our successors will carry on. . . . [Theodore] Dreiser is his older brother, and Mark Twain is the father of them both" (249–250). He added, "People will read *Huck Finn* for a long time" (56).

Faulkner's most revealing discussion of *Adventures of Huckleberry Finn* can be found in comments he made to the English Club at the University of Virginia in 1958 (Gwynn and Blotner 241–248). The remarks on Twain's novel appear in the context of Faulkner's extended lament that in the modern world of organizations and bureaucracies and dogmatic creeds citizens have been robbed of their individuality and uniqueness. The accepted "mythology" of the modern world, Faulkner says, is an almost universal belief "that one single individual man is nothing, and can have weight and substance only when organized into the anonymity of a group where he will have surrendered his individual soul for a number" (242). In such a world, human beings are "desouled as the stallion or boar or bull is gelded" (245), and individual values such as "honesty and pity and responsibility and compassion" (242) are displaced by

> factional regimented group[s], both filling the same air at
> the same time with the same double-barreled abstractions
> of "peoples' democracy" and "minority rights" and "equal
> justice" and "social welfare"—all the synonyms which take
> all the shame out of irresponsibility by not merely inviting
> but even compelling everyone to participate in it. (242)

Primary among those who stand against such dehumanizing tendencies in the modern world, Faulkner claims, are the artists—not only writers but also painters, musicians, sculptors, and architects—who know the value of individuality because their work is the result of individual, not corporate, effort. Faulkner also commends President Eisenhower's People-to-People Program (for which Faulkner served as co-chairman of the Writers' Committee) as an attempt, flawed though it proved to be, to inject a degree of individuality and personhood into the conformist, impersonal modern state. But neither artists nor even presidents, in Faulkner's view, can be successful in their reforming efforts so long as the powerful, controlling mindset of the collectivist society remains the accepted and desirable norm.

To underscore his point about the loss of individuality in the modern world, Faulkner contrasts J.D. Salinger's *Catcher in the Rye* with *Huckleberry Finn*. For Faulkner the story of Holden Caulfield is the narrative of a character who "loved man and wished to be a part of mankind, humanity, who tried to join the human race and failed" (244). But the cause of Holden's failure rests not so much in the character as in the milieu he inhabits. "His tragedy," Faulkner says, "was that when he attempted to enter the human race, there was no human race there" (244). Faulkner sees Caulfield's situation as typical of many of the characters in the books written by the young writers of the mid-century. Instead of living "in myriad company [with] the anguishes and hopes of all human hearts in a world of a few simple comprehensible truths and moral principles," these characters "exist alone inside a vacuum of facts which [they] did not choose and cannot cope with and cannot escape from like a fly inside an inverted tumbler" (244). In terms of the philosophical and literary history of the first half of the twentieth century, Faulkner, like Joseph Wood Krutch and other humanists of the period, is deploring how deterministic theories of human behavior have displaced the traditional belief in free will, how such forces as circumstance, environment, and heredity are believed to overrule individual choice and control.

In contrast to the dilemma of Holden Caulfield and his compatriots, Faulkner offers the example of Huckleberry Finn:

> ... another youth already father to what will some day
> soon now be a man. But in Huck's case all he had to
> combat was his small size, which time would cure for
> him; in time he would be as big as any man he had to
> cope with; and even as it was, all the adult world could do
> to harm him was to skin his nose a little; humanity, the
> human race, would and was accepting him already; all he
> needed to do was just to grow up in it. (244–245)

Both Huck and Holden are young individuals seeking meaning in their relationship to the larger world. However, according to Faulkner, Huck succeeds because his quest takes place within a community of shared values and beliefs that are compatible with and prize individuality, whereas Holden fails because his quest takes place "not in individuality but in isolation" (244). In other words, Huck lives and functions in relationship to society (even when he is rebelling against it), while Holden exists, metaphorically at least, in solitary confinement.

Let's examine how this theme plays out in Twain's novel. Huck's adventures are often viewed as a rebel's quest for freedom, but it is not freedom *per se* that Huck desires. An orphan who has faked his own death to escape his abusive father, Huck goes in search of the father he has lost. Though he does not know it for most of the book, he has found that father in Jim, the runaway slave who is also in need of the family he has lost. Rightly understood (and it is sad that readers obsessed with political correctness cannot get past the n-word to recognize the fact), *Huckleberry Finn* is a love story, one of the finest in all of our literature. Jim's ecstatic embrace of Huck after fearing that Huck is dead, and Huck's refusal to turn Jim over to the authorities and then later risking his life to steal Jim out of slavery (to Tom Sawyer, of course, this action of the novel is a mere charade, since he knows that Jim is already free) clearly demonstrate the love that develops between these two rejects and escapees of a society given over to abstractions and platitudes. Though the union is threatened at every point along the river, both Huck and Jim are seeking freedom not for its own sake but for the sake of relationship, acceptance, family, and love.

Too little attention has been paid to Jim's role as mentor to Huck as their relationship develops. All readers note Huck's role as "a low-down Abolitionist" (Twain 43) in defense of Jim's freedom, but the benefits of the relationship are reciprocal. Along with the great river and the whole of nature, Jim teaches Huck things that go much deeper than "sivilization" and the community's *mores*. As Richard Chase noted, *Huckleberry Finn* is a novel about "exorcism" (in Lettis, McDonnell, and Morris 405), and just as Jim instructs Huck about the use of hair balls and other magical objects to counter witches and other malignant forces of the universe, so too does Jim's example of simple, authentic humanity instruct Huck about the hypocrisies and injustices and cruelties of conventional society. Jim's counter to Huck's French lesson, "'Is a Frenchman a man? . . . *Well*, den! Dad blame it, why doan' he *talk* like a man?'" (78), expresses more than a naïve theory of language. From Jim, the "nigger" and slave at the beginning of the book but friend and father to Huck later on, Huck learns what is required of him to be truly "a man." But Huck is a slow learner, and he comes to understand only gradually the lessons Jim teaches him; still, we can easily trace the key points of Huck's moral and humanistic development.

Hints of that development appear as early as Chapter 11 of the novel, when Huck reports to Jim that "'They're after us!'"—showing by those words, as Leo Marx has pointed out, that Huck is already—instinctively if not consciously—identifying with Jim's flight for freedom (Lettis, McDonnell, and Morris 352). A further point in Huck's initiation occurs when he observes Jim's homesickness for his wife and children and concludes: "I do believe he cared just as much for his people as white folks does for their'n" (150). Another comes when Huck struggles with his conscience over not turning Jim in to the authorities. On one occasion, heading to the shore to report Jim to the authorities but remembering Jim's expression of gratitude to him ("'I'se a free man, en I couldn't ever ben free ef it hadn' ben for Huck'" [86]), Huck lies to the vigilantes about the identity of his companion on the raft: "'He's white,'" Huck says (87). Huck's moral (to him, ironically, immoral) education reaches its climax when he destroys the letter he has written informing Miss Watson of Jim's whereabouts: "'All right, then, I'll *go* to hell,'" he says, tearing up the letter (206). From this point on, Huck actively and unrepentantly works to steal Jim out of slavery. Huck now accepts his role as rebel and outcast, but in the process of losing the world, he has saved his soul. And the catalyst in this conversion experience has been Jim.

Not surprisingly, given his high regard for Twain's novel and its main character, Faulkner created a number of characters who seem modeled at least in part on the relationship of Huckleberry Finn and Jim. Let's briefly consider three pairs of them: Ike McCaslin and Sam Fathers of "The Bear," Chick Mallison and Lucas Beauchamp of *Intruder in the Dust*, and Lucius Priest and Ned McCaslin/Uncle Parsham of *The Reivers*. In each of these cases, a young white boy's cultural and ethical education is conditioned and influenced by a black mentor.

In "The Bear" the youthful Ike McCaslin serves his novitiate as a woodsman and hunter under the direction of Sam Fathers, whose name suggests the role that he plays not only for Ike but for all the participants in the annual hunt for the legendary bear, Old Ben. Part Native American as well as black, Fathers, like Jim, is a primitive in touch with truths that lie beyond the boundaries of civilized society. "'You aint in town now,'" the camp cook tells Ike; "'you in the woods'" (323); and Sam Fathers teaches Ike that he must divest himself of the symbols of civilization—the gun, the watch, the compass—in order to gain a vision of Old Ben, the deity that reigns over the wilderness. But it is not only courage and respect and responsibility that Ike learns under Fathers's guidance; he learns also to accept the tragic realities of mutability and death: the eventual loss of the wilderness and the deaths of its heroes—Old Ben, the great hunting dog Lion, and Sam.

Faulkner's woods are the equivalent of Twain's river; and life, values, and relationships there are different from the ways of the settlements. And the lessons Ike learns in the woods under the tutelage of Sam Fathers he later applies to his decision to forfeit his inheritance of the family plantation. What Vernon L. Parrington said of *Huckleberry Finn*—that it is "a drama of the struggle between the individual and the village *mores*" (Lettis, McDonnell, and Morris 306) —may also be said of "The Bear," with Ike's decision to relinquish the plantation being the equivalent of Huck's tearing up the letter to Miss Watson. And it is Sam Fathers who has brought Ike to this decision: "'Sam Fathers set me free'" (300), Ike tells his cousin Cass.

In *Intruder in the Dust*, Faulkner's Huck and Jim are Chick Mallison, a young white town-boy, and Lucas Beauchamp, a black farmer. As in the case of Twain's novel, Faulkner's Huck begins by sharing the racial prejudices of his community. This point becomes abundantly clear in the initial encounter between Chick and Lucas. While hunting on Lucas's property, Chick falls into a frozen creek and winds up in Lucas's house, where the binary oppositions of white and black are reversed when Chick is ordered by Lucas to strip off his wet clothes and later to eat the food that a Negro woman has prepared for him. Unaccustomed to being bossed about by a "nigger," Chick tries to regain the ascendancy by offering to pay Lucas for his trouble. Thus begins a series of actions in which Chick tries to lure Lucas back into the traditional Southern role of "nigger." But each time Lucas declines the gambit.

Gradually, however, as in the case of Huck and Jim, Chick comes to recognize and accept Lucas's humanity and, like Huck, actively works to secure the black man's freedom. In Lucas's case it is freedom from jail and a threatened lynching after Lucas is charged with a murder he did not commit. Eventually Chick (with the aid of his black friend Alex and an elderly spinster, Miss Habersham) proves Lucas's innocence by putting himself in danger by digging up a grave in a country cemetery. As a result of his experience, Chick not only comes to appreciate a black man's pride, dignity, and independence but also finds himself in rebellion against the traditional racial attitudes and actions of the white citizens of his community. In both cases he is following in the footsteps of Huckleberry Finn.

The Reivers is the Faulkner novel that is most nearly like *Huckleberry Finn*. The central focus of both novels is a journey—Twain's a raft trip down the Mississippi River, Faulkner's an automobile trip to Memphis. And each novel places its protagonist in the midst of disrespectable and immoral characters and forces: Huck must deal with robbers, cutthroats, con men, and fighters of feuds; while Lucius traffics with thieves, gamblers, and prostitutes. But just as Jim assists Huck to discover his humanity amid the chaos of their world, so does a black mentor (first Ned and then Uncle Parsham) help Lucius come to terms with his.

Not only does each of Faulkner's Hucks go through an initiation experience in which a black man serves as both catalyst and teacher, but each of them, like Huckleberry Finn, also learns to prize deeds over words. Ever the pragmatist, Huck finds himself continually in conflict with the bombast and inflated rhetoric of Tom Sawyer, the Widow Douglas, Pap, Emily Grangerford, and the King, to name only a few. Similarly, Ike must find his way to a sense of conscience and duty through the jungle of compromising logic expressed by his cousin Cass Edmonds; Chick Mallison must reject the rationalizations about race and states' rights politics spouted by his Uncle Gavin; and Lucius Priest must learn to trust his own experiences more than the platitudes and pieties of his family and community. Like Twain's prototypical character, Faulkner's Hucks learn to trust their hearts and not their heads, and they learn that lesson through the influence of black mentors who reprise the role of Twain's Jim.

Still, while there are many strong similarities between Twain's Huckleberry Finn and Faulkner's imitations, there is one monumental difference. At the conclusion of his experiences downriver with Jim, Huck determines "to light out for the territory ahead of the rest, because Aunt Sally she's going to adopt me and sivilize me, and I can't stand it. I been there before" (281). Huck's last act of the novel, therefore, is to plan to keep running. By contrast, Faulkner's Hucks choose family, community, and civilization over freedom and the frontier. Ike McCaslin lives out his life in Jefferson, though he continues to make frequent trips into the Big Woods. Chick Mallison, as his role in later Faulkner novels will reveal, becomes more and more a townsman, with little adult involvement with either hunting or blacks. Lucius Priest ends his Memphis adventure by becoming very homesick and longing to return home, even if that means punishment for his misdeeds.

Part of the explanation for this difference in Huckleberry Finn and Faulkner's Hucks is that Twain was writing in the context of a United States that still had an open frontier, whereas Faulkner's setting (even in "The Bear") is that of a closed frontier. As Harold P. Simonson has noted, the existence of the open American frontier of the nineteenth century promoted a national belief in "political democracy, human infinitude, and philosophical idealism" (5)—all of which found expression in the expansionist policy known as Manifest Destiny. Thus Huck's rejection of society is tempered by his ongoing faith in the West, where Tom can find adventures among the "Injuns" and Huck and Jim presumably will continue their quest for dignity, equality, and freedom. Faulkner's characters, on the other hand, inhabitants of the closed frontier, are denied such opportunity for escape and must confront their problems and conflicts *within* society. The disappearance of the physical frontier has significantly narrowed the choices available to Americans of Faulkner's day.

They had been narrowed even more significantly, Faulkner thought, in Salinger's day.

Works Cited

Faulkner, William. *Go Down, Moses*. New York: Random House, 1942.

———. *Intruder in the Dust*. New York: Random House, 1948.

———. *The Reivers*. New York: Random House, 1962.

Gwynn, Frederick L., and Joseph L. Blotner, eds. *Faulkner in the University: Class Conferences at the University of Virginia, 1957–1958*. Charlottesville: U of Virginia P, 1959.

Hemingway, Ernest. *Green Hills of Africa*. New York: Scribner's, 1935.

Lettis, Richard, Robert F. McDonnell, and William E. Morris, eds. *Huck Finn and His Critics*. New York: Macmillan, 1962.

Meriwether, James B., and Michael Millgate, eds. *Lion in the Garden: Interviews with William Faulkner, 1926–1962*. New York: Random House, 1968.

Simonson, Harold P. *The Closed Frontier: Studies in American Literary Tragedy*. New York: Holt, 1970.

Twain, Mark. *Adventures of Huckleberry Finn*. 1884. New York: Bantam, 1981.

The Mulatto Avenger in Twain and Faulkner:
Miscegenation and Identity in the South

"Every lady tells you who is the father of all the mulatto children in everybody's household, but those in her own she seems to think drop from the clouds . . ."
Mary Boykin Chestnut, March 18, 1861

When one end of a binary enjoys sole access to power, it becomes necessary for that society to clearly and immediately establish each individual's status within that binary (above all others) and all social interaction, and thus our sense of self/social identity, henceforth is determined by that status. In *Narrative of the Life of Frederick Douglass*, the author recalls being educated as well as better clothed and fed than some white children in Baltimore, yet laments to them, "'You will be free as soon as you are twenty-one, but I am a slave for life'" (Douglass 189). At this time in his life, Douglass lived in a larger house, wore nicer clothes, and ate better food than many whites. Also, unlike most slaves, he was learning how to read and write. In these categories, Douglass occupies a privileged position, yet he envies his young white friends' position in the more important binary of racial identity. He finds himself unable to follow Chestnutt's advice to the "genuine negro" to be satisfied with "the acquisition of wealth, and pursuit of learning" (5). For Douglass, who must be read as a voice for the multitude of enslaved men whose stories were not recorded, being black fundamentally defines his sense of identity; wealth and education pale in comparison.

Power distribution so one-sided cannot survive anomalies. As regimented as Southern society was along racial lines, its society and its structures could not cope with individuals who were neither white nor black. American Indians, Asians, and Latinos generally found no place within the discourse, arguably because their numbers constituted so small a percentage of the South's population, they didn't show up on the radar. But perhaps another factor was that the American South simply could not cope with the existence of groups outside the Black/White binary and so either lumped them in with the diminished term (black) or ignored their existence entirely.

Enter into this dichotomy the "mulatto," a term originally employed for individuals produced from a union of a European and an African parentage and later used as a classification for anyone whose racial heritage was not understood to be "pure."[1] My interest is in exploring the impact of racial uncertainty on the identity and self-conception of these individuals but not necessarily how society viewed them. Some of the most insightful explorations of racial and biracial identity issues in the South, either during or after slavery, can be found in the works of Mark Twain and William Faulkner. The racial consciousness of these two authors has long been scrutinized, and the attention is well founded. Race, specifically interaction between characters separated by the racial divide, is a vein through which each of these writers channeled his critique of Southern society. The implications and interpretations of these critiques provide fodder for critics and scholars that is not limited to either the original texts' time frames or topical content. For example, contemporary readings of Twain's *Adventures of Huckleberry Finn* can range from the speculative proposition of a homosexual relationship between Huck and Jim to Shelley Fishkin's intense research into the genesis of the text itself in *Was Huck Black?: Mark Twain and African-American Voices.* I believe that this resilience in the critical interest in Twain and Faulkner offers evidence that when these men wrote about race in their society, they tapped into a nearly subconscious racial awareness and conflict that persists in America to this day. An examination of four biracial characters—two in Twain's *Pudd'nhead Wilson* and two in Faulkner's *Go Down, Moses*—provides an intriguing portrait of the identity conflicts of biracial individuals in Southern society. It is important to see this portrait as separate from both white and black identity consciousness. Indeed, we can extrapolate DuBois's concept of a "double consciousness" and its impact on identity in *The Souls of Black Folks* and apply the theory to biracial characters. Such application suggests Twain and Faulkner's biracial characters would have struggled with perhaps as many as four competing senses of identity, as the two consciousnesses already inherent in their blackness would have striven with their "white" and "mulatto" identities. However, it is also understood that how a person is viewed by society impacts self-identification, and the condition of such individuals, as it was understood in their society, must briefly be examined before moving to an examination of the individuals themselves.

In his 1889 survey, "What Is a White Man?," Charles Chesnutt surveyed some of the ways in which the law worked to determine to which of the two groups (Black/White) a mulatto would be assigned. Chesnutt concludes that, while slight variation in state laws existed, ultimately a mulatto individual was more likely than not to be declared black under the law. Specifically, one needed to be at least 7/8 part (three consecutive generations of all-white parentage) white in order to "remove the disability of color" (5). This ratio would have been very difficult to apply in real time as there was obviously little or no way to identify the father in most cases. Fundamental conflicts in the structure of Southern society were seen by its citizens in daily paradoxes such as the ability of a white woman to bear black children contrasted with the inability of a black woman to have a white child.

The end of the Civil War brought the abolishment of slavery and, for a period lasting largely until the early 1890s, the suspension of most laws that prohibited interracial intercourse and "miscegenation"[2] (Wallenstein). However, as is the case in most civil-rights legislation, the societal reaction to interracial relations lagged far behind. Martha Hodes notes that societal judgment against and punishment of interracial couples increased dramatically in the years following 1865. Such liaisons had always remained largely anonymous as far as the law was concerned. Where they did occur, and were brought to court, testimony revealed that most members of the household as well as the neighborhood at large were well aware of such relationships and had been, in some cases, for several years (Hodes 3). Prevailing notions concerning the sexuality of blacks coupled with escalating insecurities of whites, especially those whose poverty matched or exceeded that of newly emancipated slaves, fueled the perception that even the modest social elevation of blacks brought with it a lowering of the white citizens' own positions. Thus there was a strong resistance to blacks entering the various facets of white society. Emancipation swept this constructed superiority away, and it was reaction to this shift in the power structure that led to the reinstatement of miscegenation laws, segregation, Jim Crow, and other forms of racial discrimination that had not existed in the antebellum South. In response to the change in legal status, the white population often felt that "extralegal control in the form of lethal violence now seemed the only way to retain that power" (Hodes 174). A reminder of the well-established increase in public lynching, largely absent from the slavery era, provides illustration enough on this point.

During work on *An American Dilemma*, Gunnar Myrdal and colleagues summarized the contrasting priorities that Americans held concerning these laws. It was found that "the white man's rank order of discriminations" had sexual relations between races at the top of the list of concerns followed in order by social interactions, segregation in schools, access to public forums (courts, churches, public transportation), and finally financial advancement. Wallenstein points out that when black men were surveyed for opinions in the same areas, their responses are almost completely reversed, with jobs coming first and interracial marriage dead last (67). These priorities led to escalating opposition to interracial relations and, in the case of black men consorting with white women, deadly violence. This violent opposition characterized the late nineteenth and early twentieth centuries in the post-war South.

It is generally agreed that miscegenation in the South, both before and after emancipation, involved white men and black women with far greater frequency than black men and white women, despite the fact that little or no official documentation of this exists. Explanation for the phenomena can take many forms. Essentially, white slaveholding men enjoyed a cultural, economic, political, and societal monopoly in the antebellum South. Few societal interactions could take place between such disparate parties as these men and their female slaves and be understood as anything other than manipulation. The end of slavery affected this monopoly in the power structures only in ending the condition of ownership of human beings. Instead of a fixed system there was now the possibility of access, but daily social interactions in the rural South were largely unaffected as the sharecropper replaced the slave. Although the plantation owner no longer had legal right to the physical body of another, he still controlled virtually all cultural resources and exercised this dominance within society much as he had in the previous century. And so the prevailing cultural attitudes and interactions remained relatively stable with regard to the primary binaries of race, class, and sex in the South despite the transition from slavery through Reconstruction and into the early twentieth century.

Miscegenation in the South was a reality that could not be faced, as illustrated by Mary Boykin Chestnut's observation which prefaces this study. Sex between slaves and masters of either race undermined religious and secular justifications for slavery. Transgression of the taboos of fornication (interracial marriage was not legal and so all interracial sexual contact was necessarily illicit) and racial purity offended Southern sexual beliefs long after emancipation. Biracialism, by its very existence, exposed the South's regimented society as a lie. The effect of this status on the identity of individuals already struggling to reconcile their own heritage must have been profound.

Twain and Faulkner

Mark Twain and William Faulkner used fiction as a vehicle of social commentary, as a way of ridiculing society for its faults by pointing out absurdities through a brand of fiction in which separations between tragedy and comedy are merely matters of perspective. William Clark observes that Faulkner and Twain both had a "genius for subjecting even the darkest social and personal concerns to transfiguring comic scrutiny" (97). Superiority is inherent in their mockery, as if it removed and set them above their society. In such writing emerges a "myth" of miscegenation, "in which the prostitution of black women's bodies and the subsequent exploitation [through slavery] of one's own flesh and blood become metaphors for the South's legacy of racial guilt" (98). Also emerging from this literature is the "mulatto avenger" who comes, through crises of self and societal identity, to symbolize the universality of human desire and the struggle for recognition, ultimately providing a damning critique of Southern race relations.

Pudd'nhead Wilson

Pudd'nhead Wilson was published, after heavy revision, in 1894, the same year that Louisiana became the last Southern state to reinstitute laws banning interracial sex and marriage. Originally begun as a comedy about a pair of Siamese twins touring rural Missouri, *Pudd'nhead* was redirected by the characters of Dawson's Landing and the social injustices with which Twain himself struggled. Through the exploration of race, society, and the residual trauma of slavery, Twain "anticipates one of the obsessive themes of Southern writing in the twentieth century" (Pettit 335). Even in his exploration into the tragedies that surrounded slavery, Twain's comedy is revealed in exaggeration and juxtaposition. The historical research of Paul Wallenstein reveals a South in which ⅞ white heritage qualified one as white under the law. Still, Twain's Roxana is 1/16 black and still a slave while her son, fathered by a white man so highly placed in the new Southern aristocracy that "'Dey ain't another nigger in dis town dat's as high-bawn,'" is blue-eyed and so indistinguishable from his "white" counterpart, whom Roxana serves as wet nurse following the mother's death, that Roxana succeeds in switching the two infants (Twain 55). The "white" child grows into a life of slavery and does not affect the narrative, while the "black" son grows up as Tom Driscoll, Twain's representation of the "American morally compromised by his associations with a fundamentally immoral system of slaveholding" (Ladd 120). He is a caricature of every negative consequence of privilege. He is cruel and boastful despite being physically inept and a coward. He is wealthy with a coming inheritance but also a petty thief. Pompous, spiteful, and arrogant, he enjoys others' embarrassment and discomfort. He actually sells his own mother down the river. He is Twain's comic "mulatto avenger," exposing the tragedy of a slave society not through suffering or endurance but through active participation that can only engender disgust from the reader. His identity crisis upon learning he is a mulatto is an episode rather than a lifelong condition. Through Tom's lamentations of the "awful difference made between black and white," Twain poses the most obvious and unanswerable question of how it is possible for a human to be "created" into slavery (55). The exaggerated comedy of Tom soon returns in subsequent barn-loft scenes as he, and his mother, come to believe that all of the character flaws learned during the privileged life of a Southern slaveholding man stem from the fact that "'thirty-one parts o' you is white, en on'y one part nigger, en dat po' little part is yo' *soul*'" (88). Twain chooses to make the proportion of racial blending so absurdly one-sided in order to expose the tragedy of this belief while maintaining Tom's status as a comic "mulatto avenger."

Through this exposure, even Twain cannot help but create the tragic "mulatto avenger" in Roxana. The tragedy of Roxana is not only that she is a slave and unfortunate enough to be Tom's mother but that she has internalized the power structure of her society and believes it is the "nigger" in Tom that causes him to refuse to duel Luigi and disgrace his birth. She consistently holds to this belief whereas Tom is allowed to question whether or not a fundamental difference existed. She refers to Tom's father, Cecil Essex, in unquestionably favorable terms and even constructs an elaborate genealogy for Tom, drawing from the highest ranks of European, African, and Native American societies, while her indignation at his behavior is not for her own sake as a mother but for the absent white father. Tom and Roxana are placed on opposite sides of the binary and it wasn't blood that determined the difference for Twain; it was society, the social interactions that create identity, in this case creating a contemptible white man and a tragic slave woman. This tragedy is evident throughout the novel as Roxana's initial attempt to subvert the power structure results in the protracted suffering of not only herself and her child but the "white" child, and illustrates that Twain "was convinced that the greater tragedy of the South was not miscegenation, but the curse that white Southerners had placed upon it" (Pettit 322). If Twain truly believed that the curse of miscegenation had its origin with the white Southerner, Faulkner exposed how this curse came to be internalized and perpetuated by black Southerners as well.

Go Down, Moses

William Faulkner incorporated biracial characters into the framework of many stories and novels and was able to develop them more intricately because his literary focus remained more regionalized than Twain's. In *Go Down, Moses* (1942), the addition of the nearly universal taboo of incest to the Southern taboo of miscegenation serves to link the two in the reader's consciousness.

Among other themes, the novel traces the history of the McCaslin plantation and the genealogy of the white McCaslin/Edmonds family and the slaves/sharecroppers whose heritage is linked first by the miscegenation occurring between the patriarch Lucius Quintus Carothers McCaslin and Eunice, a mulatto slave purchased from New Orleans for the implicit purpose of concubinage, and then by a case of incest involving Lucius and the daughter of that union (Faulkner 259). Faulkner constructs his narrative so that the male children of both the black and white members of Lucius's patronage are frequently born in the same year, and the death or absence of the white mother leads to the two boys growing up together as brothers (111). The heightened awareness of familial relationships, always a noteworthy factor in Faulkner's work, creates an environment in which the self/societal identity of the mulatto son becomes especially provocative.

Faulkner uses the neighboring Beauchamp plantation to illustrate the cultural context surrounding miscegenation in the novel. Terrel (Tomey's Turl), the son of Tomasina and her father, Lucius Quintus Carothers McCaslin, and owned by his half-brothers/uncles Buck and Buddy, runs off to Hubert Beauchamp's plantation to see Tennie, a slave he is later allowed to marry. While discussing Terrel with Buck, Hubert Beauchamp says he "not only wouldn't buy Tomey's Turl, he wouldn't have that damn white half-McCaslin on his place even as a free gift" (6). Terrel's nickname comes from the fact that, officially, his father is unknown and so he is named after his mother (Tomey a shortened Tomasina). But the neighbor, Hubert, fully understands the situation and, while he is not going to report his neighbor to the police, he wants nothing to do with it himself. Years later, when a relationship he has with a mulatto "cook" is exposed, Beauchamp protests, "'They're free now! They're folks too just like we are!'" but his sister is inconsolable: "'Even in my dress . . . That's why! My mother's house! Defiled'" (289). Sexual relations that crossed the Black/White societal boundary remained taboo long after emancipation, and Beauchamp's appeal to the woman's legal status is especially hollow as she is ejected from the household with no name and no voice. Although legally equal, she receives only the benefit of anonymity: she will escape punishment. This woman and her treatment are presented as the typical or culture-wide treatment of these individuals. Together they present the larger Southern context that Faulkner is able to subvert through the subsequent portrayal of the McCaslin plantation.

Terrel and Tennie marry and have two sons that survive infancy. The youngest is named Lucas Quintus Carothers McCaslin Beauchamp. His paternal grandfather's plantation has passed into the hands of his cousin "Cass" Edmonds whose son "Zack" Edmonds is born in the same year as Lucas. Lucas's naming is important in that it implies his father, had his character's story been elaborated, would have experienced the same identity conflicts Faulkner presents in Lucas. Faulkner also alludes to the generational impact of miscegenation when Lucas and Zack have sons born in the same year, anticipating another revolution in the cycle. His name assures that Lucas will be aware of his white blood, and his struggle to reconcile how he is both wronged and better for it dominates his interactions with Zack and Southern society as a whole.

Lucas, like Roxana, believes in the power of blood and derives a sense of pride, superiority even, from his close blood association with Lucius McCaslin, even over Zack because Lucas's McCaslin blood comes to him in an all-male, direct line. Yet there is conflict in his conception of his grandfather as Lucius McCaslin exercises his power monopoly on society like no other character. Lucius is presented as a mythic figure of nearly biblical supremacy, first obtaining the land itself, and its native son in the character of Sam Fathers, from the native population, and then populating that land with those he begat, or owned, or both. Lucas's respect for this use of power is revealed as he remembers that Zack's father, Cass, is a better man than Zack if only because he was "a McCaslin only by the distaff yet having enough of old Carothers McCaslin in his veins to take the land from the true heir [Ike] simply because he wanted it and knew he could use it better and was strong enough, ruthless enough, old Carothers McCaslin enough . . ." to take it (44). Later, after the fight with Zack, Lucas reflects, "*So I reckon I aint got old Carothers' blood for nothing, after all. Old Carothers,* he thought. *I needed him and he come and spoke for me*" (57).

Yet Lucius McCaslin also represents the power structures of white society that allow, in even the absence of slavery, Zack McCaslin to take Lucas's wife and, without a word spoken between the three, institute her into his house upon the death of his wife and keep her there for six months. Lucius McCaslin as the head of the family, the instigator of miscegenation, and the representative of white power in the South becomes symbolic of the structures of race and identity, the absence of which Lucas knows would see him occupying Zack's position of power in the patrilineal hierarchy. Despite this familial linkage between Zack and Lucas, Lucas understands that there is nothing his unacknowledged McCaslin blood can do for him within the power structure that blood created when he asks, "How to God . . . can a black man ask a white man to please not lay down with his black wife? And even if he could ask it, how to God can the white man promise he wont?'" (58). He is not only despairing of his situation but exposing Faulkner's awareness of prevailing Southern notions of race and sexuality in which he recognized a fundamental inequality that persisted long after legalized inequality.

Ultimately, Lucas does confront Zack and demand the return of his wife on the basis that "'I'm a nigger. But I'm a man too. I'm more than just a man. The same thing made my pappy that made your grandmaw'" (46). Through this demand and Zack's obedience, Lucas asserts himself against Zack as a brother or an equal would. But he still has to contend with Zack's role as Lucius's heir and the two men's positions within the overall cultural dynamic. Lucas is aware of the larger conflict as he states, "'I know you aint going to [run]. Because all you got to beat is me. I got to beat Old Carothers'" (53). Zack is facing a man; Lucas is facing an entire system. To Lucas, Zack is no longer an issue to himself because, "'I done already beat you. . . . It's old Carothers. Get your pistol, white man." It's Carothers, the symbol, the white man whom Lucas is facing, and he addresses him appropriately. Zack, the man Lucas had "accepted as his peer to the extent of intending to kill him" is no longer his foe. And Zack accepts this role, embraces the power system that transcends the humanity of both men, men born in the same year, raised together as brothers, as their sons would also be, when he stands opposite his bed from Lucas, the pistol lying between them, and orders Lucas to "come on then" as a white man orders a "nigger that's got out of hand" (54). The physical struggle is one-sided; Lucas's superiority over Zack is unquestioned. Though Lucas cries at the onset, both men understand that he cries "not to the white man" but at the history and society that have brought the men to this point. And as Lucas checks the breech of the revolver to ensure he has a bullet for himself as well, Zack realizes fully for the first time that "he cant even see me right now" and he knows that Lucas is not facing him but the specter of his grandfather, the curse of his blood (55). Standing opposite Zack, holding the pistol, Lucas admonishes him, "You thought to beat me with old Carothers, like Cass Edmonds done Isaac: used old Carothers to make Isaac give up the land," but Lucas doesn't own any land:

> "All I got to give up is McCaslin blood that rightfully aint
> even mine or at least aint worth much since old Caroth-
> ers never seemed to miss much what he give to Tomey
> that night that made my father. And if this is what that
> McCaslin blood has brought me, I dont want it neither.
> And if the running of it into my black blood never hurt
> him any more than the running of it out is going to hurt
> me, it wont even be old Carothers that had the most
> pleasure." (55)

This passage reveals that the fundamental conflict for Lucas is the stock he places in his white heritage, despite knowing it meant nothing to its provider. His anger stems from understanding he is totally devalued in the system which he buys into and so he tries to find a way out of it, thinking, "'Say I just uses the last one and beat you and old Carothers both,'" indicating that he will commit suicide there in Zack's bedroom, a mulatto avenger exposing the South through an act of despairing agency by taking the last course left available to the slave as he plans to "'leave you something to think about now and then'" (56). Zack realizes what Lucas's suicide would mean to the legitimacy of his societies' Hegelian structure, or maybe by this point he has transcended the binaries that Lucas is struggling with and again sees Lucas as his kinsman and neighbor of nearly a quarter century. Whether it is to prevent Lucas from murder or suicide is unknown, but Zack begins to spring across the bed, and as they grapple again for the pistol, Lucas "jammed the pistol against the white man's side and pulled the trigger and flung the white man from him all in one motion, hearing as he did so the light, dry, incredibly loud click of the miss-fire" (56).

Whether the miss-fire is interpreted as Lucas's ultimate helplessness against the system or Faulkner's underlying belief in the random and careless way the universe deals with all men, it ends the crises for Lucas and Zack, as if pulling the trigger is enough for Lucas to destroy Old Carothers from his mind and still allow his heir to live. The men do not speak of the encounter again. The issue seems to die away so completely that Roth, Zack's son, is left to guess at what has transpired between the two men years after his father dies. Within that reflection Faulkner presents a Lucas far-removed from the panting animal-eyed youth in the bedroom striving to the point of death with his heritage: "it was as if he were not only impervious to that blood, he was indifferent to it. He didn't even need to strive with it. He didn't even have to bother to defy it. . . . Instead of being at once the battleground and victim of the two strains, he was a vessel." He also recalls that Lucas, whose name was so deliberately chosen, always "referred to his father [Zack] as Mr. Edmonds, never as Mister Zack, as the other negroes did" and how he deliberately avoided having to address him "by any name whatever" when they spoke directly (101).

Later in pagination, but earlier by far in chronology, Faulkner returns to the issue of Lucas's name, as Ike and Cass note the shift from "Lucius" to "Lucas," and Ike concludes that he was "not refusing . . . not denying, declining . . . because he used three quarters of it; but simply taking the name and changing . . . making it no longer the white man's but his own, by himself composed, himself selfprogenitive and nominate" (269). Isaac "Ike" McCaslin is the character through which is voiced most completely the belief that the individual could transcend the identity conflicts represented in the mulatto avenger—both through this explanation of naming and through his interaction with Sam Fathers.

Sam Fathers acts as an example of the earlier-noted tendency to label biracial individuals black rather than white despite obvious indications that neither category fits. As the son of Ikkemotubbe, a Chickasaw chief, and a "quadroon slave woman,"[3] Sam is a slave despite being only ⅛ black by virtue of his mother's status, and the two of them are sold to Carothers McCaslin by the boy's father when Sam is two years old; however, the character doesn't enter the narrative until he is already an old man (160). Sam occupies a singular position among the former slaves on the McCaslin plantation in that he resides among them but rarely associates with them and is occasionally openly hostile toward them.

Sam is not a sharecropper or day laborer and operates, at his apparent leisure, as a blacksmith/carpenter in a shop at the back of the plantation. Sam and Lucas are linked together not only in their privileged status within the community but also by the way they interact with the plantation owners. Lucas wouldn't address Zack Edmonds by a name which would honor his privileged position. Sam seems to go even further in Ike's memory and treats Major de Spain and all white men with "gravity and dignity and without servility" and Cass Edmonds especially "not only as one man to another but as an older man to a younger" (164). At the same time, the plantation owner, as well as Uncle Buck and Uncle Buddy before him, seem also willing to accept that no one "ever told him [Sam] to do or not do anything that he ever paid any attention to" or ever dared demand "I want this finished by sundown" (162).

At the same time, Sam does not wholly escape the type of conflicts that characterize Lucas and Tom Driscoll. When he enters the house for the first time in Ike's memory, he does so as a "house servant would have done" and of course his hat is in his hand (166). More striking is Sam's reference to Major de Spain as "master" after the bear hunt—a verbal submission Lucas universally avoided (234). The implication is that despite having never been subject to treatment as a slave by the McCaslin family, Sam has nevertheless adapted to the structure. The assumption of a privileged status must now be questioned given these contradictions in the interactions between Sam and white men such as Cass Edmonds and Major de Spain. I believe these contradictions arise from the contradictions within Sam himself.

Sam's Chickasaw heritage is openly acknowledged as the reason for his privileged position as Cass Edmonds refers to him as a primitive whose subconscious rebels against domestication as a caged bear would (161). In Cass's estimation Sam derives not only power but shame from his blood. In statements that link Sam to Twain's Roxana, Cass tells Ike that Sam feels "betrayed" by his blood, that the blood of his fathers and chiefs had been betrayed unintentionally by his mother. His blood has not been betrayed by the "black blood" alone but even by the "white blood" that enslaved it. Like Lucas, Sam is "himself his own battleground, the scene of his own vanquishment and the mausoleum of his defeat" (162). Cass's primitivistic elevation of Sam's "Chickasaw blood" over his black and white blood unfortunately leads him back into the same misrecognition that Zack and Lucas experienced and prevents him from understanding the deeper source of Sam's conflict.

In an interesting presentation of the "Noble Savage," Sam becomes Ike's mentor, turning the boy into the type of white-native frontiersman common in American literature and folklore. What sets this education apart from other literary relationships of the type is that Ike acquires not only physical skills but an understanding of the deep structure of Southern society. That same insight which allowed him to understand the implications of Lucas's name beyond any other character lets him see something more in Sam than the "wild man" Cass Edmonds sees. Instead, Ike attributes the betrayal of Sam's blood directly to Sam's father. The connection with the land that is a necessary component of Cass's conception of Sam as primitivism's "Noble Savage" is broken because "on the instant when Ikkemotubbe discovered, realized that he could sell it [the land] for money . . . it ceased ever to have been his forever" (246). Ike sees the connection to "the land which they had all held and used" as the bond between him and his people "not only whites but the black too" and that his grandfather, Carothers McCaslin, has been effectively "penalizing his own sons" not only through human bondage they had to inherit, but the burden of "owning" land itself (256–258). It becomes the underlying reason why Sam only once in his life approaches Cass's house and why Lucas and Zack cannot successfully coexist, despite the existence of slavery, without a final confrontation. Ike is then able to link his own family's conception of ownership, and being owned by the land and in sense by landowning itself, with the South as a whole during the Civil War by concluding,

> "Who else could have declared a war against a power
> with ten times the area and a hundred times the men and
> a thousand times the resources, except men who could
> believe that all necessary to conduct a successful war was
> not acumen nor shrewdness nor politics nor diplomacy
> nor money nor even integrity and simple arithmetic but
> just love of land and courage." (276)

The identity conflicts which arise from mulatto characters in these works have the tendency to radiate from the characters themselves and impact other characters in the novel. Characters whose personal racial identities are fixed and immutable are thrown off in their interactions with these characters. These interactions lead Ike to forsake his inheritance and live the ascetic life of a huntsman/hermit despite residing in a town home with a faceless wife. He becomes, in a sense, even more removed than Sam could ever have been exactly because of the absent excuse of racial separation. He becomes unable to connect with members of his own family. And so Sam Fathers ultimately remains a specter in the woods in which the McCaslin men hunt, no more real than the semi-mystical buck Sam shows to both Ike and Cass in their youth (180). Despite his obvious association with the idea of the "mulatto avenger," Sam also seems unable to totally reconcile his blood with his self-identity, and so it seems Lucas becomes a more complete picture of the fully developed biracial character.

Lucas's transformation and eventual triumph over his blood gives his story in *Go Down, Moses* a much more satisfying ending for the reader than *Pudd'nhead Wilson* allows, because the main problems posed by Twain were never resolved. The defeat of a mulatto criminal by the established white power structure does more to reinforce frustrations with that society than a closer examination may yield. In Faulkner, we see that Zack and Lucas were very much caught in the same system, and Zack remains a far more sympathetic character than Tom Driscoll ever could be, even after Tom is exposed as mulatto. At the same time, Lucas, by confronting and triumphing over his inherited identity conflicts, avoids the tragedy inherent in a character like Roxana.

Notes

1. There is some argument about the term's genesis, but it is generally agreed to be of Spanish or Portuguese origin, meaning "a small mule." The term, as it is used in America to describe persons with both black and white heritage, was widely accepted in American culture, literature, and law for generations, but has fallen out of favor in recent years as some now consider it, its origins and past applications, pejorative. Terms such as "biracial," "multiracial," or "mixed heritage" are preferred. For the sake of clarity, I use the term used in the source material being examined.

2. For all its association with the South, the genesis of miscegenation, the term at least, took place in the North as part of a Democratic propaganda campaign against the re-election of Lincoln. However, it soon gained popularity with segregationists and white supremacists which continues to this day. It is understandable then that many politically correct scholars have abandoned it as a term. The word itself comes from the Latin *miscere*, "to mix," and *genus*, "race," and has consistently retained that meaning. For this reason, as well as the lack of a more accurate/acceptable term, I use it in this study.

3. "Quadroon" is a term of Spanish origin designating ¼ black heritage.

Chesnutt, Charles W. "What Is a White Man?" *The Independent* 41 (May 1889): 5–6.

Clark, William Bedford. "Twain and Faulkner: Miscegenation and the Comic Muse." In *Faulkner and Humor: Faulkner and Yoknapatawpha*, edited by Doreen Fowler and Ann J. Abadie. Jackson: UP of Mississippi, 1984. 97–109.

Douglass, Frederick. *Narrative of the Life of Frederick Douglas.* In *A Norton Anthology: The Literature of the American South*, edited by William L. Andrews. New York: Norton, 1998. 189.

Faulkner, William. *Go Down, Moses.* 1942. New York: Vintage, 1991.

Hodes, Martha. *White Women, Black Men: Illicit Sex in the Nineteenth-Century South.* New Haven: Yale UP, 1997.

Ladd, Barbara. *Nationalism and the Color Line in George W. Cable, Mark Twain, and William Faulkner.* Baton Rouge: Louisiana State UP, 1996.

Myrdal, Gunnar. *An American Dilemma: The Negro Problem and Modern Democracy.* New York: Harper & Bros., 1944.

Pettit, Arther G. "The Black and White Curse: *Puddn'head Wilson* and Miscegenation." In *Mark Twain: Pudd'nhead Wilson and Those Extraordinary Twins*, edited by Sidney E. Berger. New York: Norton, 1980. 322–336.

Twain, Mark. *Pudd'nhead Wilson.* 1894. New York: Oxford UP, 1992.

Wallenstein, Peter. "Reconstruction, Segregation, and Miscegenation: Interracial Marriage and the Law in the Lower South, 1865–1900." *American Nineteenth Century History* 6.1 (March 2005): 57–76.

Can Affectation Lead to Freedom?:
Faulkner's *Absalom, Absalom!* and Twain's *Pudd'nhead Wilson*

American authors in the nineteenth century created characters who "are significant in that they are social and sociological indices" (Bullock 78) of the struggles they faced. Many American authors were imaginatively nourished by the culture they experienced, even when they were politically opposed to its ideology or practices. The use of mulatto characters by William Faulkner and Mark Twain brings the issue of affectation, or passing, to the forefront and exposes the complications of racism and the miscegenation anxieties of the South. Before the Civil War and the emancipation of slaves, the "one drop" rules of the 1830s relegated anyone with African "blood" to slave status, regardless of their outward appearance. In the face of these racist views, slaves who could pass for white attempted to use deception and affectation to improve their status in society and gain freedom. William Faulkner and Mark Twain examine the issue of race and status as well as the destructive consequences that arise when mulattos attempt to subvert the power of whites through affectation. *Absalom, Absalom!*'s Eulalia Bon and *Pudd'nhead Wilson*'s Roxy are two characters that use their sons for such endeavors. Thomas Sutpen's abandonment of Eulalia Bon and their son Charles in *Absalom, Absalom!* and Roxy's subjugated status in *Pudd'nhead Wilson* act as catalysts for these women's decision to challenge, albeit subversively, the societal conventions of the South. Unfortunately, for their sons, this subversion does not yield the positive results they intend; instead, Chambers/"Tom" murders Judge Driscoll and is sold "down the river," and Charles Bon is murdered by Henry Sutpen, his half-brother.

In Twain's original conception of *Pudd'nhead Wilson*, "Tom Driscoll is the *white* child of Percy Driscoll" (Ladd 106) with all the negative characteristics that remain in the final version of the novel: gambling, drinking, and moral indecision, but without the "fatal drop" (Ladd 106) of Roxy's slave blood. In the second stage of writing, the focus shifted from the story of Siamese twins to "Tom's racial classification, his indebtedness, Judge Driscoll's murder, the ensuing trial, and the final revelation of Tom Driscoll's racial identity to the townspeople" (Ladd 106). Twain's final addition to the novel was David Wilson's story and the use of fingerprinting to prove that Roxy had switched the babies. In switching her son with the son of her master, Roxy subverts the Southern ideals of racial segregation and sets a series of events into motion that only she can alter. Roxy's treatment of Chambers and Tom reflects the social conventions of not only Dawson's Landing but the South as a whole:

> Tom got all the petting, Chambers got none. Tom got all the delicacies, Chambers got mush and milk, and clabber without sugar. In consequence Tom was a sickly child and Chambers wasn't. Tom was "fractious," as Roxy called it, and overbearing; Chambers was meek and docile. (Twain 935)

Roxy succeeds in "[e]nacting the central tenet of her community; Roxy treats the ostensible black child as property and satisfies the 'white' child's every whim" (Mitchell 302). In treating the children as she does, not only does Roxy fail to escape the racist standards of society, she actually legitimizes them. Lee Mitchell asserts, "The novel's power is that her [Roxy's] trick tricks her much as racial assumptions trick everyone" (302). Over time, Roxy is faced with the realization that "the little counterfeit rift of separation between imitation-slave and imitation-master widened and widened, and became an abyss" (Twain 936). This abyss becomes complete and she is later relegated to the position of chattel when Tom plans to sell her down the river to keep her from revealing the truth of his parentage. Tom feels no inherent loyalty toward Roxy; she complains: "'En he's al'ays callin' me nigger-wench, en hussy, en all dem mean names, when I's doin' de very bes' I kin. Oh, Lord, I done so much for him—I lift' him away up to what he is—en dis is what I git for it'" (939). Roxy's plan to improve her child's position in life has not resulted in any benefit for her; instead, her son has become the embodiment of the racist white mentality, which Tom developed while being raised in white privilege.

However, Tom has not made the most of the advantages his position has offered him. He does poorly at Yale, develops an unctuous attitude, and becomes a reckless gambler. Twain uses Tom's progressive degeneration to bring the nature-nurture dilemma to the forefront of the reader's mind. Barbara Ladd references an excised portion of text from *Pudd'nhead Wilson* in which Tom contemplates the knowledge of his "slave" and "bastard" designations. Tom concludes: "the nigger blood degraded from original courage to cowardice by decades and generations of insult & outrage inflicted in circumstances which forbade reprisals, & made mute & meek endurance the only refuge & defense" (114). Tom's thoughts point to the dominant white belief that Negro blood was polluted, and the justification for the "one drop" designation was sufficient to classify one as a slave with all its negative implications of savagery. However, Tom also condemns his white blood in this excised portion of the novel:

> Whence came that in him which was high, & whence that which was base? That which was high came from either blood, & was the monopoly of neither color; but that which was base was the white blood in him debased by the brutalizing effects of a long-drawn heredity of slave-owning, with the habit of abuse which the possession of irresponsible power always creates & perpetuates, by the law of human nature. (Ladd 114)

Although not present in the final text of *Pudd'nhead Wilson*, this passage points to Twain's position on the nature-nurture issue and the contention that Tom's downfall was not an issue of his Negro blood but the result of his upbringing as a white slave owner in a society of privilege that indulged his every whim.

Tom's life changes almost immediately after Roxy reveals his true parentage. He struggles with his identity and what this new knowledge means: "'A nigger! I am a nigger! Oh, I wish I was dead'" (Twain 968). He begins processing what this revelation means for him in the global world as well: "'Why were niggers *and* whites made? What crime did the uncreated first nigger commit that the curse of birth was decreed for him? And why is this awful difference made between white and black?'" (968). After killing Judge Driscoll, because he fears being excluded from the Judge's will, Tom accepts his fate and is sent to prison before eventually being sold "down the river." Meanwhile, Chambers must find a way to adjust to his new position in society as the true Driscoll heir and a white man.

Faulkner's mulatto, Charles Bon, is a more mysterious creation because his racial identity is based on the projections of various characters. While Bon's designation as "white Negro" may be logical in light of Sutpen's abandonment of Creole Eulalia Bon after discovering that she contains African-American blood, there is no discussion to substantiate Bon's designation as such until Quentin's narrative imagines the conversation between Henry and Charles toward the novel's conclusion. Henry Sutpen's exact motivation for killing Charles Bon also remains unclear: "whether the 'purity' that Henry is seen as protecting is constructed in terms that are nationalistic, familial, or racial depends on who the speaker is or, rather, *when* he is" (Ladd 141). Rosa, Jason, and Quentin each have their own visions of Bon based on their view of society as events evolved prior to and after the Civil War. At first, Bon is labeled "a mysterious French Creole, but as Quentin's story unfolds, Bon is transformed from colonialist Creole, into Sutpen's elder son, into 'the nigger that's going to sleep with your sister'" (Ladd 149).

Charles Bon wants to be recognized, by Sutpen, as his son and is more intent on claiming his rightful place at Sutpen's Hundred than in the actual love affair with Judith. She has become, for Charles, a means of acquiring some portion of the estate to which he is entitled. Bon's use of Judith to gain access to Sutpen's Hundred, and the legitimacy he feels belongs to him, is reminiscent of Sutpen's own determination to marry Ellen and solidify his place in Jefferson society. Bon demands recognition as Sutpen's son and the benefits of that designation, for which he will abandon his relationship with Judith. However, Bon's ultimatum is not successful and leads to a Christmas argument between Henry and Sutpen when Sutpen reveals that Charles Bon is not white. This revelation changes the course of the novel because "Bon's claims to the white estate are rendered absolutely monstrous, and Bon is transformed from alienated son into 'the nigger who's going to sleep with your sister,' an agent for the destruction of the white estate" (Ladd 150). Charles Bon represents what was feared most by the white Southerner after 1890: "the gradual usurpations of political, familial, and economic purity—that is, legitimacy, recognition by the national body, or father—by a mulatto brother or brother-in-law, a usurpation almost always associated with the degeneration of a proud civilization into a 'mongrel' future" (Ladd 151).

The possibility that an unrecognized and unrecognizable black son might "pass" unknown into the white family and violate laws against miscegenation as well as incest was a central concern for many Southerners. Faulkner finally provides the reader with insight into the conversation between Henry and Charles, as Quentin sees it, toward the end of the novel:

> —So it's the miscegenation, not the incest, which you can't bear.
> Henry doesn't answer.
> —And he sent me no word? He did not ask you to send me to him? No word to me, no word at all? That was all he had to do, now, today; four years ago or at any time during the four years. That was all. He would not have needed to ask it, require it, of me. I would have offered it. I would have said, I will never see her again before he could have asked it of me. He did not have to do this, Henry. He didn't need to tell you I am a nigger to stop me. He could have stopped me without that, Henry.
> —No! Henry cries—No! No! I will—I'll—(285)

Bon continues to question Henry by explaining that he has no other choice, other than to return to Sutpen's Hundred and marry Judith because he had waited long enough. Henry, with a gun pointed at Charles, pleads with him: *"You are my brother,"* to which Charles replies: *"No I'm not. I'm the nigger that's going to sleep with your sister. Unless you stop me, Henry"* (286). Sutpen's refusal to acknowledge his mulatto son and give him a name is exactly what precipitates the dual threats of incest and miscegenation and results in the ultimatum with which Bon challenges Henry. In this climactic scene between Henry and Charles at the gate to Sutpen's Hundred, the segregationist ideal is enforced when Henry kills Charles and saves his sister and the family from miscegenation. However, this preservation does not lead to "the laying of foundations for a sunny future" (Ladd 153) for the Sutpens, as radical racist ideology would envision it. Ladd comments: "Instead of progress, redemption from the sins of the fathers, and transcendence of history, one is left with degeneration, damnation, and submergence into history" (153). Henry acts on behalf of his white family to protect his father's design and what he envisions as the purity of the bloodline with tragic results that cement the destruction of Sutpen's design.

Faulkner and Twain create the characters of Charles Bon and Tom Driscoll to elucidate the South's miscegenation anxieties. Barbara Ladd says, "The consequence—in . . . these works—is the exile or death of . . . 'imitation white'" (112). Charles Bon meets his end at the hands of Henry Sutpen who must protect his sister, not from the potentially incestuous relationship with Charles Bon but from a relationship with a mulatto. This prompts him to murder Charles Bon, despite their friendship and previous allegiance. Twain's novel concludes with Tom's life sentence for the murder of Judge Driscoll and his subsequent sale "down the river." Despite the intentions of their mothers, neither of these characters is able to improve his life or usurp the power of the South, which remained officiously impregnable and immune to manipulation long after these novels were written.

Works Cited

Bullock, Penelope. "The Mulatto in American Fiction." *Phylon (1940–1956)* 6.1 (1945): 78–82.

Faulkner, William. *Absalom, Absalom!*. 1936. New York: Vintage, 1990.

Ladd, Barbara. *Nationalism and the Color Line in George W. Cable, Mark Twain, and William Faulkner*. Baton Rouge: Louisiana State UP, 1996.

Mitchell, Lee Clark. "'De Nigger in You': Race or Training in *Pudd'nhead Wilson?" Nineteenth-Century Literature* 42.3 (1987): 295–312.

Twain, Mark. *Mississippi Writings*. New York: Library of America, 1982.

Step Right Up:
Spectacle and Showmanship in *Pudd'nhead Wilson* and *The Hamlet*

In the preface to his first autobiography in 1855, Phineas Taylor Barnum began with the obligatory authorial statement expressing modesty and reluctance in writing his life story. He then offered a lengthy list of his accomplishments to date:

> I have been a farmer's boy and a merchant, a clerk and a manager, a showman and a bank-president. I have been in jails and in palaces; have known poverty and abundance; have travelled over a large portion of two Continents; have encountered all varieties of men, have seen every phase of human character; and I have on several occasions been in imminent personal peril. (*Life of P.T. Barnum* n.p.)

Though designed to sell himself as a representative striving American and pillar of Yankee virtue, *The Life of P.T. Barnum* exalts in equal measure the conventional pursuit of wealth through the mercantile system and the high adventure of travel, intrigue, and danger. Though even he could not have anticipated it, Barnum's well-publicized life bridges two key literary depictions of showmanship and spectacle. The rise of Flem Snopes in William Faulkner's *The Hamlet* uncannily follows Barnum's professional path and upward mobility. The son of an itinerant farmer with a reputation for incinerating landlords' barns, Flem assumes a job at a country store, rising from clerk to supervisor before moving to the county seat and, after a series of legally dubious deals, taking over the presidency of a local bank in the sequel *The Town*. (He even does Barnum one better by marrying the boss's daughter.) Less obviously, Snopes accomplishes all this with a sense of silent showmanship, built on rumor and speculation, that seems the polar opposite of Barnum's extroverted bravado and ballyhoo.

Likewise, Barnum's much-dramatized series of ups and downs resembles the figurative and literal trials of the Capellos, the Italian twins who excite the denizens of Dawson's Landing in Mark Twain's *Pudd'nhead Wilson and Those Extraordinary Twins*. Like performers in a traveling show, Angelo and Luigi arrive in town suddenly, for no discernible reason, to great fanfare. They thrill their new neighbors with tales of "jails and palaces," "poverty and abundance," and the perils they have faced around the world. Their presence is alternately celebrated, debated, and complicated by questions of citizenship, until they find themselves on the wrong end of a gun in a farcical duel and the wrong side of the law in a murder trial.

Like Flem, the ultimate success of the twins is predicated on the dynamics of innuendo, and what Neil Harris termed the "operational aesthetic." As Barnum related in his autobiographies, popular audiences did not mind trickery—or even the occasional outright hoax—if it was delivered with panache and followed up quickly by an opportunity to discuss the spectacle with their peers. Once immersed in the event, paying customers could apply their technical knowledge in an attempt to either solve the enigma or decry the hoax. Barnum's genius was in encouraging the masses to actively question the machinery behind his spectaculars; they could ponder the creation, enactment, and effect of their entertainment, and then come back for more.

In his first extant letter home, dated August 24, 1853, seventeen-year-old Samuel Clemens writes to his mother from New York City, having decided on a whim to leave St. Louis, escape the printing shop run by his brother Orion, and seek his fortune. After assuring his mother of his safety and well-being, Clemens spends the majority of the letter remarking, with undisguised wonder, about a "curiosity" he has seen on the streets of Gotham. "I don't know what to call it," he writes.

> Two beings, about like common people, with the exception of their faces, which are more like the "phiz" of an orang-outang, than human. They are white, though, like other people . . . They were found in the island of Borneo (the only ones of the species ever discovered,) about twenty years ago . . . . I watched them about an hour and they were "tramping" the whole time. (Twain, *Letters* 4)[1]

If the signature trope of the young man on the make in the big city is Benjamin Franklin entering Philadelphia with a few coins in his pocket and two loaves of bread tucked beneath his arms, the young Clemens represents himself as Franklin's ironic twin. Rather than exhibit the behaviors of the model citizen—saving his money, obeying his elders, laboring long hours at the printing press—young Samuel prefers to spend a seemingly unproductive hour gawking at the "tramping" of a low-rent street performance, making note of the Wild Men spectacle for use in the letter. In this extraordinary description of his entry into urban life, the apprentice/author spells out his fascination with human oddities and their liminal space in a rapidly industrializing world. Initially, he assures his mother (and himself) that the performers are "like common people" and "white . . . like other people." Then he exhaustively lists their alien features and notes the staged performance of primitivism and difference between the two Borneo brothers: "One is the best natured in the world, while the other would tear a stranger to pieces," while observing they "look like one mass of muscle" (Twain, *Letters* 4). Other than brief mentions in his message of the Crystal Palace anchoring that year's World's Fair and the colossal Marble Palace store, the street show is the sole New York landmark Clemens deemed worthy of writing home about.[2]

This fascination with popular spectacle re-emerges throughout Twain's career: in occasional newspaper pieces, the travel writings of *Following the Equator*, the short stories "The Man Who Corrupted Hadleyburg" and "The Stolen White Elephant," and woven in the narrative fabric of *Pudd'nhead Wilson*. In the persons of *Wilson*'s Capello twins, Twain constructs an imaginative composite of the Italian conjoined twins Giacomo and Giovanni Tocci, Barnum's original Siamese twins Chang and Eng Bunker, the Corsican Brothers of legend, and feuding brothers going back to Cain and Abel. The Toccis were an especially timely choice; the Italian twins ceased their touring of Europe and the United States and "retired" from performing in 1891, at the age of sixteen. (Their father first put them on display when they were a month old.) Their differences were the stuff of legend (and farce). While, like Angelo and Luigi, the Toccis had their wildly different personalities brought out by alcohol, it was in fact Giacomo, the teetotaler of the pair, who had the explosive temper, to the consternation of the imbibing, well-mannered Giovanni (Hartzman 92–93). Twain may also have recalled the most celebrated version of the "Wild Men from Borneo" act he viewed in New York City. In his letter to Jane Clemens, Samuel offers a catalog of the brothers' physical attributes and feats of strength. Yet he elides an important facet of their presentation: though born to English parents as Hiram and Barney Davis, impresario Lyman Warner dubbed his Wild Men "Waino" (good) and "Plutano" (bad) and exaggerated the natural differences in their demeanors to enhance conflict, as Twain would do in his Angel-and-Lucifer dyad (Hartzman 99).

In place of the Wild Men attracting the gawkers in the big city, the two cultured, well-traveled Capellos charm the odd unincorporated village of Dawson's Landing. With little prodding, the twins assume their roles as "natural" performers, meeting and greeting their audience before performing a party piece on the piano. While Twain scaled back their more outrageous traits in his revisions, Angelo and Luigi share "one mass of muscle" (for most of the story) and periodically engage in the same combativeness that captivated Twain on that New York street. In a comic subversion of the Franklinian self-made man, the brothers seek their fortune in a small town. Though they possess little in the way of work ethic and have no trade to speak of outside of displaying their extraordinary bodies, their European manners and pedigree allow them to win the town's approbation and "cross over" from human curiosities to aspiring citizens.

It falls to Judge Driscoll to guide the twins through Dawson's Landing, in his role as "first citizen," an undisputed title acceded largely through his lineage from the First Families of Virginia. Judge Driscoll commences the twins' indoctrination into civic life with a tour of the town's key sites, including the jail, the town hall, several churches, and the graveyard. In contrast to the straitlaced, semi-exiled Pudd'nhead Wilson, the Capello twins, despite their uncanniness and sordid tales of the Berlin freakshow, are welcomed into Dawson's Landing. The twins are initially incorporated into town life and marked as "white" in a way never attempted with the Tocci twins or Chang and Eng Bunker. With their whiteness affirmed, Angelo and Luigi earn key rights: imminent citizenship, the possibility of marriage, the chance to run for office, and competent legal defense. Within thirty days of their arrival, they seek election as alderman in Dawson's Landing, as the townsfolk marvel at their "stock of rare and curious accomplishments" (Twain, *Pudd'nhead Wilson* 80).

The town's debate also surrounds the comic duel between Judge Driscoll and Luigi, offering a glimpse of the operational aesthetic at work. The duel (which is only narrated through town gossip) demonstrates no real sense of justice and serves little purpose except as a spectacular opportunity for the town to discuss issues of race and honor. Campaigning against the twins soon afterward, the first citizen's choice of epithets against them is telling. No longer a civic mentor, the Judge slanders them as "sideshow riff-raff" and "dime-museum freaks" (89). By reminding the community of their two years on display in Berlin—a period Angelo pointedly refers to as "slavery"—the Judge strips them of freemen's rights and the chance to assimilate. He dismisses the tale of their lost knife as nothing more than "humbug." With the insinuation of a criminal past, the Judge suggests the twins have no civic honor to defend and are nothing more than crafty transients, "organ-grinders bereft of their brother-monkey" (89). Driscoll's invocation of difference and his conflation of human oddity with sub-humanity put an end to the twins' election chances. Overnight, their extraordinary bodies make them suspect, as they descend from emerging citizens to pariahs.

It is up to Pudd'nhead Wilson to re-grant the twins their freedom and citizenship. In Wilson's uncharacteristically lengthy case for the defense, his sense of showmanship—which has lain dormant for twenty-three years—comes to the fore. Rather than express himself in modest, Poor Richard-type aphorisms, Wilson indulges in the language of dramatic legal oratory. As both Dawson's Landing's mayor and the twins' attorney, he entrances the courtroom audience with the unlikely, almost freakish tale of Tom's elaborate deceptions. The crowd pays rapt attention, then applauds Wilson's "act," composed equally of scientific reasoning and divination. Presenting his fingerprint studies and findings of fact to the gallery, Pudd'nhead Wilson emerges as the anti-huckster, offering a wild narrative based on logic and actual science, rather than the crowd-pleasing tricks of hype and pseudo-science. Rather than disrupt the values of native honor and racial typecasting underlying the lawsuit, Wilson's courtroom performance restores order, albeit to a flawed system. In winning the case, Dawson's Landing's putative mayor finally completes his own long-delayed incorporation into the body politic by declaiming on the twins' behalf as half attorney/half carnival barker, selling the twins to the community as much as proving their innocence. After his successful defense, he leaves the crowd buzzing and commiserating, like after a successful tent show.

Wilson's ostentatious framing of truth through technology parallels the mode of showmanship that emerged after Barnum's death in 1891. Early twentieth-century performers like Harry Houdini were aware of the heightened public skepticism Barnum engendered. Houdini routinely prefaced his most daring acts with elaborate demonstrations of his props and accessories, often inviting skeptical audience members onstage to test locks, chains, and the like. In this way, John F. Kasson writes, "Houdini's operational aesthetic . . . appealed to the amateur's desire to understand technical processes. . . . He invited viewers to look inside the works of his escapes and to match wits with him, all the better to astound them" (Kasson 123).

Seeking to astound his mass audience, Barnum was as adept at fostering genuine debate as provoking outrage. He took enormous pride in the success of his American Museum in New York City and his role as middlebrow impresario, and criticized traveling shows that made no pretensions of educating or enlightening the paying customers. Historians and biographers agree that Barnum could not have sustained a half-century career had he engaged solely in rip-offs and hoaxes. His sponsorship of Jenny Lind's massively successful 1850 United States tour and his promotion of popular museum displays and melodramas exemplified his devotion to affordable diversions delivered at face value. Barnum enjoyed extraordinary personal popularity, becoming something of an attraction himself.

In every version of his autobiography, he related the tale of the man who traveled to Barnum's American Museum, immediately sought out the proprietor, gazed at him momentarily, then left the premises, claiming "I have got the worth of my money" (Barnum, *Struggles* 161).

While we commonly associate Barnum's spectacular showmanship today with the display of human oddities and exoticized freaks, many of Barnum's attractions were offered to the masses with an uplifting, patriotic sheen. Robert Bogdan has termed the clash of unusual appearances and exalted presentation the "aggrandized" mode, with Charles Stratton (stage name: General Tom Thumb) as its exemplar.[3] Beginning in 1835 with his first "star" attraction—Joice Heth, the enslaved, allegedly 161-year-old former nurse of George Washington—Barnum foregrounded race in the presentation of his performers, even as he pandered to his audience's patriotism.[4] In his recounting of his first meeting with Heth, Barnum claimed that with the sight of the old woman, "I had at last found my true vocation" (*Struggles* 83). Significantly, Barnum never "owned" Joice Heth, nor did he exert his influence in attempting to manumit her. In the contract reprinted in full in *The Life of P.T. Barnum*, he assumed "sole right of exhibiting" Heth for a one-year term, but she remained property of her previous owner, with whom Barnum split the profits. Contractually, Heth was leased property. Barnum's display of Heth both ignited a spark of Revolution-era nostalgia and reinforced the half-slave/half-free dichotomy of 1830s America. This arrangement also preempted any bad publicity Barnum would have received, especially in the North, as a slaveowner (Barnum, *Life* 150–151).[5] In Heth, Barnum found a potent symbol, one that celebrated the tradition and unity inherent in nationhood while tacitly accepting the race and class assumptions fundamental to the slave system.

This heightened attention to nationality and racial categorization was central to the commodification of "exotic" performers. Significantly, Barnum was publicly silent on the politics of race, even during the period of *Uncle Tom's Cabin* fever. His dedication of his *Life* to "The Universal Yankee Nation, of which I am proud to be one," was written as a statement of regional, rather than political, commitment. Race marked both those he presented as exotic curiosities—like the "Fejee Mermaid" (a hideous manmade fusion of a monkey and a fish) or "Siamese Twins" Chang and Eng Bunker—and those he privileged and elevated as performers, such as General Tom Thumb, who often commanded the stage in Union military garb, and "Swedish Nightingale" Jenny Lind. Intuiting that a heavily concentrated display of the exotic may disrupt or threaten middle-class mores and alienate paying customers, Barnum frequently updated his autobiography and added melodramatic stage performances to push teetotaling and Prohibition as his pet social causes, aligning himself with a more respectable platform of nineteenth-century "family values."

It also led Barnum to make ludicrous moves to uphold the symbolic order: in one instance, Barnum, unable to find a suitable blackface minstrel, insisted that an African-American man "blacken up" with greasepaint and an oversize wig before a performance (Harris 284). If no willing performer was available for a minstrel olio, Barnum himself would assume the role and, in his own recollection, excite the crowds with his dancing and "plantation melodies" (Barnum, *Life* 189). Barnum was less forthcoming with the fact that he became a slaveowner on one trip South in the 1830s, owning a woman and her child and a young man who served as his *valet de chambers*. Accusing the valet of theft, Barnum asserted his legal rights as a slaveowner, had him whipped, and arranged to have him sold in New Orleans, quite literally selling him down the river.[6]

Of course, Twain followed Barnum's public life, read his autobiography, and had a casual friendship with him. That familiarity, and their comparable stature among the most famous men of their time, undoubtedly humanized him (to a degree) in Twain's eyes (Harris 282–285). Twain's audience read his depictions of human oddity through the lens of Barnum's spectacles; the *Springfield* (Massachusetts) *Republican*'s review of *Pudd'nhead Wilson* characterized the Capellos as "a freak of the Barnum variety" (Budd 368). William Faulkner's generation, on the other hand, knew "Barnum" as a synonym for the shady proprietors of traveling shows, conflating his presentations—lowbrow and middlebrow alike—with the cheap carnivals and sideshows that visited the outskirts of small towns like Oxford, Mississippi. The South has had a history of mistrust toward the traveling show and has attempted to contain its seductive power through legislation. Nestled between regulations regarding tobacconists and pool rooms, the "Laws of Congress In Regard to Taxes, Currency, and Conscription," passed by the Confederate states in February 1864, included provisions that taxed circuses one hundred dollars up front, plus ten dollars for every performance (Section 4, XV).[7] Jugglers and sleight-of-hand artists were levied fifty dollars. Perhaps unsurprisingly, the tax law allowed for states' rights to approve the content of traveling shows and determine which exhibitions were proper.

Likewise, during Faulkner's formative years in Mississippi, traveling shows were still perceived as threats from the outside (Yankee threats, to give it its proper emphasis) and harbingers of unstable modernity. In his book *Faulkner's County,* Don H. Doyle notes that Lafayette County played host to all manner of traveling entertainment around the turn of the century: circuses, minstrel shows, animal shows, melodramas, and, eventually, moving pictures. So as to keep such stimulating fare in check, the city fathers imposed a daily tax on these and other exhibitions deemed not to carry a "religious, benevolent or educational" purpose (334). In short, any diversion deemed to be outside the realms of official culture—church, charity, or school—had to at least pay monetary tribute to the old order it was undermining.

In his memoir *My Brother Bill*, John Faulkner recalls one of the more unusual spectacles surrounding the county fairs that took place in Oxford each fall. On the Square, in the shadow of the courthouse and the Confederate monument, alongside the town's stores and displays of the county's finest produce, a small sideshow featured "a wild man from Borneo, that some English explorer had caught in a net. The scene of his capture was always depicted on the front of his tent. We stared at it and believed and paid our dimes to go inside and stare at the wild man, seated in a cane-bottomed chair with one leg chained to the stand on which he sat, and gnawing at the bones scattered about him" (109). John Faulkner's description tactfully refuses to speculate on the authenticity of the Wild Man, probably with good reason. Of course, the sideshow act he and his brothers enjoy demonstrates the taming of nature crucial to what Robert Bogdan calls the "exotic mode" of display and the overarching narrative of whiteness. The act exhibits a simulacrum of unknown places and dangerously uncivilized beings; the scene is only complete with the dramatic painted depiction of the Wild Man's capture by the brave White Hunter. John Faulkner reflexively assumes that the capturer is English, acting in the colonial role of "explorer."[8] The chains and gnawed bones go even further in reifying the binary between primitive and civilized, white and nonwhite.

By now a carnival and circus mainstay, the Wild Man from Borneo act had barely evolved since Mark Twain's apprehension of it in New York over half a century earlier.[9] The act itself required little more than pigmentation (real or artificial), a few basic props to signify "the Primitive," and an audience that, to borrow John Faulkner's apt phrase, "believed and paid [their] dimes." As in 1850s New York, the setting shapes the belief. In the enclosed, quasi-domestic public space of the Square, Nature (and its "wild" inhabitants) are tamed and overcome by Civilization and its contents: law, agriculture, capitalism, and exciting, affordable entertainment. As Rachel Adams notes about such dubious spectacles, "spectators' desire to unmask the racial freak as a hoax did not mean that they questioned the exhibit's underlying assumption of white supremacy" (163). The sideshow tableau both announces and affirms a belief in race as immutable, hierarchized, and inassimilable.

Faulkner dramatizes the disharmony between the fading old order and the seductions of the transient, carnivalesque world in *The Sound and the Fury*. The younger Jason Compson, embittered scion of the Old Order (and, like *Pudd'nhead Wilson*'s Tom Driscoll, a thieving wastrel), watches with scorn as folks from the country—black and white—set aside their Good Friday chores to enjoy a traveling show while he works in his own fashion. Not content simply to begrudge Luster a quarter to attend the show, Jason bemoans the excitement of the townsfolk who try to bargain over hame strings to save money, "so they can give it to a bunch of Yankees that come in and pay maybe ten dollars for the privilege" (Faulkner, *Sound* 230). Yet such Yankees often had to put forth an effort to swindle Southerners; in his autobiography, Barnum's gladhanding democratic stance is only interrupted by his bitter remembrances of the difficulty in getting Southerners to pay for the privilege of bamboozlement. Characterizing his early itinerant shows in the South as the low point of his career, his recriminations toward tight-fisted Southern gawkers anticipate Jason's bitterness (Barnum, *Struggles* 91). The country folk who bedevil Jason with their haggling and the musicians who entice them away from the fields with the siren song of the musical saw chip away what little remains of the Compsons' inherited authority. The division between legacy and carnival is underscored through Miss Quentin's final escape with her money and the mysterious Con Man in the Red Tie in tow.

This division became even more pronounced when the traveling show expanded into the now-familiar three-ring circus around the turn of the century. Commencing with the ritual of the preshow parade, the circus broadly announced its difference from middle-class domestic and economic life, making it the real-life analogue to the rapturous reception the Capellos received at Dawson's Landing. The circus wagons' processional through town announced the arrival of the big show while signaling the temporary disruption of everyday life. In her study *The Circus Age*, Janet M. Davis notes the lengths to which towns once wary of traveling amusements would now greet the larger circuses that traveled by railroads: businesses, factories, even schools would close (2). When incorporated into civic life, the circus occasioned a temporary diversion from labor and responsibility and a momentary, carnivalesque upending (and ultimate reinforcement) of social order. A second parade, at the beginning of each performance, underlined the multiethnic, stratified character of the circus; Davis cites one Ringling Brothers show that claimed performers from twenty-two countries (5). Barnum, not content to let the performers stand on their own as nonwhite Others, had inaugurated this spectacle in the 1880s, arranging his performers in a quasi-humanistic "Ethnological Congress," a human ark "forming a collection, in pairs or otherwise, of all the uncivilized races in existence . . ." (B. Adams 181).[10] Again, the topsy-turvy nature of the circus forged a break in civic and racial thinking—while "uncivilized" performers were cynically presented as human oddities or ethnic curiosities, a few, following Joice Heth and Charles Stratton, were elevated not simply to "star" status but granted a degree of honored citizenship.

To symbolize the unanticipated coming of the "uncivilized" to Jefferson, Faulkner employs the trope of the wagon parade both in *Absalom, Absalom!* and *The Hamlet*. In the former case, Thomas Sutpen spurs speculation with his caravan and accompanying men. The narrator denotes the French architect's "theatrical clothes" and describes his team of unassimilated, French-speaking black men as "wild men" (26–27), perhaps a nod to what young Billy Falkner and his brothers once saw in the town square. Like the arrival of the Snopeses, their grand entrance into Yoknapatawpha County life parodies the wide-eyed Franklinesque arrival of the young, white, self-made man to his promised land. The "talk" of the town serves as Sutpen's best advertisement, as residents collectively debate and confirm the grandiosity of the stranger's design.

In analyzing Flem Snopes's own design and conquest of Yoknapatawpha County in *The Hamlet*, critics have long noted his uncanny adaptability, but few have recognized the performative aspect of his rise. Flem's strange appearance at Varner's store enacts the aggrandized mode to some degree, his starched, unnaturally white business shirt belying his family's reputation as a "soiled," almost animalistic clan of "white-trash" barn-burners. Like the Barnumesque huckster, Flem patterns himself after the "first citizen" of the town yet undermines authority through an unwavering, unemotional allegiance to profit. Barnum's first autobiography features a series of comic vignettes set in New England country stores, illustrating the rural marketplace as a cutthroat battleground of wits, as shrewd consumers face off with profit-driven shopkeepers, each suspecting the other of cheating while artfully concealing their own trickery; the storekeeper's profit, then, is his hard-fought reward for "vanquishing" his customers.

Flem also seeks gain, but only by allowing himself and his clan to fulfill the role of despised Other, like Wild Men on display. From almost the moment he arrives in town, Jeffersonians unite to see the curious interloper; women fix their stares on Flem, while the men who populate the gallery in front of Varner's store gaze at the "strange beast" (57). Townsfolk rush to the quasi-public space of the store to see the spectacle for themselves: "By the end of that first week they had all come in and seen him . . . the men, the women, the children . . . the sick and the aged . . . coming on horses and mules and by wagonsful" (58). Like Samuel Clemens's gaze upon the Wild Men in New York, Jeffersonians cannot quite reconcile the Snopeses' obvious whiteness with their inscrutability. Like the sight of the Wild Man and the explorer described by John Faulkner, the hamlet's citizens converge on a site of commerce to gawk at their supposed inferior, spend their nickels and dimes, and leave, secure in their place in the community. Standing alongside Will Varner as the storeowner adds up the debts of his tenant farmers, Flem and his "civilized" partner are depicted in the language of colonialism, underscoring their mutual interests and antipathies: "Varner and Snopes resembled the white trader and his native parrot-taught headman in an African outpost. That headman was acquiring the virtues of civilization fast" (67). The "virtues of civilization" in this case have more to do with ledger-keeping and the unforgiving, if not exploitative, economics of sharecropping than anything cultural or civic in nature. The town seems mesmerized by Flem's lack of emotion and his "act" of being uncanny and unforgiving with figures. Flem meanwhile seeks the social standing, if not the respectability, of landed gentry. With the arrival of more Snopeses in Flem's wake, the Wild Man/headman slips his bonds, moves out of his circumscribed space, and, in collaboration with the town's chief citizen, seeks a dominant role in the town's economic life.

As the culminating book of *The Hamlet* opens, Ben Quick spies Flem's gaudy caravan, resembling a scene from a circus poster. "Howdy, Flem," he calls in half-jest. "Starting you a circus?" (300). With spotted horses barely in tow, Flem is indeed ringmastering a scheme to separate Jeffersonians from their money and destabilize the body politic of Yoknapatawpha County. Flem's horse-sale breaks down to a simple capitalist equation Barnum would have appreciated: a mysterious commodity plus Flem's enigmatic nature equals pandemonium. Drawn to the spectacle of the horse auction, an unnamed gawker asks in anticipation, "So this here is the Snopes circus, is it?" (309). It takes Flem's assumed power and understated showmanship to spur the desire for these commodities, allowing the operational aesthetic to do its insidious work.

Faulkner's depiction of the horse auction, deliberately or not, reads as a clever subversion of a famous Barnum "humbug," the Great Buffalo Hunt of 1843. Upon transferring a herd of docile, nearly dead buffalo to New Jersey, Barnum advertised, with exaggerated descriptions and illustrations, a Western-style buffalo hunt. Excited by the possibilities of the exhibition (and perhaps stirred up with a little bloodlust), New Yorkers converged upon the ferries to Hoboken that Barnum had chartered. (While admission to the hunt was free, tolls to and from the event were not.) Though the "hunt" offered little excitement, Barnum claimed the deception became a shared joke among all present, who "gave three cheers for the author of the humbug, whoever he might be" (Barnum, *Life* 355). Though self-serving, his description of the event does underscore how he orchestrated his spectacles as living exposés of Yankee cleverness, wild rumor, and basic human greed. Though tricked out of some money, the spectators, under the operational aesthetic, could recover their standing and essentially get their money's worth by collectively uncovering just how the "author" of the scheme had outwitted them once again. Ultimately, the revelations of such humbugs galvanized Barnum's audience, even if just momentarily, into a community.

In his own humbug, Flem's choice of livestock, of course, differs wildly from Barnum's. The spotted horses brought in from Texas exemplify the exotic. As freakish genetic crazy quilts, defying every law of heredity and evolution, they stand "larger than rabbits and gaudy as parrots . . . calico-coated, small-bodied, with delicate legs and pink faces in which their mismatched eyes rolled wild and subdued, they huddled, gaudy motionless and alert, wild as deer, deadly as rattlesnakes, quiet as doves" (300). As was the case in classic Barnum hoaxes like the Fejee Mermaid and humans advertised as "Missing Links," Flem's reputation has taken on such superhuman proportions that gawkers expect him as a matter of course to possess, if not outright create, new and exotic species. The Texan Buck Hipps acts as the perfect confederate, complementing Flem's ominous silence with overstated Barnumesque hyperbole. Making a show of getting the horses in line, Hipps barks at them, "'Get up, you transmogrified hallucinations of Job and Jezebel'" (302). As auctioneer, Hipps brilliantly suckers the crowd, from his patently untrue overture—"'Come up boys . . . You're just in time to buy a good gentle horse cheap'"—to his hectoring and effective style of salesmanship (315).

In the hysteria, the men of the hamlet forget Ratliff's repeated warnings against trusting Flem. Following the chaotic horse sale, Lump Snopes has the last laugh at his social betters, telling Ratliff: "'If Flem had knowed how quick you fellows was going to snap them horses up, he'da probably brought some tigers. Monkeys too'" (342). Lump's pointed observation has special resonance. He suggests that while Flem designed the horse sale to swindle the townsmen who once underestimated him, even he never anticipated their gullibility and zeal to be tricked. (With barely disguised self-satisfaction, Barnum frequently noted in his autobiographies his surprise at the success of his more outrageous endeavors.) The carnivalesque excitement surrounding the horse-sale humbug ultimately weakens Ratliff's resistance, as he falls prey along with Armstid and Bookwright to Flem's staged "salting" of the Old Frenchman place. Once able to detach himself from the Snopesian spectacle—as in his brilliant comic set piece in which an impassive Flem beats the Devil—Ratliff now takes his place among the rubes, sharing the curious pleasure that accompanies outrage.

The showmanship surrounding Flem's sale of the spotted horses and the Old Frenchman Place recalls Barnum's most cynical manipulations of the public trust. Like Flem, Barnum at his most roguish often resorted to the grayer areas of the law when pressed on the particulars of his ownership. Allegedly "shocked" to find out that Joice Heth was about half of her advertised age of 161, with no possible first-person connection to George Washington, Barnum cited a "forged bill of sale" for Heth that he had trusted "in perfect good faith." Using quasi-legal language, Barnum implicitly argued that he, not Heth, was the exploited party (Harris 21–22). Picking up on the notion of "bad faith," Faulkner satirizes the incompatibility of law and spectacle in the aftermath of the spotted-horse caper: Armstid and Tull can bring their claims against Flem to court but cannot receive a judgment—much less justice—since Snopes simply denies ever owning the horses and has left no paper trail to prove otherwise. Since Hipps verbally bequeathed one particularly destructive horse to Eck without ever claiming or demonstrating possession, Flem cannot be held responsible.

Barnum resorted to the same legal fiction in his 1842 display of the Fejee Mermaid. According to his own account (against which there are no surviving documents to the contrary), the showman procured the doctored specimen through his business partner Moses Kimball from an unnamed sailor, who claimed he purchased it from Japanese sailors while docked in Calcutta. Barnum widely publicized the monstrosity as a feature attraction in his American Museum and ignited the debate on its authenticity. Reprising his Joice Heth ruse, Barnum took great care never to own the Mermaid, merely leasing it from Kimball for the nominal sum of twelve dollars and fifty cents a week and frequently relating (and embellishing) the tale of its strange provenance (Barnum, *Struggles* 110; Harris 63–64). In this way, Barnum could garner all the publicity of ownership while deflecting any claims of fraud onto a subordinate. Likewise, Buck Hipps, though an itinerant "carny" figure, has enough conscience (or remorse) to offer Mrs. Armstid a refund of the five dollars her husband has squandered on a wild horse. Flem's own act of "charity"—pocketing the five dollars, then offering a nickel's worth of candy to the Armstid children—stands as a final patronizing gesture to the citizenry he has swindled.

Like any other traveling show, the Snopeses exit Jefferson as they came, in a trail of wagons, with the townsfolk still debating what just happened, comparing their relative losses, and speculating on what schemes Flem will unleash next (403–405). In Flem's absence, with "the rapt interest of a crowd watching a magician at a fair," Jeffersonians congregate around the Old Frenchman place to watch Armstid's futile dig (404). The hapless Armstid becomes the last resident to understand that Flem simply cannot be beat. In a neat coincidence, Flem's last words in *The Hamlet*, "Come up," underscore not only his impending rise of fortune but echo Buck Hipps's come-on to the potential horse buyers and the carnival barker's time-honored invitation for gullible townsfolk to "step right up" and engage in a predetermined game of rigged chance.

Half a century ago, Leslie Fiedler noted the sympathy between the Snopes trilogy and Twain's more uproarious works, with their concentration on the "humor of the freak" (250). Both Twain and Faulkner find their richest vein of humor in the pleasurable yet shameful act of staring at the Other, and both lampoon the irrational obsessions of communities ignoring the fissures of race and class that threaten true and equal citizenship. The farcical comedy of the Capello twins derives from their efforts to incorporate into the body politic, despite the intrusive interests of the town and a skewed system of justice. The dark satire of *The Hamlet* arises from the Snopes circus coming to town and refusing to pay tribute or submit to any social boundary or preexisting hierarchal order. Lump Snopes rationalizes Flem's swindling of Jefferson in an aphorism worthy of Barnum: "'If a man ain't got gumption enough to protect himself, it's his own look-out'" (345). The odd sights of the extraordinary twins, the wild Snopeses, and their untamed horses create spectacles and rumors so outrageous that staid citizens become gawkers, awestruck by the proximity of the Other. While Twain relents and allows the keen legal reasoning and civic rectitude of Pudd'nhead Wilson to restore order in the former case, the riotous horse sale and Flem's unjust vindication in court suggest that Faulkner was more inclined than his predecessor to illustrate a carnivalesque upheaval of legal and community standards and end on a note of ambivalence. Their unique adaptations of Barnum's brand of mass entertainment suggest that the great showman had an influence on both authors' conception of race, culture, and community and hint that—just maybe—the labors of a novelist and a huckster may be more alike than we realize.

Notes

1. See also Ron Powers, *Mark Twain: A Life* (New York: Free Press, 2005), 62–64.

2. The following year, Barnum bought the failing Crystal Palace but never followed up on plans to make it a permanent exhibit hall.

3. A semblance of the aggrandized mode lives on in the Snopeses. Throughout the Snopes Trilogy, the rising family's self-aggrandizement results in such fake-noble marquee names as Colonel Sartoris, Admiral Dewey, and Saint Elmo Snopes. Perhaps the young author who bestowed upon himself a properly regal "U" to his last name and seemed to tolerate

the title "Count No 'Count" understood the significance of naming rituals and lofty presentation.

4. Coincidentally, Barnum burst on the American scene with the Joice Heth hoax in 1835, the same year Twain was born.

5. For a broader discussion of Barnum and Heth, see Benjamin Reiss's *The Showman and the Slave: Race, Death, and Memory in Barnum's America*.

6. Outside of a few private letters, Barnum revealed very little about his slaveholding, omitting it entirely from his autobiographies, so further details on Barnum's slaveholdings are difficult to uncover. Discussion and context can be found in Peter Kunhardt et al., *P.T. Barnum: America's Greatest Showman* (New York: Knopf, 1995) 74; and A.H. Saxon, *P.T. Barnum: The Legend and the Man* (New York: Columbia University Press, 1989) 82–85.

7. The younger Jason Compson invokes this type of taxation in *The Sound and the Fury*, 230.

8. The traditional reference to Borneo is deliberate; in the mid-1850s, when showman Lyman Warner inaugurated the act, Borneo was a highly contested colonial outpost (Bogdan 122).

9. The term was an evocative bit of exploitation and marketing, but the original "Wild Men" touted by Lyman Warner, Hiram and Barney Davis, were born to English parents, diminutive, and anything but ferocious. See Bogdan 121–127.

10. In his amended autobiography *Struggles and Triumphs*, Barnum refines his ark concept further, applying the language of Darwinian "fitness": "I meant to secure a man and woman, as perfect as could be procured, from every accessible people, civilized and barbarous, on the face of the globe" (170).

Works Cited

Adams, Bluford. *E Pluribus Barnum: The Great Showman and the Making of U.S. Popular Culture*. Minneapolis: U of Minnesota P, 1997.

Adams, Rachel. *Sideshow U.S.A.: Freaks and the American Cultural Imagination*. Chicago: U of Chicago P, 2001.

Barnum, P.T. *The Life of P.T. Barnum, Written by Himself.* 1855. Urbana: U of Illinois P, 2000.

———. *Struggles and Triumphs.* 1869. Edited by Carl Bode. London: Penguin, 1981.

Bogdan, Robert. *Freak Show: Presenting Human Oddities for Amusement and Profit.* Chicago: U of Chicago P, 1988.

Budd, Louis J., ed. *Mark Twain: The Contemporary Reviews.* New York: Cambridge UP, 1999.

Davis, Janet. *The Circus Age: Culture and Society Under the American Big Top.* Chapel Hill: U of North Carolina P, 2002.

Doyle, Don H. *Faulkner's County: The Historical Roots of Yoknapatawpha.* Chapel Hill: U of North Carolina P, 2001.

Faulkner, John. *My Brother Bill: An Affectionate Reminiscence.* New York: Trident P, 1963.

Faulkner, William. *Absalom, Absalom!* 1936. The Corrected Text. New York: Random House, 1987.

———. *The Hamlet.* 1940. The Corrected Text. New York: Random House, 1990.

———. *The Sound and the Fury.* 1929. The Corrected Text. New York: Random House, 1987.

Fiedler, Leslie. "As Free as Any Cretur. . . ." *New Republic* 15 and 22 Aug. 1955: 130–139. Rpt. in *Pudd'nhead Wilson and Those Extraordinary Twins,* edited by Sidney E. Berger. 2nd ed. New York: Norton, 2005. 248–257.

Harris, Neil. *Humbug: The Art of P.T. Barnum.* Chicago: U of Chicago P, 1973.

Hartzman, Marc. *American Sideshow.* New York: Tarcher/Penguin, 2005.

Kasson, John F. *Houdini, Tarzan, and the Perfect Man: The White Male Body and the Challenge of Modernity in America.* New York: Hill and Wang, 2001.

Kunhardt, Philip B., Jr., Philip B. Kunhardt III, Peter W. Kunhardt. *P.T. Barnum: America's Greatest Showman.* New York: Knopf, 1995.

"Laws of Congress in Regard to Taxes, Currency and Conscription." *Documenting the American South*. 2001. U of North Carolina, Chapel Hill. 18 Oct. 2006. <http://docsouth.unc.edu/imls/lawsofcong/lawsofcong.html>.

Powers, Ron. *Mark Twain: A Life*. New York: Free P, 2005.

Reiss, Benjamin. *The Showman and the Slave: Race, Death, and Memory in Barnum's America*. Cambridge: Harvard UP, 2001.

Saxon, A.H. *P.T. Barnum: The Legend and the Man*. New York: Columbia UP, 1989.

Twain, Mark. *Mark Twain's Letters: Volume 1: 1853–1866*. Edited by Edgar Marquess Branch, Michael B. Frank, and Kenneth M. Sanderson. Berkeley: U of California P, 1988.

———. *Pudd'nhead Wilson and Those Extraordinary Twins*. 1894. Edited by Sidney E. Berger. 2nd ed. New York: Norton, 2005.

Absorbed in Reading the "Worst Heart of the World": Faulkner, Twain, and Their "Failed Detectives"

There are no "real" detectives either in Dawson's Landing, Missouri, or in Jefferson, Mississippi: To put it another way, no "professional" detectives appear either in Twain's *Pudd'nhead Wilson* or in Faulkner's Yoknapatawpha novels. There are, however, characters in both Twain's and Faulkner's works who act like "private eyes" trying to search out the truth in some mystery they are forced to face. David Wilson, "ATTORNEY AND COUNSELOR-AT-LAW" (Twain 7) in *Pudd'nhead Wilson* is one such figure, while Faulkner's fiction presents not only the always inquisitive Gavin Stevens, "the District Attorney, a Harvard graduate, a Phi Beta Kappa"(*Light in August* 444) but also several other characters—such as Byron Bunch and Hightower[1] in *Light in August*; Mr. Compson, Quentin, Shreve, and even Rosa Coldfield in *Absalom, Absalom!*;[2] Ike McCaslin in *Go Down, Moses*; and Ratliff in the Snopes trilogy. All of these may be included in the category of "pseudo" or "amateur" detectives, attempting a "reading" of something mysterious which attracts their attention.

Even Jason Compson, who appears to bear no resemblance to any of the characters mentioned above, seems to qualify for membership of this group when he complains, "I says if I've got to spend half my time being a dam [*sic*] detective, at least I'll go where I can get paid for it" (*The Sound and the Fury* 238). He compares himself to "a dam detective" because he has to chase his niece Quentin, who cuts school, rides the streets of Jefferson with an obscure man wearing a red tie—probably a "man from the show"—and runs away with him after she has stolen (or, to be correct, recovered her or her mother Caddy's) money from Jason's safe. Since this is the only occasion when an explicit reference to a detective is made, it may easily be overlooked. But we should note that the reference appears shortly after his habitual saying—"Like I say blood always tells. If you've got blood like that in you, you'll do anything." Though the "blood" has no connotation of race but refers to Caddy's "licentious" life which Jason condemns in his equally habitual malicious and sexist way, "Once a bitch always a bitch, what I say," (180),[3] the reference to "blood" reminds us of Gavin Stevens's infamous speech about Joe Christmas's "white blood" and "black blood."[4] And Stevens's remark further takes us to Roxana's harsh words toward her real, black son, "Tom," in *Pudd'nhead Wilson*— "'Thirty-one parts o' you is white, en on'y one part nigger, en dat po' little one part is yo' *soul*'" (Twain 70). The mystery of "blood" and a detective-like performance connect these characters from different texts.

Jason fails, however, both in identifying the man and in recovering the money, and returns from his pseudo-detective work only to face another problematic situation created by his younger brother's wailing in the middle of the town, and although by the end of the novel he has stopped Benjy's making the "sound" and thus achieved a temporary and superficial restoration of "peace" and "order," few readers will be persuaded that he has cleared his family's reputation by making Benjy quiet or that he has restored everything "in its ordered place."[5] On the contrary, the last scene increases the readers' uneasiness by presenting, so to speak, two different Jasons[6]—one who "failed" at his detective work and another who "succeeded" in restoring quiet. Unlike ordinary detective stories in which some kind of resolution is presented and the readers experience catharsis, *The Sound and the Fury* leaves them suspended, unable to find a way out. Jason is not the only Faulknerian pseudo-detective who fails in his attempt. Nor is he the only one who strikes readers as ambiguous, representing two different or oppositional values in one. Such figures are in fact destined to fail, since the whole point of such episodes lies not so much in the attempt to solve the mystery and arrive at the truth as in the fact that the truth is ultimately elusive or impossible to be arrived at.

Faulkner's world never suffers from a dearth of "failed detectives" in this sense[7] and such "failures" may well remind us of the similar "failure" experienced by the narrator in Poe's "The Man of the Crowd" (1840), the story with which, according to Charles J. Rzepka, Poe's crime and detective writing began (74).[8] Following an initial allusion to "a certain German book" said to be one which "does not permit itself to be read" ("*er lasst sich nicht lesen*"), a mysterious sentence is presented: "There are some secrets which do not permit themselves to be told" (Poe 475). That these "secrets" seem to be concerned with some criminal acts is indicated by the narrator's going on to say that "the essence of all crime is undivulged" when "the conscience of man takes up a burden so heavy in horror that it can be thrown down only into the grave." But in the story the narrator actually begins telling, no crime—no murder or theft or arson—appears. There seems at first nothing problematic in his sitting at the window of a coffeehouse in London, observing the pedestrians outside, and having his attention drawn to one particular figure:

> With my brow to the glass, I was thus occupied in
> scrutinizing the mob, when suddenly there came into view
> a countenance (that of a decrepit old man, some sixty-five

or seventy years of age)—a countenance which at once
arrested and absorbed my whole attention, on account of
the absolute idiosyncrasy of its expression. . . . I felt singularly aroused, startled, fascinated. "How wild a history," I
said to myself, "is written within that bosom!" Then came
a craving desire to keep the man in view—to know more
of him. (Poe 478)

The narrator's pursuit then begins and continues to the second day,[9]
until "the shades of the second evening came on." During this time both of
them keep walking, but finally, grown "wearied unto death," the narrator
stops "fully in front of the wanderer, gaz[ing] at him steadfastly in the
face" (481). But the old man does not, as the narrator (and the reader with
him) might have expected, show any reaction but keeps walking while the
narrator, giving up the pursuit, "remain[s] absorbed in contemplation."
Frustrated in his desire to get to "know more of him," the narrator admits
that "*He is the man of the crowd*" and it "will be in vain to follow," since the
"worst heart of the world is a grosser book than the 'Hortulus Animæ,'[10]
and perhaps it is but one of the great mercies of God that '*er lasst sich nicht
lesen*,'" that is, "it does not permit itself to be read."

The reader may feel uneasy, not only with the strange old man who
tirelessly keeps walking the city conscious or unconscious that he is
followed by the narrator, but also with the narrator himself who maintains
his pursuit and keeps walking as energetically, or frantically, as the old man.
The old man is, without doubt, strange, but nobody except a detective or
someone with some secret purpose—perhaps of attacking the old man or
trying to steal something from him—would act the way the narrator does.
In fact, as Rzepka says, adapting Vidocq,[11] the old man could easily be
imagined as a suspected criminal:

> To loiter among crowds like the anonymous "Man of the
> Crowd" is, according to Vidocq, the sure sign of a "*tireur*"
> or pickpocket, while if one entered "shop after shop, priced
> nothing, and looked at all objects with a wild and vacant
> stare," as the narrator's quarry does at one point, Vidocq
> would immediately recognize the traits of the "*détourneur*"
> or shop-lifter. In short, Poe's "Man of the Crowd" would
> be presumed guilty until proven innocent by nearly any
> of Vidocq's plainclothes subordinates, regardless of the
> personal inscrutability of his features. (41)

If, then, the old man's walk among the crowd is nothing but his "professional" act, a routine, seeking opportunities to steal, he must be quite conscious of what he is doing. On the other hand, the reader should be aware that the narrator may well be very unreliable, far from being an ordinary, rational, or commonsensical man as he is presented, or rather as he presents himself, at the beginning of the story. Noting the strange actions of the narrator, Rzepka points out that he is one of Poe's familiar narrators:

> Objectively considered, the man following the man of
> the crowd seems as legitimate a target of suspicion as
> his quarry. As in many other tales by Poe with unstable
> or unreliable narrators, such as "The Black Cat" or "The
> Tell-Tale Heart," the "locked room" of the mind that most
> stoutly resists our imaginative ingress here is located in the
> sub-basement of the narrator's soul. And he himself seems
> unaware of what is down there. (42)

But what makes the story and the suspicious narrator of "The Man of the Crowd" unique among Poe's stories and narrators is surely that no actual criminal act seems to have been committed and that the narrator, however suspicious and unreliable, is nevertheless a "reader." He may well be "unaware of what is down there," what is concealed in his "locked room," but the story does not end with the narrator's confession that he is "the one who did it" as in "The Tell-Tale Heart" or "The Black Cat"; rather, it ends with his admission that it is impossible for him to "read" the "worst heart of the world" since "it does not permit itself to be read." If, as in the cases of the narrators in "The Tell-Tale Heart" or "The Black Cat," what he tells us at the very end of the story is a confession, a pouring out of his true heart, then the narrator of "The Man of the Crowd" can be said to disclose his true self, not as a criminal, as do the narrators in other stories, but as a reader, or rather a failed reader, of a book. In addition, therefore, to Poe's usual intriguing twist by which the detective-like pursuer turns out to be himself a shady and suspect figure, there is in "The Man of the Crowd" the unique feature that the narrator's pursuit constitutes an act of reading and ratiocination which will inevitably fail. Much as *The Sound and the Fury* ends with Jason as a failure in his detective-like work of pursuit and yet a success in making Benjy at least temporarily[12] quiet, so "The Man of the Crowd," another story of pursuit, ends with a narrator who "succeeds" in arriving at the realization that he will inevitably "fail."

Careful readers of *Pudd'nhead Wilson* will notice that the act of reading is again the central issue. The story begins with an act of reading that fixes one man's fate and replaces his real name with a nickname, an anticipation of the exchange of the babies that constitutes the main plot of the whole novel. On his first day in town, a "homely, freckled, sandy-haired" young man, "with an intelligent blue eye that had frankness and comradeship in it and a covert twinkle of a pleasant sort," is "gauged"[13] by the townspeople on the basis of "his fatal remark" that he would have owned "half" of a dog because he can "kill [his] half":

> "I wish I owned half of that dog."
> "Why?" somebody asked.
> "Because, I would kill my half."
> The group searched his face with curiosity, with anxiety even, but found no light there, no expression that they could read. They fell away from him as from something uncanny,[14] and went into privacy to discuss him. One said—
> "Pears to be a fool."
> "Pears?" said another. "*Is*, I reckon you better say."
>
> . . . Within a week he had lost his first name; Pudd'nhead took its place . . . That first day's verdict made him a fool . . . and was to continue to hold its place for twenty long years. (5–6)

Like the narrator of "The Man of the Crowd," the onlookers turn into readers and "[search] his face with curiosity, with anxiety even." Failing in their attempt, they "gauged" him as "something uncanny," a mystery, an unreadable text, and their misreading results in an exchange of two first names, David and Pudd'nhead, that in turn foreshadows another exchange of two first names and two distinct identities, "Tom" and "Chambers."

It is not only the townspeople, however, who commit themselves to the act of reading. Interestingly enough, their "text," Wilson, is also an out-and-out "reader" of a collection of fingerprints of the people of the town:

> He often studied his records [of fingerprints], examining and poring over them with absorbing interest until far into the night; but what he found there—if he found anything—he revealed to no one. Sometimes he copied on paper the involved and delicate pattern left by the ball of a finger, and then vastly enlarged it with a pantograph so that he could examine its web of curving lines with ease and convenience. (7)

Like the narrator of "The Man of the Crowd," absorbed in pursuing the mysterious old man, Wilson follows the records of fingerprints: as Tom says, "he'll read your wrinkles as easy as a book, and not only tell you fifty or sixty things that's going to happen to you, but fifty or sixty thousand that ain't" (49). Tom continues, unknowingly:

> "Why, a man's own hand is his deadliest enemy! Just think of that—a man's own hand keeps a record of the deepest and fatalest secrets of his life, and is treacherously ready to expose him to any black-magic stranger that comes along. But what do you let a person look at your hand for, with that awful thing printed in it?" (52).

As if echoing the mysterious sentence in Poe's short story—"There are some secrets which do not permit themselves to be told."—Tom ironically predicts his own fate, one which, until the last moment, seems safely hidden from Wilson's eyes. Temporarily, at least, there is every reason to believe that "the conscience of man takes up a burden so heavy in horror that it can be thrown down only into the grave. And thus the essence of all crime is undivulged" (Poe 475). But of course, unlike in "The Man of the Crowd," where no actual crime is committed, Tom murders his "uncle," and Wilson successfully spots the offender by reading "a man's own hand [which] keeps a record of the deepest and fatalest secrets of his life," as the murderer himself had earlier and unwittingly admitted.

A similarly devoted "reader," attracted to and absorbed in his single-minded pursuit of the mysterious, can be found in Faulkner's *Absalom, Absalom!*. At the beginning of the second chapter, we are told that Quentin and his father, Mr. Compson, "sat on the front gallery after supper until it would be time for Quentin to start," responding to the request of Miss Rosa Coldfield that he accompany her to Sutpen's Hundred (23). Mr. Compson starts telling the story, or rather, his version of the story, of the Sutpens to his son, who has been chosen by Miss Rosa for a reason he does not understand and therefore keeps saying, "But why [does she] tell me about it?" (7). At the beginning of Chapter 4, Mr. Compson interrupts his story in order to fetch a letter from inside the house. Whose letter it is and why it is significant is not explained until later: he simply starts telling his son about Henry, Judith, and Charles Bon, while sitting under the dim porch light with "the letter in his hand and the hand looking almost as dark as a negro's against his linen leg" (71). This comparison effectively emphasizes the relative nature of "color." Since even the hand of a white man from a distinguished Southern family could "look black" when contrasted with the linen, it is ironic that Mr. Compson's reasoning should be faulty from the beginning because of his not realizing the possibility of Charles Bon's being Sutpen's son and nonetheless (according to Southern ideology) a black.

The irony, however, is delayed, hence largely retrospective. Mr. Compson's telling continues from Chapter 2 to 4 and then forms a basis for Miss Rosa's monologue in the fifth chapter and for the four final chapters in which Quentin and his roommate, Shreve, create their own version of the story in the iron-cold of a Massachusetts winter. What is important is that Mr. Compson is not a mere reteller of an old story handed down from his father; it is rather that, by actively re-living a story shared by the community, he becomes a reader/interpreter of a text/object to which he is strongly attracted. In his absorbed pursuit of this object of fascination, he strongly resembles the narrator of "The Man of the Crowd" who is "singularly aroused, startled, fascinated" by the old man's face and by the way in which it "at once arrested and absorbed [his] whole attention" and compels him to follow the old man with "a craving desire . . . to know more of him":

> [Bon] is the curious one to me. He came into that isolated puritan country household almost like Sutpen himself came into Jefferson . . . who seems to have seduced the country brother and sister without any effort or particular desire to do so . . . [and who] seems to have withdrawn into a mere spectator, passive, a little sardonic and completely enigmatic. He seems to hover, shadowy, almost substanceless, a little behind and above all the other straightforward and logical . . . It was as if he found the whole business, not inexplicable of course, just unnecessary; that he knew at once that Sutpen had found out about the mistress and child and he now found Sutpen's action and Henry's reaction a fetish-ridden moral blundering which did not deserve to be called thinking, which he contemplated with the detached attentiveness of a scientist watching the muscles in an anesthetized frog. . . . (Faulkner, *Absalom* 74)

Not knowing the "real" relationships involved, Mr. Compson establishes Bon as "a mere spectator . . . completely enigmatic," who transcends the "straightforward and logical," yet who "contemplated with the detached attentiveness of a scientist." He speculates that Sutpen tried to get rid of Bon as his daughter's suitor because of Bon's octoroon mistress and their child. But such speculation does not solve the mystery of why it was Henry, Judith's brother and Bon's bosom friend, who finally killed him:

And yet, four years later, Henry had to kill Bon to keep them from marrying. . . .Yes, granted that . . . the existence of the eighth part negro mistress and the sixteenth part negro son, granted even the morganatic ceremony . . . was reason enough, which is drawing honor a little fine even for the shadowy paragons which are our ancestors born in the South and come to man- and womanhood about eighteen sixty or sixty one. It's just incredible. It just does not explain. Or perhaps that's it: they dont explain and we are not supposed to know. We have a few old mouth-to-mouth tales. . . . Yes, Judith, Bon, Henry, Sutpen: all of them. They are there, yet something is missing; they are like a chemical formula exhumed along with the letters from that forgotten chest, carefully, the paper old and faded and falling to pieces, the writing faded, almost inde-cipherable, yet meaningful, familiar in shape and sense, . . . you bring them together in the proportions called for, but nothing happens; you re-read, . . . making sure that you have forgotten nothing, made no miscalculation; you bring them together again and again nothing happens: just the words, the symbols, the shapes themselves, shadowy inscrutable and serene, against that turgid background of a horrible and bloody mischancing of human affairs. (79–80)

In his agonizing struggle to make a clear explanation, solve the mystery, "divulge" the secret, Mr. Compson is trapped in a difficult situation in which he can only exclaim that "something is missing" and admit his failure only by complaining that "they dont explain and we are not sup-posed to know."

Here, it is difficult not to see the similarities between Mr. Compson and Pudd'nhead Wilson who also suffers in an obsessive hunt for the something missing, in his case "the missing confederate," the one that he believes really murdered Tom's uncle, Judge Driscoll. Wilson "mooned around, thinking, thinking, guessing, guessing, day and night, and arriv-ing nowhere" (Twain 98), and when the day of trial finally comes, it is "the heaviest day in Wilson's life, for with all his tireless diligence he had discovered no sign or trace of the missing confederate" (99). But Wilson's predicament shifts from a simple spotting of the murderer to something more complicated. When Tom visits him and leaves "the new finger-marks unintentionally" on the glass on which Roxy's mark is kept, Wilson's "trained eye" does not fail to see that they coincide with "the tracings of the marks left on the knife handle"(104), the weapon used in the assault.

However, one solution leads to another mystery. Wilson gets more confused than ever when he compares Tom's fingerprints at the age of twelve and as a baby with the one just left by him a few minutes before and finds out that "the baby's don't tally with the others!":

> He sat down and puzzled over these things a good while, but kept muttering, "It's no use; I can't understand it. They don't tally right, and yet I'll swear the names and the dates are right, and so of course they *ought* to tally. I never labeled one of these things carelessly in my life. There is a most extraordinary mystery here."
>
> He was tired out, now, and his brains were beginning to clog. He said he would sleep himself fresh, and then see what he could do with this riddle. He slept through a troubled and unrestful hour, the unconsciousness began to shred away and presently he rose drowsily to a sitting posture. "Now what was that dream?" he said, trying to recall it; "What was that dream?—it seemed to unravel that puz—"
>
> He landed in the middle of the floor at a bound, without finishing the sentence, and ran and turned up his light and seized his "records." He took a single swift glance at them and cried out—"It's so! Heavens, what a revelation! And for twenty-three years no man has ever suspected it!" (Twain 104)

Like Mr. Compson, who complains that all is there and yet he cannot reach the truth, that "you bring them together and again nothing happens: just the words, the symbols, the shapes," Wilson deplores that he cannot solve the mystery. What should be noted, however, is that, unlike Mr. Compson, Wilson gets a flash of revelation by a dream which brings him to the truth about the changed identities of the babies. Though Wilson and Mr. Compson share the predicament of not being able to "read"—the finger-marks in the one instance and "the words, the symbols, the shapes" in the other—their similarities seem to end there, given that the one finally sees the light while the other does not. Interestingly, however, there are several other important characteristics which are common not only to *Absalom, Absalom!* and *Pudd'nhead Wilson* but also to "The Man of the Crowd."

Not surprisingly, Robert H. Byer suggests that in "The Man of the Crowd," the "narrator's experience of viewing the crowd takes the form, we might want to say, of a dream or nightmare of the city's everyday life, a dream that is the life of the old man," a dream into which the narrator enters "by way of a feverishly enhanced appetite for the world and from which he reawakens to the mysterious conditions of his own mortality"(Byer 239). Citing Freud's remark about a dream as an illustration of "an indeterminate (or unreadable) content of deeper wishes," Byer proposes that the story can be read in terms of Freud's argument that "every dream [has] some link with a recent daytime impression—often of the most insignificant sort" (562). It could be said, in fact, that "The Man of the Crowd" is only a prototype, "almost an abstract of the detective sub-type of surveillance, flight, and pursuit" (Rzepka 74), and not yet an "authentic" detective story such as "The Murders in the Rue Morgue," "The Mystery of Marie Roget," or "The Purloined Letter"—the three "tales of ratiocination" in which Dupin tries to solve the mystery. It is a story like "William Wilson" or "The Tell-Tale Heart" in which a narrator confines himself within a closed space of his own deepest desires; as Rzepka says,[15] "the 'locked room' of the mind that most stoutly resists our imaginative ingress" is "located in the sub-basement of the narrator's soul" (42).

Dreaming is certainly an important element both in "The Man of the Crowd" and *Pudd'nhead Wilson*. In the former the narrator, in his dream-like pursuit through the phantasmagoric city—which in fact may be a "locked room"[16] of his mind, both literally and symbolically—confronts the old man/unreadable text and comes to the "failed" understanding that the "worst heart of the world is a grosser book than the 'Hortulus Animae,'" and that "it does not permit itself to be read." In the latter, Wilson, in his dream, examines the fingerprints and gets a revelation, as if literally following Freud's remark that "every dream [has] some link with a recent daytime impression—often of the most insignificant sort." Even so, however, their similarities appear to end there, given that in their analogous attempts at "reading," the one "succeeds" while the other does not: Wilson arrives at the solution to the question of the murderer and subsequently at the true identities of Tom and Chambers, while the narrator of Poe's story "fails" in his attempt. But such an interpretation does not contribute to the solution of the controversial question as to whether Wilson—who in the end comes to be successful in gaining his original first name and in becoming a celebrity and the Mayor of Dawson's Landing—can be identified with the man who is the author of the Pudd'nhead Wilson's Calendar, particularly the one which belongs to the "Conclusion." It is hinted by some critics, for a variety of different reasons, that the ending of the novel suggests, perhaps inadvertently, that Wilson's is an ambiguous nature which "does not permit itself to be read" in simple either/or terms. And it may therefore throw some light on the questionable characterization of David Wilson, at once a popular celebrity among his townspeople and a cynic who despises the very people who admire him, to consider him in relation to the situation of Quentin and his father in *Absalom, Absalom!*, another novel with a famously ambiguous ending.

At the beginning of "The Man of the Crowd," the narrator observes the pedestrians with "my brow to the glass," the window pane of a coffeehouse. It is through the glass window that he catches sight of the old man who attracts his attention—"I felt singularly aroused, startled, fascinated"—and starts his pursuit. It is also by examining the glass(es), the "strips of glass five inches long and three inches wide" (Twain 7), that Wilson observes the fingerprints which he collects among the people of the town, "poring over them with absorbing interest until far into the night." Interestingly, there is another character whose attention is obsessively attracted to a glass of a windowpane, not in a coffeehouse in London but in a dormitory room in Cambridge, Massachusetts. The ninth and last chapter of *Absalom, Absalom!* starts with Quentin and Shreve, after their long talk from Chapter 6, finally in bed in their dark, cold room in which "the iron and impregnable dark had become one with the iron and icelike bedclothing lying upon the flesh slacked and thin-clad for sleeping." Despite the darkness, "the window which Shreve had opened became visible against the faintly unearthly glow of the outer snow," and Quentin, who "lay watching the rectangle of window," started "to jerk all over, violently and uncontrollably" (288), for reasons that Quentin does not understand and in fact remain a mystery to the end.

As Shreve and Quentin resume their talk, Quentin recollects the occasion when he accompanied Miss Rosa Coldfield to Sutpen's Hundred in Mississippi the previous year and "faced" Henry Sutpen on his deathbed. Like the narrators of "The Man of the Crowd" and *Pudd'nhead Wilson*, Quentin has to enter into a dreamlike situation before he is brought to face the last phase of his pursuit,[17] and the unexpected—or perhaps the unconsciously expected—meeting of two heirs from the old families of the South is itself remembered as having taken place in a dreamlike or sleepwalking-like manner.[18] As he recalled the interview with Henry, Quentin "lay still and rigid on his back . . . breathing hard but slow, his eyes wide open upon the window, thinking 'Nevermore of peace. Nevermore of peace. Nevermore. Nevermore. Nevermore'" (298–299), an invocation of the famous refrain from Poe's "The Raven."

There are also subsequent references to Quentin watching the window, lying in the dark, cold room, as if imitating the reiterative performance.

When Shreve is talking about the day when Sutpen's Hundred was burned to ashes and Sutpen's family, except Jim Bond, the "idiot boy," perished in fire, Quentin is staring at the window, listening to Shreve telling what he, Quentin, himself has told Shreve, somehow assuming a task at which his father had previously failed. As he does so, Quentin observes a mysterious transformation of the shape of the window which he was watching:

> He just lay there staring at the window without even
> blinking, breathing the chill heady pure snowgleamed
> darkness. "And she went to bed because it was all finished
> now, there was nothing left now, nothing out there now
> but that idiot boy to lurk . . . and howl . . . . And so she
> died."
> . . . Quentin did not answer, staring at the window;
> then he could not tell if it was the actual window or the
> window's pale rectangle upon his eyelids, though after
> a moment it began to emerge. It began to take shape
> in its same curious, light, gravity-defying attitude—the
> once-folded sheet out of the wisteria Mississippi summer,
> the cigar smell, the random blowing of the fireflies. "The
> South," Shreve said. "The South. Jesus. No wonder you
> folks all outlive yourselves by years and years and years." It
> was becoming quite distinct; he would be able to decipher
> the words soon, in a moment; even almost now, now,
> now. . . .
> Now he (Quentin) could read it, could finish it—the
> sloped whimsical ironic hand out of Mississippi attenu-
> ated, into the iron snow . . . (301)

The quotation is complicated and mysterious: the windowpane metamorphoses into the shape of a letter from Mr. Compson; though not described
as such, "it," that is, the letter, has been "obscure" until it becomes "distinct"
at this point; the letter needs to be "deciphered" before it is simply read
even though it seems not to be written in any form of secret language or as
a cryptogram. Before getting any answers to such questions, however, the
reader faces another mysterious situation in which, as if to imitate Quentin,
s/he must "decipher" the most esoteric words that bring the novel to an
end:

> " . . . Now I want you to tell me just one thing more.
> Why do you hate the South?"

"I dont hate it," Quentin said, quickly, at once, immediately; "I dont hate it," he said. *I dont hate it* he thought,
panting in the cold air, the iron New England dark: *I dont.
I dont! I dont hate it! I dont hate it!* (303)

As in the case of Poe's "Nevermore," Quentin's refrain is presented in
the negative; but there is, of course, no explanation as to why he responds
in the negative, or answers "quickly, at once, immediately," or repeats the
word in his thoughts in a very emotional way. Suspended in a sort of
middle ground, the frustrated reader may struggle to find some kind of a
solution: whether to accept naïvely that Quentin is just telling the truth,
that he answers in the negative simply because he does not hate the South,
or to "read" more shrewdly between the lines and realize that Quentin
answers in the negative and repeats it emotionally because Shreve's question touches the core of that suppressed ambivalent feeling toward the
South which was hidden deeply in his soul. Since no reader may accept the
first answer, such an either/or preposition sounds meaningless. However,
it may not be totally wrong to say that Quentin is, in a sense, telling the
truth, or at least not telling a lie, when he says that he doesn't hate the
South. In other words, Quentin is telling the truth but not telling the
"whole truth": his feeling toward his native land is too complicated to be
expressed in terms of a simple yes/no response, so that he cannot help
but answer in the negative, that he does not hate the South. In so doing,
he can negate not only Shreve's assumption that he hates the South but
also the type of question which decides everything, even the most delicate
personal feelings, in terms of a binary opposition of either/or. Ideally,
therefore, the reader's task is not so much to follow Shreve in seeking to
find out whether Quentin does or does not hate the South, and in what
way or to what degree, but rather to imitate Quentin himself by rejecting a
binary-opposition and accepting the depth and complexity of an ambiguous ending which "does not permit itself to be read" in any either/or type of
reading.

That the ending of *Absalom, Absalom!* does not permit an easy or com-
mon-sense type of reading represented by Shreve's conclusion and requires
a more complex decipherment brings us back to the problematic ending
of *Pudd'nhead Wilson*, where there is no clear basis for deciding whether
David Wilson is a fraud, a snob, a social climber, or a cynic, a pessimist, a
scoffer of the corrupted, deceptive, hypocritical society. By correctly "reading" the fingerprint, Wilson recognizes Tom as the murderer and a sham
and a black. But the reader knows that while the reading of a fingerprint
can identify the individual, it does not identify that individual's race, which
is socially constructed and not biologically defined. It is also clear that

Tom's situation is exceptional because Roxana admits the exchange of the babies and because she is, by her community's standard, black.

So the success of Wilson's reading is based on the community's social norms and not on scientific method in any real sense. Critics have expressed uneasiness about the final part of the novel. Eric Sundquist points out that Twain's "use of the metaphor of the revealing hand in *Pudd'nhead Wilson* seems rather to mock the theory that segregation was rooted in organic laws susceptible to proof by the new scientific and sociological study of heredity"(63). Michael Cowan agrees with Sundquist by saying that "it is perfectly possible for Twain . . . to cast an ironic eye on the convention itself" (173). Susan Gillman claims that "what is on trial in the courtroom conclusion is Wilson's method of deducing identity, his 'scientifics,' the fingerprinting system" (97). "Wilson's conclusion," she continues, "though strictly 'the truth,' is also illogical and arbitrary, almost more confusing than clarifying" (99). George E. Marcus is more critical of Wilson, saying that he

> is not the social progressive that we (mistakenly, it
> appears) associated with his intelligence. His prideful
> exposure of his own magic—the fingerprinting as the
> effective proof of his intelligence—is the final move
> toward his acceptance by the community, and he turns out
> to be just as distasteful as they are. (205)

Judging by such standards it becomes clear that Wilson is similar to another intellectual, Faulkner's Gavin Stevens, who in *Light in August* shares the white townspeople's prejudices and characterizes in racial terms Joe Christmas's final action before his death.

The key to the understanding of this puzzling situation is to "decipher" the phrase in the Calendar, "*October 12, the Discovery*. It was wonderful to find America, but it would have been more wonderful to miss it" (Twain 113), the very phrase which creates the discrepancy between the successful Mayor Wilson and the cynical "Pudd'nhead" Wilson. One possible reading is to paraphrase it as follows: "It was wonderful for Wilson to have not only spotted the murderer but revealed his true identity as a 'black' son of a slave, but it would have been more wonderful if there were no slavery, no racial discrimination, in an America which was supposed to have been established with the idealism that all men are created equal." Had America been "missed," there would then have been no institution of slavery, and if no slavery, then no occasion for a Civil War which turned the nation into a "House Divided" and caused the deepest wound, the worst trauma, to fall upon Southerners such as Quentin Compson.

Such a reading, however, does not fill the gap between the two contradicting images of Wilson; rather, it would confirm the difference more clearly and leave the reader without any resolution. An alternative would seem to lie in accepting Wilson's contradictions and seeing him as both Wilson the cynic and Wilson the mayor, a character who resists a definite identity and "does not permit [himself] to be read" in any either/or type of reading. To put it differently, David Wilson's identity is insecure, though not in terms of race as in the case of Tom or Chambers. But this does not mean that the insecure identity of Wilson and the changeable identities of Tom and Chambers represent totally different problems. The ambiguous nature of their identities may rather remind us of a phrase in "The Man of the Crowd" to the effect that "the essence of all crime is undivulged," that we will never be able to get to the "truth." And when the "crime" is specifically "Southern," whether a murder committed by Tom or Thomas Sutpen's desertion of a wife and a son whose "whiteness" is doubtful, that "crime" is rooted not only in the institution of slavery but also in the fear of miscegenation among the white population. In a society where the "One Drop Rule" has a strong influence, nothing is more horrible than a "discovery" that a "white" person has turned out to be "black."

The uneasiness at the end of *Pudd'nhead Wilson*, where Wilson's own identity becomes insecure, and Quentin's highly emotional negation at the end of *Absalom, Absalom!* can be explained by comparing them to a "metaphysical detective story," which, according to Patricia Merivale, is "likelier to deal with a Wakefield, a Missing Person, a person sought for, glimpsed, and shadowed, gumshoe style, through endless, labyrinthine city streets, but never really Found—because he was never really There, because he was, and remains, missing" (105). It may be possible to say that Wilson, Quentin, and the reader with them, follow the path, "reading" the fingerprint or Mr. Compson's letter or the novels, only to find that one is "only following one's own self" (Merivale 105) like the narrator of Poe's story. At the same time, however, we should not forget that "the essence of all crime," both literally and symbolically, in *Pudd'nhead Wilson* or in *Absalom, Absalom!* is "Southern." In the society where race decides people's destiny—where "the conscience of man takes up a burden so heavy in horror"—"white" people will never be sure whether they are "pure" or not—"it can be thrown down only into the grave." Though there is no question as to their "whiteness," David Wilson and Quentin Compson suggest the problematic, "Southern" situation either by implying a "divided" identity with a puzzling remark about a dog—"half" of a dog David wants to own in order to "kill [his] half"— or by repeating a painful and silent cry—"I dont hate it!"—in a cold dormitory room in Massachusetts.

Notes

1.   There are significant similarities between Hightower and David Wilson: both live in the verge of town; both hung a sign outside their house/office; and both are rejected, or in Hightower's case even attacked, by the people of the community due to their misbehavior. In Wilson's case, he "bought a small house on the extreme western verge of the town" (Twain 6) and "hired a small office down in the town and hung out a tin sign with these words on it: DAVID WILSON / ATTORNEY AND COUNSELOR-AT-LAW / SURVEYING, CONVEYANCING, ETC." And "his deadly remark had ruined his chance—at least in the law. No clients came" (7).

2.   Even Thomas Sutpen could be included in this group since, after the famous scene in which he is driven away by a "monkey nigger" from an plantation owner's front door, he runs to the woods and ratiocinates, so to speak, trying to find out the meaning of his experience. Since this shocking experience with the black butler of the mansion triggers the course of his future life, and since his "reading"(understanding) of its meaning turns out to be wrong, as he confesses, in Mr. Compson-like manner, "where did I make mistake," it is possible to say that Sutpen fails in "reading" the black man's words and thus in making his "design" complete.

3.   However, Jason's expression could easily be replaced by a racial one. As Carolyn Porter suggests, "Once a slave, always a slave. Once a 'nigger,' always a 'nigger'—even to the fifth generation in Tom's case," since "the exchange of 'A' for 'B,' as David Wilson later refers to the original Tom and Chambers, is no simple act of turning 'A' into 'B' and 'B' into 'A' so that the two can be returned to their original condition by a legal decision" (Porter 128–129).

4.   Stevens says, "It would not be either one or the other and let his body save itself. Because the black blood drove him first to the negro cabin. And then the white blood drove him out of there, as it was the black blood which snatched up the pistol and the white blood which would not let him fire it. And it was the white blood which sent him to the minister . . ." (Faulkner, *Light* 449).

5.   John Scaggs suggests, quoting Scott R. Christianson's argument about *The Waste Land*, that "The poet's attempts to order experience, mirrored in the actions of the Fisher King and Tiresias in Eliot's poem, also describe the narrative efforts of the hard-boiled private eye." Scaggs continues that the Fisher King's plea at the end of *The Waste Land* draws "a clear link

between 'making meaning' and restoring order that is central to the private eye's attempts to restore social order and justice by making sense of the crimes that have disrupted it" (Scaggs 75). Jason's action, then, supports his sarcastic description of himself as a "detective," a modern antihero who attempts to restore, in his case, not a social but a personal and sterile, since temporary, order.

6.   The expression—"two different Jasons"—reminds us of a reference to Quentin in the early part of *Absalom, Absalom!*. Listening to Rosa Coldfield, the narrative voice says that "[Quentin] would seem to listen to two separate Quentins now—the Quentin Compson preparing for Harvard in the South ... and the Quentin Compson who was still too young to deserve yet to be a ghost ... the two separate Quentins now talking to one another in the lost silence of notpeople in notlanguage ...." (Faulkner, *Absalom* 4–5).

7.   An element common to Gavin Stevens and Mr. Compson is their reference to pseudo-scientific remarks, or "black-magic" science, as Sundquist calls Pudd'nhead Wilson's fingerprinting (Sundquist 63). Gavin Stevens, in *Light in August*, famously comments on why Joe went to Hightower's house in profoundly racial "blood" language, and Mr. Compson, in *Absalom, Absalom!*, confesses that the mystery of the Sutpen family is "like a chemical formula" which he will never be able to figure out. Gavin Stevens and Mr. Compson are good examples of failed detectives in this sense. Neither Gavin nor Mr. Compson succeeds in finding a solution to his respective "problem" either.

8.   To be precise, Rzepka says, "The canon of Poe's crime and detective stories begins with 'The Man of the Crowd' (1840) and extends over the next five years to include 'The Murders in the Rue Morgue' (1841), 'The Mystery of Marie Roget' (1842), 'The Gold Bug' (1843), 'Thou Art the Man' (1844), and 'The Purloined Letter' (1844). All of these tales influenced the later course of detective fiction. 'The Man of the Crowd,' with its debt to Vidocq, is almost an abstract of the detective sub-type of surveillance, flight, and pursuit." In general, however, as John Scaggs says, it is "The Murders in the Rue Morgue" which is "often identified as the first detective story" (Scaggs 19).

9.   The narrator's obsessive pursuit reminds us of Jason's similarly obsessive pursuit after "the man with a red tie" and Quentin. He also chases them for "two days," though not continuously like the narrator; he follows them on April 6 and April 8, the first and the last day/section of the three sections set in the present time of 1928.

10. The note to the word reads as follows: 'The *Hortulus Animæ cum Oratiunculis Aliquibus Superadditis*' of Grünninger" (Poe 481).

11. Rzepka introduces Vidocq as follows: "In the literature of crime as it had evolved up to 1840, identifying criminal types from physical traits was already common. The 1828 *Memoirs* of Eugène-François Vidocq (1775–1850), first head of the Parisian Sûreté (the French equivalent of Scotland Yard), contains lengthy explanations of how to identify different types of thieves, and Poe knew the *Memoirs* well" (41).

12. The word reminds the readers of Quentin; in the last hours of his life, the word "temporary" repeatedly appears in his stream of consciousness.

13. According to *Oxford Thesaurus of English*, to "gauge" is to "assess, evaluate, analyze, judge, rate, determine, estimate," etc. In an ironic turn, the person "gauged(=judged and determined as a fool)" here will clear his name by "gauging(=analyzing)" his "record" of fingerprints.

14. The reference to "uncanny" links *Pudd'nhead Wilson* to "The Man of the Crowd" which, according to Robert H. Byer, "provides a text in which certain seminal explorations of 'modernity' have taken their bearings." As was suggested by Walter Benjamin, Byer continues that modernity appears in the "figure of the *flâneur*, the urban context of capitalism, the world of the private citizen, the poetry of material life, the social production of the 'uncanny'" (221). Stephen Rachman also notes that "The old man is a purely phrenological man, an aggregation of physiognomic traits construed as whole, and this makes him uncanny or 'scary'" (80).

15. Rzepka refers to the narrators of "The Black Cat" and "The Tell-Tale Heart" and not to "William Wilson." But I chose "William Wilson" because, as a story of doppelgänger, or a double, it has some relation to *Pudd'nhead Wilson* in which the problem of identity is a significant theme.

16. The coffeehouse itself is like a library: "With a cigar in my mouth and a newspaper in my lap, I had been amusing myself for the greater part of the afternoon, now in poring over advertisements, now in observing the promiscuous company in the room, and now in peering through the smoky panes into the street" (Poe 475). It is as Stephen Rachman correctly indicates, "more like a library in that it is not a place of public literary discourse but one of private exchanges in public. No conversation takes place at all; in fact, with the exception of a clock striking the hour, Poe's London is largely a silent city" (78–79). In other words then, we can say that the crowded city of London is a phantasmagoria, nothing but a reflection of the narrator's inner world.

17. However, unlike the narrator of "The Man of the Crowd" who obsessively follows the old man or Pudd'nhead Wilson who tries to spot the culprit, the object of Quentin's pursuit is not clearly presented. Yet it is not difficult to see that the kind of pursuit he is involved in and what he will get in the end is one of the main themes of the novel.

18. Quentin confesses, "there was no difference" whether he was "waking or sleeping it was the same" (Faulkner, *Absalom* 298).

Works Cited

Byer, Robert H. "Mysteries of the City: A Reading of Poe's 'The Man of the Crowd.'" In *Ideology and Classic American Literature*, edited by Sacvan Bercovitch and Myra Jehlen. New York: Cambridge UP, 1986. 221–246.

Cowan, Michael. "'By Right of the White Election.': Political Theology and Theological Politics in *Pudd'nhead Wilson*." In *Mark Twain's* Pudd'nhead Wilson*: Race, Conflict, and Culture*. Edited by Susan Gillman and Forrest G. Robinson. Durham, NC: Duke UP, 1990. 155–176.

Gillman, Susan. "'Sure Identifiers': Race, Science, and the Law." In *Mark Twain's* Pudd'nhead Wilson*: Race, Conflict, and Culture*. Edited by Susan Gillman and Forrest G. Robinson. Durham, NC: Duke UP, 1990.

Faulkner, William. *Absalom, Absalom!*. 1936. New York: Random House, 1990.

———. *Light in August*. 1932. New York: Random House, 1985.

———. *The Sound and the Fury*. 1929. New York: Random House, 1990.

Freud, Sigmund. *The Interpretation of Dreams*. Trans. James Strachey. 8th ed. 1930. New York: Basic Books, [1955].

Jehlen, Myra. "The Ties that Bind: Race and Sex in *Pudd'nhead Wilson*." *Readings at the Edge of Literature*. Chicago: U of Chicago P, 2002.

Marcus, George E. "'What did he reckon would become of the other half if he killed his half?': Doubled, Divided, and Crossed Selves in *Pudd'nhead Wilson*; or Mark Twain as Cultural Critic in His Own Times." In *Mark Twain's* Pudd'nhead Wilson*: Race, Conflict, and*

Culture. Edited by Susan Gillman and Forrest G. Robinson. Durham, NC: Duke UP, 1990. 190–210.

Merivale, Patricia. "Gumshoe Gothics: Poe's 'The Man of the Crowd' and His Followers." In *Detecting Texts: The Metaphysical Detective Story from Poe to Postmodernism*, edited by Patricia Merivale and Susan Elizabeth Sweeney. Philadelphia: U of Pennsylvania P, 1999. 101–116.

Poe, Edgar Allan. "The Man of the Crowd." In *The Complete Tales and Poems of Edgar Allan Poe*. New York: Modern Library, 1965.

Porter, Carolyn. "Roxana's Plot." In *Mark Twain's* Pudd'nhead Wilson: *Race, Conflict, and Culture*. Edited by Susan Gillman and Forrest G. Robinson. Durham, NC: Duke UP, 1990. 121–136.

Rachman, Stephen. "'Es lässt sich nicht schreiben': Plagiarism and 'The Man of the Crowd.'" In *The American Face of Edgar Allan Poe*, edited by Shawn Rosenheim and Stephen Rachman. Baltimore: Johns Hopkins UP, 1995. 49–87.

Rzepka, Charles J. *Detective Fiction*. Cambridge: Polity P, 2005.

Scaggs, John. *Crime Fiction*. London: Routledge, 2005.

Sundquist, Eric J. "Mark Twain and Homer Plessy." In *Mark Twain's* Pudd'nhead Wilson: *Race, Conflict, and Culture*. Edited by Susan Gillman and Forrest G. Robinson. Durham, NC: Duke UP, 1990. 46–72.

Twain, Mark. *Pudd'nhead Wilson and Those Extraordinary Twins*. 1894. Edited by Sidney E. Berger. New York: Norton, 1980.

From Unreadable Experience to Initiation: The River in Twain's *Life on the Mississippi* and Faulkner's "Old Man"

The generic identity of *Life on the Mississippi* (1883)—a travelbook that is meant to be both historical and autobiographical—and "Old Man" (1939)—a tale the chapters of which are alternated with those of "Wild Palms" within the contrapuntal structure of *The Wild Palms*—can make it incongruous to compare these two discontinuous texts; yet, the main protagonist, the River, can but lead the reader to probe into their depths. The genesis of *Life on the Mississippi* can be explained by Twain's wish for self-(re)construction, since it was written after a five-week pilgrimage to the Mississippi Valley in 1882. As many critics have pointed out, this retrospective narrative was no creation *ex nihilo* and incorporates the sketches he had published in 1875 in the *Atlantic Monthly* and entitled "Old Times on the Mississippi."[1] The multiple textual fragments that generate a cumulative effect make the swelling narrative widen in the same way that the Mississippi flows into the Delta. This return to the source of the Mississippi experience in both Twain's life and the nation's history can also be read as an initiation story, for the young man, Samuel Clemens, learns how to become a pilot, an avatar of the storyteller.

Initiation is one of the topics "Old Man" shares with *Life on the Mississippi*, for the convict is snatched away by the River from the Parchman penitentiary he was sent to at the age of nineteen. He is entrusted with the mission of rescuing a man he will never find and a woman he regards all the more as a burden because she is pregnant. Thus "flooded into" the realities of a symbolical nuclear family, he has to find his way through the metamorphoses and anamorphoses of the treacherous, unreadable River. Whereas *Life on the Mississippi* is built around the anecdotal and the circumstantial, "Old Man"—the characters of which remain anonymous—takes on an allegorical and nearly mythical dimension, for "Old Man" is meant to throw a light on "Wild Palms" and Harry Wilbourne's initiation into love by Charlotte Rittenmeyer. Faulkner said he "wrote the two stories by alternate chapters" and used "Old Man" for "background effect," thus expressing the need for "contrapuntal quality like music" (Gwynn and Blotner 171). Although "Old Man" is apparently subservient to "Wild Palms," the reference to music is all the more significant as music

154

inevitably suggests fluidity, liquidity, and, thus, water. The major role of the River is to turn the convict's life topsy-turvy in the same way as Charlotte turns Harry's life topsy-turvy by snatching him away from his doctor's dormant and comfortable life. The River is the very space for apprenticeship and gives both Twain and Faulkner the opportunity to problematize the question of knowledge and truth. Initially appearing unreadable, the River is a baroque stage for a quixotic quest: whereas Mark Twain yearns after what he calls "the petrified truth" through his paradoxical initiation into the past in a liquid and unsteady medium, the convict unwittingly goes through ritualistic hardships and refuses to undertake any quest whatsoever, preferring to go back into a world of shadows. Far from petrifying the truth, both authors seem to be trapped in the form and flux of their texts, and the River that overflows its banks is so resistant to definition and interpretation that it is either too written over, or "overwritten," or it cannot be written over—it is "unwritable."

The Unreadable River: From Kronos to Chaos

The continuity and linearity of rivers have turned them into symbols of Time/Kronos and its irreversibility, the Heraclitean flow generating constant metamorphoses. In *Life on the Mississippi* and "Old Man," what should be linear, continuous, and chronological is winding, whirling, and spiralling, so that protagonists get lost in such vorticist labyrinths. Mark Twain pokes fun at the arbitrariness of the state boundaries, written off by the eccentric and unpredictable River. He is typically obsessed with the disappearance of marks and traces which compels him to revise his cartography of the Mississippi and testifies to the unreliability of all scientific measurements—and maybe to his own unreliability as the writer Mark Twain. The River defamiliarizes the map-reader and plays tricks on pilots when they are plunged into the *heart of darkness*, faced with randomness and uncertainty: "I was appalled; it was a villainous night for blackness, we were in a particularly wide and blind part of the river, where there was no shape or substance to anything . . ." (Twain, *Life* 40). The Flood distorts the pilot's familiar vision, for the River in spate is a stage for metamorphoses and anamorphoses: "As I have said, the big rise brought a new world under my vision. By the time the river was over its banks we had forsaken our old paths and were hourly climbing over bars that had stood ten feet out of water before" (52). Samuel Clemens, a pioneer figure, is amazed at the River's potentialities; this North-South axis is a new frontier to be conquered, a pristine world that sends the reader back to the primitivism of "Old Man": "The dense, untouched forest overhung both banks of the crooked little crack, and one could believe that human creatures had never intruded there before" (53). This vision of the ever-transforming flux illustrates Bergson's equation of motion with creation in *La Pensée et le mouvant*: like the River, reality is growth, expansion, and invention, and can be compared to a balloon taking unpredictable shapes.[2] Although the River symbolizes the American nation's expansion, the pilot, who is also a budding writer, is nonetheless aghast at the hermeneutic problems that gush out from its treacherous configuration: "Now I had often seen pilots gazing at the water and pretending to read it as if it were a book; but it was a book that told me nothing" (43). The surface thus problematizes the possibilities of interpretation as well as its limits. The catalogues that clot up the text here and there, in the same way that steamboats and people are carried along by water, contribute to such obstructionism. The surface is no transparent window or mirror, but an opaque screen which the convict also feels unable to read in "Old Man."

In "Old Man," indeed, the River is referred to as the cosmic joker which shrinks man to the inhuman status of a toy or a pawn. Ironically enough, like the Twain's cub-pilot, the convict does not manage to make out the outlines of the hostile water expanse:

> Wild and invisible, it tossed and heaved about and
> beneath the boat, ridged with dirty phosphorescent foam
> and filled with a debris of destruction—objects nameless
> and enormous and invisible which struck and slashed at
> the skiff and whirled on. He did not know he was upon
> the river. (Faulkner 114)

Blinded by the surface, caught in the indomitable stream, the convict, who seems to suffer from aphasia, is shackled by the river—a river or the River?—which is Faulkner's equivalent of Plato's cave. The convict never acquires the knowledge of this rhizomatic labyrinth of rivers and basins and channels, never distinguishing the River from other rivers such as the Yazoo River, before he finds safety on the Indian mound, "that earthen Ark out of Genesis" (163). The Flood brings about universal destruction and dissolution, and the River becomes an allegory of the chaos depicted in Genesis and of the origins of mankind: he did not know "whether the river had become lost in a drowned world or if the world had become drowned in one limitless river" (117). This absolute space-and-time represents some primordial time when the earth was only chaotic swampland inhabited by saurian monsters and inarticulate people. Oxymorons and the play with negatives often convey the difficulties in defining and describing the elements: "the aqueous earth" (51), "the curling wall of water" (112), "that flat fecund waste, neither earth nor water" (17). The River is beyond language and makes the convict unable to articulate his experience when faced with this spatial projection of the human body.

This projection of the body is also difficult to convey. In order to portray the River's bowels, the narrator interweaves similes suggesting suction, digestion, or defecation, and conveying the convict's repulsion towards "some forty hours' constipation of the elements" (113): " . . . the skiff made one long bounding lunge as the convict's native state, in the final paroxysm, regurgitated him on to the wild bosom of the Father of Waters" (113). Although water is usually associated with womanhood, the River's body is that of an "old man," a patriarch such as Abraham and the figure of an initiator who embraces the newborn, as shown by the Native Americans' periphrasis, the Father of Waters. This father figure stands for Kronos or Saturn, also identified as the God of Time, Time over which the convict can have no control when he is outside his monastic cell at the penitentiary. The anaphoric use of the adjective "wild" actually reveals the extent of the elemental subversion: the father figure is endowed with a carnivalesque force that erects a Dionysian (dis)order and shows the vulnerability of civilization by breaking the levees during the famous 1927 flood. Yet, the chaos is followed by a return to order, and the Father embodies law once again: "But four weeks later it [the River] would look different from what it did now, and did: he (the old man) had recovered from his debauch, back in banks again, the Old Man . . ." (194).

Faulkner plays upon the ambiguities so that the convict, now grown old because of his epic journey similar to that of Odysseus, and the River, one of the founders of the nation, seem to be interchangeable after this regenerating episode of festivities which was not, however, perceived as such by the convict. The carnivalesque Time spits out the convict into some Styx or Acheron: in his skiff he can be compared to Charon, the ferryman conveying souls to Hades. Yet Faulkner inverts the symbols, for the skiff becomes a crib for the woman's baby and the convict will find death-in-life in the ascetic life he comes back to after he says "farewell to flesh." At the end of the story, he is portrayed as "saturnine" and thus associated with Saturn, the god of Time; he has explored Time and gone through the cycle of life and death.

The carnival implies the subversion of signs, and Mark Twain's humorous account of the River's eccentricities is also pervaded by the carnivalesque mode—and, tellingly, he gives a lengthy description of the New Orleans carnival. His vision of the River itself turns out to be subversive: he disparagingly borrows "Captain Marryat's rude name for the Mississippi—'the Great Sewer'" (Twain, *Life* 5), which becomes "the great common sewer" (124). The convict's anthropocentric vision of the River also leads him to curse "that risible and concentrated power of water" (Faulkner 175). His ceaseless nose-bleeding, usually interpreted as a symbol of castration, can be construed as a comic echo or replica of the River's absurd flow towards the Unknown.

This tragic and comic approach to the "*immensity of water, of waste and desolation*" (Faulkner 192), reminding the reader of Coleridge's "The Rime of the Ancient Mariner," conveys the dual perception of the River in each text. In spite of its power, the River is tamed and cannot withstand the intrusion of the machine, and especially of the railroad symbolized by the railway bridge across the river: "all the towns out there are railway-centers now" (Twain, *Life* 277). Mark Twain's pilgrimage down the River constitutes an initiation into modernity and the future as well, as if he were a kind of prophet; the former pilot, who denounces the disappearance of aristocratic steamboating, adopts the posture of the champion of progress. The exploration of the country that the River affords in a photographic and nearly cinematic form leads him to discover the potentialities of the American nation and a new "reading grid" unfurls over the formerly chaotic River. Yet, Twain, like Faulkner later in "Old Man," remembers the destructiveness of the River that killed his brother Henry in a steamboat accident involving a kind of elemental struggle between fire and water.[3] Such destructiveness is also experienced by the convict, aghast at the unreality of a burning plantation or people drifting on the River's shores. Parallels can be drawn between the depiction of the wasteland born out of the Flood in each text. Destruction links this wasteland to Babylon, the "debauch" the convict wants to run away from: "Remarking that the story of the Tall Convict takes place by or on the Great American River has no real relevance in the search for Biblical analogies, but a taste, an odor, of the Biblical Babylon may be perceived in the atmosphere of the richly rotting New Orleans by the river" (Pitavy 118).

The symbolical perception of the River is actually subject to change and the relativity of one's perceptions. To the uninitiated, it is an unreadable book; even in "Old Man," the river-as-book metaphor is spun on, and the surface is compared to paper or a palimpsest the convict cannot decipher: it is "a flat still sheet of brown water," "a single, perfectly flat and motionless steel-coloured sheet" (Faulkner 46). Although he often holds phallic symbols such as the paddle, the convict cannot pierce the mysterious screen of the waters or probe their different strata:

> It was as if the water itself were in three strata, separate
> and distinct, the bland and unhurried surface bearing a
> frothy scum and a miniature flotsam of twigs and screen-
> ing as though by vicious calculation the rush and fury
> of the flood itself, and beneath this in turn the original

stream, trickle, murmuring along in the opposite direction, following undisturbed and unaware its appointed
course, and serving its Lilliputian end, like a thread of ants
between the rails on which an express train passes, they
(the ants) as unaware of the power and fury as if it were a
cyclone crossing Saturn. (47)

The River, despite its apparent linearity and continuity, combines opposite
natural forces, both conscious and unconscious, peaceful and violent, and
the paradoxes it symbolizes are also conveyed by the choice of the similes—the ants and the train referring to earth and the cyclone suggesting
wind and air—but all point out to this unreadable elemental disorder. The
Flood is an accident of carnivalesque Time but the Eternal, Heraclitean
flux is as irreversible as the motion of a train, the very symbol of modernity.
Saturn/Kronos goes on presiding adamantly over this chaos. Such imme-
morial Time, characterized by sameness and repetition, is also the circular
and cyclical Time of seasons. The River cyclically expresses its fertility and
fecundity and has impregnated "the richened soil which would not need
to be planted, which would need only to be shown a cotton seed to sprout
and make." Unexpectedly, the usual association of water with womanhood and motherhood is subverted, for the water of the Old Man, its/his
seminal liquid, is "brown and rich as chocolate" (194). The Flood is only a
regeneration ritual for Mother Earth. Years before Faulkner, Mark Twain
had joked about the Old Man's nurturing virtues in his own hyperbolic
and humorous way which contrasts with Faulkner's mythopoeic construct:
". . . there was nutritiousness in the mud, and a man that drunk Mississippi
water could grow corn in his stomach if he wanted to" (Twain, *Life* 17).
Such comic extravagance—which reminds the reader of the tall-tale
tradition—contrasts with the allegorical and philosophical dimension of
Faulkner's tale. In his miscellaneous *autofiction*,[4] Mark Twain sometimes
wears the philosopher's mask, and his journey on the Mississippi is
investigative, a quest for truth. The bartender who complains about the
disappearance of drinking facilities on the Upper Mississippi voices Twain's
concerns as a writer: "'Sounds like poetry, but it's the petrified truth'" (158).

The River as a Birthplace: The Quest for the Petrified Truth

The cub-pilot initiated into the art of piloting learns how to become
a "seer" and a "teller," and the "Father of Waters"—like the older pilots—is
the main initiator, reasserting the heuristic function of the journey on
baptismal water. Gaston Bachelard asserts that the first leap into the
Unknown is a leap into water.[5] The River becomes Samuel Clemens/Mark

Twain's birthplace: ". . . I became a new being and the subject of my own admiration" (Twain, *Life* 26). He becomes aware of the discrepancies between the layman's and the seasoned pilot's perceptions of the River. The young apprentice feels disappointed with his new scientific knowledge that has deprived him of the aesthetic pleasure he used to take in gazing at the river: "In truth, the passenger who could not read this book saw nothing but all manner of pretty pictures in it, painted by the sun and shaded by the clouds, whereas to the trained eye these were not pictures at all, but the grimmest and most dead-earnest of reading-matter" (46). The discovery of truth proves incompatible with the preservation of beauty, which corroborates the words of the bartender who opposes truth to poetry. The newborn pilot has to unveil the artifices of the River and to sort out the dilemma that haunts Twain as regards the pursuit of aesthetic and scientific ideals, the constant wavering between ornament as temptation and truth as requirement. He derides the conventional descriptions of the River, especially the "picturesque" details that are actually clichés. The depiction of sunset is one of the literary prerequisites of travelbooks, which Twain delights in parodying:

> And I remember Muscatine—still more pleasantly—for its summer sunsets. I have never seen any, on either side of the ocean, that equalled them. They used the broad, smooth river as a canvas, and painted on it every imaginable dream of color, from the mottled daintinesses and delicacies of the opal, all the way up, through cumulative intensities, to blinding purple and crimson conflagrations, which were enchanting to the eye, but sharply tried it at the same time. All the Upper Mississippi region has these extraordinary sunsets as a familiar spectacle. It is the true Sunset Land: I am sure no other country can show so good a right to the name. The sunrises are also said to be exceedingly fine. I do not know. (246–247)

The River is no longer compared to a text, but to a painting. Twain condemns the stereotyped accounts produced by the scribblers of travel literature, which is implied by the phrase "the Sunset Land," and ironically resorts to the poetic devices or the florid artistic and literary vocabulary such texts are cluttered with. So as to show his weariness about sunsets and sunrises, he dismisses the reader in a casual way. Despite this distrust of so-called romantic representations of reality, Twain often feels torn between the two poles of memory and imagination, and cannot refrain from dabbling in the picturesque: he can ambiguously surrender to the mimetic illusion and the rendering of a "picturesque spectacle" (79).[6] It is not uncommon for him to interweave pictorial terms, which makes it difficult for the reader to distinguish pastiche—neutral imitation—from parody, which is essentially ironical. Twain's modernity and belief in progress actually lie in his aspiration to be as accurate and truthful as photography: "That picture of it was still as clear and vivid to me as a photograph" (227). The pilot's visual acuity is compared to that of a photographer: "his trained faculties instantly photographed the bearings" (62). Photography is a bulwark against the writing off of marks and traces and can make up for loss of memory.

Being a seer, the pilot, an avatar of the storyteller gifted at spinning yarns, also teaches the cub-pilot how to speak and, accordingly, how to lie; initiated into the vernacular, the budding pilot learns how to read the Other, steamboating being thus a lesson in humanism: the River teaches "a kind of human relationship at odds with the vanity, selfishness, competitiveness, and hypocrisy of society" (Warren 61). The cub-pilot travels among a crowd of eccentric and marginalized people whose tricks and cock-and-bull stories throw a grim light on the human soul. It is still difficult for him to find his own voice, which is also confirmed by the anecdote he reports about his *nom de plume* or *nom de guerre*. This name, he says, was in fact used by a knowledgeable pilot, Captain Isaiah Sellers, whom the young cub-pilot Samuel Clemens admired for his fabulous memory and his "accurate and valuable" information (Twain, *Life* 213); he was, however, the target of the other pilots' irony. Clemens parodied a text by Sellers, arousing the latter's anger:

> He never printed another paragraph while he lived, and he never again signed "Mark Twain" to anything. At the time that the telegraph brought the news of his death, I was on the Pacific coast. I was a fresh, new journalist, and needed a *nom de guerre*; so I confiscated the ancient mariner's discarded one, and have done my best to make it remain what it was in his hands—a sign and symbol and warrant that whatever is found in its company may be gambled on as being the petrified truth. (214)

The name "Mark Twain" bears the mark of usurpation. Symbolically killing the father of Logos, he stole both his style and his name, and wants readers to construe this "borrowing" as a tribute and as unquestionable evidence of his own reliability as a writer. Such self-irony or self-derision shows the limits of his claim to find the petrified truth, and critics have questioned the truthfulness of this anecdote.[7] The elusiveness of marks ("mark twain" means "two fathoms" and thus refers to the art of piloting with accuracy in shallow water), their obliteration or their resurgence, conveys the writer's failure to petrify the truth, to give it a stable shape. The different hypo-texts[8] that resurface in *Life on the Mississippi* also testify to Twain's constant masquerading. Even if the River initiates him into reading and writing, in the end, the book, which is permanently inchoate and rather inconclusive,[9] is kaleidoscopic and blurs the linearity of Samuel Clemens's exploration of the River and narcissistic self-exploration. If stasis is a characteristic of truth, then this quest for truth remains subject to motion and elusiveness.

On the contrary, Faulkner's convict has grown old and his adventures on the River constitute a condensation of all the stages of life and death a human being may go through. Ironically, he did not choose the quest; the River chose and elected him, as the Nile—and God—chose and elected Moses. From the Flood to the regeneration of Nature at the end of the tale, his own epic story can be read as the genesis and odyssey of mankind. Even more than in *Life on the Mississippi*, the River turns into a psychological mirror, a mental "waterscape" and watershed. The ebb and flow of the River mirrors "the ebbing and fluxing phases of anxiety and impotent rage" (Faulkner 111); the surface is thus the mirror held up to the convict so that he can know himself, learn patience and humility, even if he refuses to look at himself in an unnarcissistic attitude or if he hardly manages to see himself in this muddy glass. This immersion into reality increases his awareness of his fear of sex and women and of his wish to return to the womb-like prison, for he is often described in a fœtal posi-tion, crouching and squatting. The role of the River—which is no amniotic liquid—consists in triggering off an anamnesis and, indirectly, the convict's own narrative: once he is back in his cell, like Mark Twain's cub-pilot, he in turn becomes a storyteller. Thanks to the River, he is born to language and the heterodiegetic narrator gradually lets him have his say: "Then, sud-denly and quietly, something–the inarticulateness, the innate and inherited reluctance for speech, dissolved and he found himself, listening to himself, telling it quietly, the words coming not fast but easily to the tongue as he required them" (234).

The word "dissolution" refers to liquidity and sends one back to the connections Bachelard established between water and fluid and continuous language.[10] The definite closure of "Old Man" contrasts with the appar-ently slapdash ending of *Life on the Mississippi*: like Robinson Crusoe, the convict is compelled to adjust to the whimsical flood for his survival, becomes a *homo faber* whom Bachelard calls "*l'homme pétrisseur*," the man who mixes earth with water and embodies creativity and practicality; this Southern Hercules also learns how to become "a matador" in his daily struggles with alligators. Last but not least, he becomes a surrogate father for the unknown woman's child. The conclusion of the story—"Women ——t!"—with the rejection that the censored word ("shit "?) implies, may suggest that the convict's initiation into life with the archetypal woman results in a reassertion of his fear of women. The latter are often referred to as flesh and meat devoid of any glamor. The River overflowing its banks is as inescapable as the burden of the female whose dim portrayal mirrors that of the vortex: she is nearly reified as "the swelling and unmanageable body before him" (Faulkner 110). Ironically the only flesh the convict yearns to be close to is that of his mule at Parchman, "the eunuch race" (113), and the animal's name is symbolically "John Henry." The tall convict and his emasculated mule form the grotesque couple that excludes all women from the mundane world.

After the carnivalesque foul play of the River comes Lent, the time of penance and asceticism during which the convict says farewell to flesh. Powerful as he may be thanks to his Herculean feats, he expresses no will to power but only aspires to an ascetic life and to ataraxia, a life deprived of emotions and sensations. Like a hermit at the end of his life, initiated into essential values such as endurance and stoicism, he chooses a life away from women, thus reasserting the manliness of the Father of Waters. One might be tempted to conclude that the reader is presented with an anthropocentric and even phallocentric image of the River. Amazingly enough, one can wonder whether Mark Twain's vision of the River does not exclude women; he exhibits a wide range of characters, but women are quite absent from *Life on the Mississippi*, as if the world of pilots initiated little Samuel into manliness only. The treatment of the Southern lady whose worship was encouraged by Walter Scott, is disparaging and ironical: "I find confirmation of the theory which I broached just now—namely, that the trouble with the Southern reporter is Women: Women, supplemented by Walter Scott and his knights and beauty and chivalry, and so on" (Twain, *Life* 197). The description of the mule-race on the same page is probably not accidental. . . . The debunking of the Southern Belle's image undoubtedly stems from Mark Twain's anti-romantic stance, and the purpose of "Old Man" is also to expose any quixotic vision of human life and any overwriting or hyperbolic writing of human experience.

The River's Un/Overwritability: Form and Flux

Mark Twain's narrative appears as inflated as the flooded River, and Faulkner's marathon sentences are so convoluted, laden with similes, anaphoras, and embedded clauses that the text, like the River, both enthralls and entraps the reader who wonders if the initiation story can be written. "Like the philosophers, the architects of the Modernist tradition explored the dialectic of form and flux, and were attached to constructs that unify concrete particulars without suppressing the differences between them" (Schwartz 7). The River enables both Twain and Faulkner to problematize this dialectic of form and flux as well as that of linear unity and textual multiplicity. Even Twain can indeed be considered as a pre-Modernist and even a pre-Postmodernist if one pays attention to the fragmentary nature of his work and the effect of dissemination it produces: "Dissemination is the state of perpetually unfulfilled meaning that exists in the absence of all signifieds" (Harland 135). In both texts, the reader is immersed in a liquid labyrinth of "bric-à-brac" (Twain, *Life* 172, 189), "odds and ends" (193) which likens the writing process to making a scrap-book. Although Twain, the autodiegetic narrator, divides his retrospective narrative into chapters and announces the composition of his personal and historical chronicle on the Mississippi, the text is definitely a palimpsest, a *collage* of fragments from travelbooks. He even adds to this patchwork an extract from his own embryonic novel known as "the raftsman episode," taken out of what was to become *Adventures of Hucklebbery Finn* (1884). He borrows material from articles, ghost stories, adventure novels, or Indian tales, wandering from one story to another and crossing generic boundaries. Such extravagance is typical of the Southern tall tale, and the failure to frame the text is as remarkable as the failure to tame the River. The narrative is flooded with anecdotes turning into digressions rife with embedded narratives which are so many replicas of the River's channels: the storyteller "branched out into a narrative that bristled all along with incredible adventures" (28).

The violation of the verisimilitude principle and the hyperbolic language are all the more detrimental to the quest for "the petrified truth" as this *mise en abyme* of the narrative process highlights the pilots' unreliability as storytellers who ensnare their audience in their lies. A pilot, indeed, masters "the noble art of inflating his facts" (Twain, *Life* 111). Entertainment, comic relief, and humiliation of one's listeners are the purposes of such lies. The imitation of the pilots' idiolect and the variety of styles—one of the characters is even called "Rob Styles"—replicate the River's inventiveness and unpredictability. "Old Man" is also a text that overflows its margins, and the heterodiegetic narrator—the typical writer of fairytales who starts his narrative with "Once . . . there were two convicts" (Faulkner 19)—introduces shifts in perspectives, tampers with the framework of his narrative, and inserts the dialogue with the other prisoners' so that the convict's narrative seeps into his tale. This narrative technique seems to be based on *collage* as well. The polyphony and the merging of voices contribute to the complexity of the narrative threads which one can hardly unravel, for the style remains as uniform as the River's surface. Moreover, the heterodiegetic narrator emphasizes the convict's limited point of view with the help of a great many modal adverbs or negatives. He parades the convict on the stage so as to underline the limits of narration. Twain and Faulkner wonder to what extent the word, written or spoken, can be relied upon as "the petrified truth."

The River proves to be a pretext for quite an iconoclastic exploration of fiction, a literary stance that can be as destructive as the Flood. Both texts can be read as relevant examples of metafiction, and even historiographic metafiction, since Twain also claims to write the history of the Mississippi, combining facts with fiction. Twain debunks romance and the romantic tradition derived from Walter Scott's novels: "There, the genuine and wholesome civilization of the nineteenth century is curiously confused and commingled with the Walter Scott Middle-Age sham civilization . . ." (Twain, *Life* 199). Truth is thus opposed to fraud and lies that caused many people during the Civil War to become quixotic adventurers, as revealed by the convict's distrust of "paper novels" or Twain's irony towards "girly-girly romance" (199). The convict was sent to Parchman because he attempted a train robbery. He took at face value what was written in the stories and paper novels he had read:

> the writers, the uncorporeal names attached to the stories,
> the paper novels—the Diamond Dicks and Jesse Jameses
> and such—whom he believed had led him into his present
> predicament through their own ignorance or gullibility
> regarding the medium in which they dealt and took
> money for, in accepting information on which they placed
> the stamp of verisimilitude and authenticity. (Faulkner 19)

There are no real heroes in Twain's *Life on the Mississippi*, although he regards pilots as aristocratic picaroons. But the latter are liars whose feats barely deserve "the stamp of verisimilitude and authenticity," and their world is doomed to vanish. The convict himself loses his heroic status when his gestures are parodied by the Cajun, a grotesque double who imitates his killing of alligators: ". . . the Cajan would perform his ritualistic victorious pantomime" (Faulkner 184). The convict is unwillingly heroic; he chooses a nihilistic life in prison and turns a deaf ear to eloquence. Twain emphasizes the dangers of "talking wild" (Twain, *Life* 22). Both stories are thus cautionary tales that initiate readers into the intricacies of literature—the metaphor of which is the River and its expanding Delta, the symbol of both "overwriting" and of the inability to encircle "the petrified truth." Such scepticism towards the truthfulness of language by two authors who write in so many words appears particularly postmodern, especially through their investigation of metafiction: "... postmodern does not aspire to tell the truth as much as to question whose truth gets told" (Hutcheon 71).

Notes

1. James M. Cox paid a lot of attention to the structuring of *Life on the Mississippi*, which critics often describe as a patchwork: "He [Twain] had, as we know, already returned to the river in his writing, having written seven sketches which William Dean Howells had published in the *Atlantic* (from January to August 1875) under the title 'Old Times on the Mississippi,' and when he came to the actual business of writing his travel book, he inserted those sketches wholesale. They constitute chapters 4 to 18 of *Life on the Mississippi* and are often referred to as the 'first half' of the book, though they constitute only one-fourth of its contents. These are inevitably the chapters critics cite as the 'strong part' of the book, whereas the remaining three-fourths are often dismissed as one more example of Mark Twain's unfortunate hauling and filling and padding for the subscription trade" (Cox, "*Life on the Mississippi* Revisited" 157).

2. "*La réalité est croissance globale et indivisée, invention graduelle, durée: tel, un ballon élastique qui se dilaterait peu à peu en prenant à tout instant des formes inattendues*" (Bergson 105).

3. According to Michel Imbert, the destructiveness suggested by fire and steam in *Life on the Mississippi* is caused by industrial mechanization and by what he refers to as "machinery of life," determinism: "Written after the Reconstruction era, in the context of devious re-enslavement of African-Americans and attuned to the unprecedented forms of alienation entailed by industrial mechanization, *Life on the Mississippi* was imbued with a grimly deterministic view of the machinery of life manufacturing a gratuitous holocaust" (Imbert 55).

4. Damien Zanone mentions in his glossary that the word "autofiction" was coined by Serge Doubrovski and designates a narrative that has the characteristics of autobiography but is close to the novel by combining fictional with real facts.

5. "*Le saut dans l'inconnu est un saut dans l'eau. C'est le* premier *saut du nageur novice*" (Bachelard 188).

6. Henry Nash Smith underlines Twain's ambiguity and thinks that the dilemma he is faced with is sheer convention: "In discussing the sunset

Mark Twain succumbs to the cliché of heart versus head always lurking in the theory of ideality. He professes to yearn for an innocence of vision that knowledge and experience have destroyed. But the elegant posture he has talked himself into is merely a stereotype" (Smith 80).

7.   "The tale, so far as the most serious Mark Twain scholars have been able to discover, cannot be corroborated from the life of Samuel Clemens. But then why should it be? For Mark Twain, even as he insists upon his extreme veracity, actually arouses comic doubt about the entire episode" (Cox, *Mark Twain* 165–166).

8.   The terms "hypotexte" and "hypertexte" are used by Gérard Genette in *Palimpsestes*. The hypertext is the text derived from another text, which is the hypotext.

9.   The last sentence sounds conventional at best, casual at worst: ". . . and there ended one of the most enjoyable five-thousand-mile journeys I have ever had the good fortune to make" (Twain, *Life on the Mississippi* 261).

10.   "*L'eau est la maîtresse du langage fluide, du langage sans heurt, du langage continu, continué, du langage qui assouplit le rythme, qui donne une matière uniforme à des rythmes différents*" (Bachelard 209).

Works Cited

Bachelard, Gaston. *L'Eau et les rêves : essai sur l'imagination de la matière*. Paris: Le Livre de Poche, Biblio Essais, 1942.

Bergson, Henri. *La Pensée et le mouvant*. Quadrige, PUF, 1938.

Cox, James M. *Mark Twain: The Fate of Humor*. Princeton: Princeton UP, 1966.

———. "*Life on the Mississippi* Revisited." In *Mark Twain*, edited by Harold Bloom. New York: Chelsea, 1986. 153–167.

Faulkner, William. "Old Man." In *The Wild Palms*. 1939. New York: Penguin Modern Classics, 1987.

Genette, Gérard. *Palimpsestes*. Paris: Le Seuil, 1982.

Gwynn, Frederick L. and Joseph L. Blotner, eds. *Faulkner in the University*. 1959. Charlottesville: U of Virginia P, 1995.

Harland, Richard. *Superstructuralism. The Philosophy of Structuralism and Post-structuralism*. London: Routledge, 1987.

Hutcheon, Linda. "'The Pastime of Past Time': Fiction, History, Historiographic Metafiction." In *Postmodern Genres*, edited by Marjorie Perloff. 1988. Norman: U of Oklahoma P, 1989. 54–74.

Imbert, Michel. "Fluctuations in *Life on the Mississippi*." *Revue Française d'Études Américaines* 98 (2003): 48–56.

Pitavy, François. "Forgetting Jerusalem: An Ironical Chart for *The Wild Palms*." In *Intertextuality in Faulkner*, edited by Michel Gresset and Noel Polk. Jackson: UP of Mississippi, 1985. 114–127.

Schwartz, Sanford. *The Matrix of Modernism: Pound, Eliot, and Early Twentieth-Century Thought*. Princeton: Princeton UP, 1985.

Smith, Henry Nash. *Mark Twain: The Development of a Writer*. Cambridge, MA: Harvard UP, 1962.

Twain, Mark. *Life on the Mississippi*. 1883. In *The Family Mark Twain*. New York: Dorset P, 1988. 1–282.

———. *Adventures of Huckleberry Finn*. 1884. In *The Family Mark Twain*. New York: Dorset P, 1988. 437–650.

Warren, Robert Penn. "Mark Twain." In *Mark Twain*, edited by Harold Bloom. New York: Chelsea, 1986. 55–82.

Zanone, Damien. *L'Autobiographie*. Paris: Collection Ellipses, 1996.

To Kill a Prejudice:
Racial Relations and the Lynch Mob
in Twain, Faulkner, and Harper Lee

Mark Twain's *Adventures of Huckleberry Finn* (1884), William Faulkner's *Intruder in the Dust* (1948), and Harper Lee's *To Kill a Mockingbird* (1960) were all novels which addressed the subject of racism in the United States and which were considered, when published, progressive and liberal statements against racial injustice. Recent revisionists, however, have suggested that they preached a doctrine of gradualism and did not go far enough towards supporting genuine equality. If placed in the contexts of their respective historic periods, however, it may be argued that each represents a forward-looking perspective that develops in progressive stages. The grace of enlightenment over prejudice comes about because of what happens in a specific place, usually a jailhouse, where a crowd has gathered. In each case, a shaming of the crowd, as well as the assertion of common human bonds and individual responsibility, bring people to their senses.

When Harper Lee's first and only novel, *To Kill a Mockingbird*, appeared in 1960, it met with immediate praise. It remained on the bestseller list for over eighty weeks, it won the author several awards in America and abroad including the Pulitzer Prize for fiction (she was the first woman to win that award in twenty years), it was translated into numerous languages, and a paperback edition has gone through hundreds of printings. The novel was immediately filmed and released in 1962 to an equally enthusiastic reception, with Gregory Peck receiving an Academy Award for his portrayal of Atticus Finch, perhaps the finest performance of his career.

Any number of prominent people have testified to the power and influence of *To Kill a Mockingbird* on their attitudes toward racism in the United States. When James Farmer, head of the Congress of Racial Equality, was arrested campaigning for Civil Rights in Jackson, Mississippi, Roy Wilkins brought him a copy of *To Kill a Mockingbird* to read and pass the time in jail, and political campaign strategist James Carville once noted that when he first read it, he knew that his whole attitude towards racial justice had been wrong (Sundquist 182–183). When Timothy Kaine, now Governor of the state of Virginia, became a white mayor of predominantly black Richmond in 1998, he testified that it was reading *To Kill a Mockingbird* as a child in an all-white Kansas town that opened his eyes to racial injustice and the need for reform (Williams A19).

A great many lawyers, including celebrity defender F. Lee Bailey and independent counsel Kenneth Starr, have admitted that it was Atticus Finch in either the book or the film, as the wise and fair-minded new conscience of the South, who caused them to decide to enter the profession (Holcomb 35). Film producer Cameron Crowe works references to the novel's characters into his films as a way of paying tribute, and when asked by the *New York Times* to discuss the one film that had the most "personal meaning" for her, Sissy Spacek selected *To Kill a Mockingbird* (Lyman E1). A 1991 survey of lifetime reading habits conducted by the Library of Congress and the Book-of-the-Month Club found that the 5,000 respondents listed Harper Lee's novel as ranking second to the Bible in influencing their lives (Johnson 14).

Coming just six years after the tradition-shattering decision of *Brown vs. Board of Education* by the Supreme Court, both novel and film were hailed for their revelations of discrimination in Southern courts against black defendants. The black writer and critic Nick Aaron Ford noted that "instead of stereotyped Negroes, this novel presents living, convincing characters—neither saints nor devils, neither completely ignorant or craven or foolish, nor completely wise or wholly courageous" (Ford 122). Yet, of late, few other critics have agreed with Ford, as the novel has come under the scrutiny of revisionists who see it as less radical or liberal than it seemed in 1960 and believe that it "represents a white view of racism that marginalizes both the lives and the pains of the very people it seeks to humanize—blacks living in the Deep south during the Depression" (Martelle A2).

Recent essays by Eric J. Sundquist and Joseph Crespino have argued that Harper Lee preached a doctrine of gradualism rather than promoting genuine immediate reform and that her point of view was paternalistic if not, indeed, racist in its own way. The black character in the novel, Tom Robinson, is seen as defenseless unless the white man, Atticus Finch, intervenes on his behalf. As Richard Yarborough has noted, in this and similar novels, "The black character is the victim and he or she becomes the test upon which any struggle for moral satisfaction on the part of the white savior is waged" (qtd. in Martelle A2). If viewed in the context of its time and place, however, and seen in the larger literary tradition to which it belongs, I would argue that *To Kill a Mockingbird* represents a major progressive step towards enlightenment in matters of race.

The literary antecedents of the novel are clear. It belongs in the tradition of Mark Twain's *Adventures of Huckleberry Finn* and William Faulkner's *Intruder in the Dust*. Both are novels which view society through the innocent eyes of a child narrator who, unblinded by pride and prejudice, discerns in startling outlines the shams and hypocrisies through which man imprisons and destroys his fellow man. Huck takes a raft down the Mississippi with his black friend Jim and discovers that a slave can be a human being and that what society legally sanctions can be immoral. Chick Mallison, in *Intruder in the Dust*, is pulled from a baptismal stream by a proud, defiant black named Lucas Beauchamp and embarks on an odyssey in pursuit of the truth, which teaches him that apparent and presumed guilt can often mask brutality, evil, and racial bigotry. In *To Kill a Mockingbird*, Scout Finch, with her brother Jem and their precocious playmate Dill, play the seemingly frightening game of making Boo Radley come out, while around them the deadly serious game of sacrificial scapegoat is played against a background of rural ignorance and hatred. Like Huck and Chick, Scout discovers that kindness and goodness reside behind a black face and that the spook of one's imagination can prove to be a source of salvation and an agent of conscience in reality.

But *To Kill a Mockingbird* is about many other things than race relations. For example, it is about the psychological and physiological growth of two children, the boy approaching puberty and manhood and breaking away from childish attachments, and his sister becoming aware of the world of femininity and the pressure to give up her tomboy ways. It is about the education of these children and suggests finally that genuine learning comes from life-experience rather than books or school, as educational philosopher John Dewey would preach. As Jem tells Scout when she complains about Miss Caroline, her first-grade teacher, "Our teacher says Miss Caroline's introducing a new way of teaching. She learned about it in college. It'll be in all the grades soon. You don't have to learn much out of books that way—it's like if you wanta learn about cows, go milk one, see? . . . It's the Dewey Decimal System" (20).

The novel is also about superstition and how fear and ignorance feed it. The treatment ranges from simple childhood beliefs and folklore to the kind of superstition that makes a lurking terror out of the recluse, Boo Radley, or that nurtures the racial myth that all black men want to violate white women. It is about reverence for life; despite the occasional necessity to shoot a mad dog, there is a respect for harmless animals like mockingbirds, which rob no one and contribute only beauty to life. Atticus tells Jem, "Shoot all the blue jays you want, if you can hit 'em, but remember it's a sin to kill a mockingbird" (103).

Finally, *To Kill a Mockingbird* is about us, the people, and reflects a positive attitude about human nature and our potential for achieving in this world a truly democratic society where people act out of love and compassion rather than hatred and contempt. It represents a stage in human development that can be traced through earlier works of fiction.

Mark Twain was one of the first to work out the formal setting for this development. It consists of a jailhouse or a building where a crowd has gathered to exact vigilante justice, but they are stalled by someone who intervenes and challenges the fury of mob rule. In *Adventures of Huckleberry Finn*, it happens in a small Arkansas town where Huck and Jim have tied up their raft. They witness a minor tragedy in which a boastful, drunken man named Boggs has challenged for the last time the town's leading figure, the aristocratic Colonel Sherburn, who coolly shoots him down in the street. A crowd collects, "a-whooping and yelling and raging like Injuns," and determines to lynch Colonel Sherburn. They gather together at the Colonel's house and call him out:

> Just then Sherburn steps out onto the roof of his little front porch, with a double-barrel gun in his hand, and takes his stand, perfectly ca'm and deliberate, not saying a word. The racket stopped, and the wave sucked back.
>
> Sherburn never said a word—just stood there, looking down. The stillness was awful creepy and uncomfortable. Sherburn run his eye slow along the crowd; and wherever it struck, the people tried a little to out gaze him, but they couldn't; they dropped their eyes and looked sneaky. Then pretty soon Sherburn sort of laughed; not the pleasant kind, but the kind that makes you feel like when you are eating bread that's got sand in it.
>
> Then he says, slow and scornful:
>
> "The idea of *you* lynching anybody! It's amusing. The idea of you thinking you had pluck enough to lynch a *man*! Because you're brave enough to tar and feather poor friendless cast-out women that come along here, did that make you think you had grit enough to lay your hands on a *man*? Why, a *man's* safe in the hands of ten thousand of your kind—as long as it's daytime and you're not behind him.
>
> "Do I know you? I know you clear through. I was born and raised in the south, and I've lived in the north; so I know the average all around. The average man's a coward. In the north he lets anybody walk over him that wants to, and goes home and prays for a humble spirit to bear it. In the south one man, all by himself, has stopped a stage full of men, in the daytime, and robbed the lot. Your

newspapers call you a brave people so much that you think you *are* braver than any other people—whereas you're just *as* brave, and no braver. Why don't your juries hang murderers? Because they're afraid the man's friends will shoot them in the back, in the dark—and it's just what they *would* do.

"So they always acquit; and then a *man* goes in the night, with a hundred masked cowards at his back, and lynches the rascal. Your mistake is, that you didn't bring a man with you; that's one mistake, and the other is that you didn't come in the dark and fetch your masks. You brought *part* of a man—Buck Harkness, there—and if you hadn't had him to start you, you'd a' taken it out in blowing.

"You didn't want to come. The average man don't like trouble and danger. *You* don't like trouble and danger. But if only *half* a man—like Buck Harkness, there—shouts 'Lynch him, lynch him!' you're afraid to back down— afraid you'll be found out to be what you are—*cowards* and so you raise a yell, and hang yourselves onto that half-a-man's coat-tail, and come raging up here, swearing what big things you're going to do. The pitifulest thing out is a mob; that's what an army is—a mob; they don't fight with courage that's born in them, but with courage that's borrowed from their mass, and from their officers. But a mob without any *man* at the head of it, is *beneath* pitifulness. Now the thing for *you* to do, is to droop your tails and go home and crawl in a hole. If any real lynching's going to be done, it will be done in the dark, southern fashion; and when they come, they'll bring their masks, and fetch a *man* along. Now *leave*—and take your half-a-man with you"—tossing his gun up across his left arm and cocking it, when he says this.

The crowd washed back sudden, and then broke all apart and went tearing off every which way, and Buck Harkness he heeled it after them, looking tolerable cheap. I could a' staid, if I'd a' wanted to, but I didn't want to. (189–191)

This is a cynical view of human nature and society, but Twain was writing in the wake of social Darwinism and scientific determinism. Twain himself had lost faith in the American dream and was entering a period of philosophic despair that would result in a series of misanthropic novels that predicted a technological apocalypse (as in *A Connecticut Yankee in King Arthur's Court*).

Mark Twain suggests in this passage that only in mindless crowds are people willing to commit violence and outrage, and that if left alone, the individual lacks the courage to act. To put it in a more positive light, Twain also suggests that we are more rational and moral when taken separately from the crowd and that violence is a senseless act performed only under the persuasion of peer pressure. Bravery and true courage reside in the ability to resist.

Obviously this is not a racial confrontation, and certainly no black man who had killed a white would have been permitted the podium taken by Colonel Sherburn. Despite the fact that the novel is largely concerned with racism and the meaning of slavery, Twain knew he could not have a black character speak these words. Thus he is working by indirection. Since the topic is lynching, no reader then or now is likely not to think of racist violence, since the black man has always been the most likely subject of such attacks.

Between 1882, when Twain was writing *Huckleberry Finn*, and 1900, the United States averaged over 150 reported lynchings per year, and from 1882 to the early 1950s, the total would climb to somewhere between 4,000 to 6,000 victims who died at the hands of lynch mobs. In the South, 84 percent of these victims were black males (Hair 174–175). That Twain was thinking of lynching as a form of racist violence is made clear in an essay which expands on his thoughts in the Sherburn episode. In his 1901 article, "The United States of Lyncherdom," blacks are primarily mentioned as victims of this form of what Twain calls "Moral Cowardice" (675).

The second confrontation occurs in a novel published over sixty years later, William Faulkner's *Intruder in the Dust*. As in *Adventures of Huckleberry Finn*, a young boy is the central consciousness who must contend with a black man who defies the conventions of a society which defines him as an object or a piece of property. Chick Mallison is on the verge of adulthood but still innocent of society's methods of moral duplicity and self-deception. He finds that what society says to be true does not always square with justice. An interesting addition to his pattern of initiation is Miss Eunice Habersham, who applies the intuitive principles of womanhood to the strictly literal principles of men. As Lucas Beauchamp, the black man accused of murdering a white man, puts it:

> Young folks and womens, they aint cluttered. They can lis-
> ten. But a middle-year man like your paw and your uncle,
> they cant listen. They aint got time. They're too busy with

facks. In fact, you mought bear this in yo mind; someday you mought need it. If you ever needs to get anything done outside the common run, don't waste yo time on the menfolks; get the womens and children to working at it. (70)

In the town of Jefferson, Mississippi, a crowd has gathered to lynch Lucas Beauchamp for his alleged crime. They have come, says the narrator, not to sit in judgment on the black man because "they had already condemned him but on Beat Four, not come to see what they called justice done nor even retribution exacted but to see that Beat Four should not fail its white man's high estate" (134).

While the sheriff is away gathering evidence that will prove the black man innocent, a lone woman in her eighties, Miss Habersham, sits between the jailhouse door and the impatient crowd, doing her knitting. No man with any pretensions to being a gentleman is likely to try to move her, thus Lucas remains safe. In Clarence Brown's faithful film adaptation, Crawford Gowrie threatens to light some spilled gasoline at her feet with a match. She faces him down and then goes to the screen door to address the entire crowd. With none of the eloquence of Colonel Sherburn, she says simply, "Go on home. You should be ashamed." While they do not disperse immediately, and only when the actual murderer confesses, the spirit of the mob has been broken as this venerable representative of Southern womanhood (which most lynchings were supposedly meant to protect) reminds them of their lack of shame and loss of individuality. She momentarily reminds them of who they are and that they should think better of themselves.

Intruder in the Dust does promote a political policy of gradualism in improving race relations. As Gavin Stevens notes:

> Someday Lucas Beauchamp can shoot a white man in the back with the same impunity to lynch-rope or gasoline as a white man; in time he will vote anywhen and anywhere a white man can and send his children to the same school anywhere the white man's children go and travel anywhere the white man travels as the white man does it. But it wont be next Tuesday. Yet people in the North believe it can be compelled even into next Monday by the simple ratification by votes of a printed paragraph. (151–52)

Later he insists, "I only say that the injustice is ours, the South's. We must expiate and abolish it ourselves, alone and without help nor even (with thanks) advice" (199). But the novel features a black man, labeled "a damned highnosed impudent Negro" (148), who not only stands up for his right to his day in court but manipulates everyone in the community to prove his innocence without once leaving his jail cell. If ever twentieth-century literature had a black character free in body, spirit, and soul, that character was Lucas Beauchamp.

The third confrontation takes place in *To Kill a Mockingbird*. This time Atticus Finch is standing guard at the jailhouse door to protect his client's life, Tom Robinson, accused of assaulting a white woman. A lynch mob arrives in pickup trucks and is about to force their way past Atticus when three children suddenly arrive and gather at the feet of Atticus. Unaware that they stand between the forces of barbarism and civilization, between unreasoning prejudice and the logic of humane rationalism, Scout Finch innocently surveys the men for their common humanity, seeking to locate a familiar face:

> "Hey, Mr. Cunningham."
> The man did not hear me, it seemed.
> "Hey, Mr. Cunningham. How's your entailment gettin' along?"
> Mr. Walter Cunningham's legal affairs were well known to me; Atticus had once described them at length. The big man blinked and hooked his thumbs in his overall straps. He seemed uncomfortable; he cleared his throat and looked away. My friendly overture had fallen flat.
> Mr. Cunningham wore no hat, and the top half of his forehead was white in contrast to his sunscorched face, which led me to believe that he wore one most days. He shifted his feet, clad in heavy work shoes.
> "Don't you remember me, Mr. Cunningham? I'm Jean Louise Finch. You brought us some hickory nuts one time, remember?" I began to sense the futility one feels when unacknowledged by a chance acquaintance.
> "I go to school with Walter," I began again. "He's your boy, ain't he? Ain't he, sir?"
> Mr. Cunningham was moved to a faint nod. He did know me, after all.
> "He's in my grade," I said, "and he does right well. He's a good boy," I added, "a real nice boy. We brought him home for dinner one time. Maybe he told you about me, I beat him up one time but he was real nice about it. Tell him hey for me, won't you?"

Atticus had said it was the polite thing to talk to people about what they were interested in, not about what you were interested in. Mr. Cunningham displayed no interest in his son, so I tackled his entailment once more in a last-ditch effort to make him feel at home.

"Entailments are bad," I was advising him, when I slowly awoke to the fact that I was addressing the entire aggregation. The men were all looking at me, some had their mouths half-open. Atticus had stopped poking at Jem: they were standing together beside Dill. Their attention amounted to fascination. Atticus's mouth, even, was half-open, an attitude he had once described as uncouth. Our eyes met and he shut it.

"Well, Atticus, I was just sayin' to Mr. Cunningham that entailments are bad an' all that, but you said not to worry, it takes a long time sometimes . . . that you all'd ride it out together. . ." I was slowly drying up, wondering what idiocy I had committed. Entailments seemed all right enough for living room talk.

I began to feel sweat gathering at the edges of my hair; I could stand anything but a bunch of people looking at me. They were quite still.

"What's the matter?" I asked.

Atticus said nothing. I looked around and up at Mr. Cunningham, whose face was equally impassive. Then he did a peculiar thing. He squatted down and took me by both shoulders.

"I'll tell him you said hey, little lady," he said.

Then he straightened up and waved a big paw. "Let's clear out," he called. "Let's get going, boys." (175–176)

Once again a lynching is averted. The faceless mob is dispersed as Scout pins on Mr. Cunningham his identity and responsibility as an individual. As Atticus later explains to Jem:

"Mr. Cunningham's basically a good man," he said, "he just has his blind spots along with the rest of us."

Jem spoke. "Don't call that a blind spot. He'da killed you last night when he first went there."

"He might have hurt me a little," Atticus conceded, "but son, you'll understand folks a little better when you're older. A mob's always made up of people, no matter what.

Mr. Cunningham was part of a mob last night, but he was still a man. Every mob in every little Southern town is always made up of people you know—doesn't say much for them, does it?"

"I'll say not," said Jem.

"So it took an eight-year-old child to bring 'em to their senses, didn't it?" said Atticus. "That proves something—that a gang of wild animals *can* be stopped, simply because they're still human. Hmp, maybe we need a police force of children . . . you children last night made Walter Cunningham stand in my shoes for a minute. That was enough." (Lee 180)

Mark Twain suggested that human beings can rise above their prejudices if they will only pay attention to their individual consciences rather than follow the persuasion of conformity found in society in general as well as in mob violence. Faulkner demonstrated that a single frail woman could raise the consciousness level of a crowd by appealing to their sense of decency and personal shame. Harper Lee argued that the assertion of common human bonds and taking responsibility for one's actions bring people to their senses, if we can but for a moment walk in someone else's shoes. While perhaps not radical enough for some modern sensibilities, all three books were clearly helpful and hopeful contributions to improved race relations. They remain works of dignity rather than despair, compassion rather than prejudice.

Works Cited

Brown, Clarence, prod. and dir. *Intruder in the Dust*. MGM Studios, 1949.

Crespino, Joseph. "The Strange Career of Atticus Finch." *Southern Cultures* 6.2 (Summer 2000): 9–29.

Faulkner, William. *Intruder in the Dust*. New York: Random House, 1948.

Ford, Nick Aaron. Review of *To Kill a Mockingbird*, by Harper Lee. *Phylon* 22 (June 1961): 122.

Hair, William I. "Lynching." *Encyclopedia of Southern Culture*. Edited by Charles Reagan Wilson and William Ferris. Chapel Hill: U of North Carolina P, 1989. 174–176.

Holcomb, Mark. "*To Kill a Mockingbird*: A Classic Revisited." *Film Quarterly* 55.4 (2002): 34–40.

Johnson, Claudia Durst. *To Kill a Mockingbird: Threatening Boundaries*. New York: Twayne, 1994.

Lee, Harper. *To Kill a Mockingbird*. 1960. Thirty-Fifth Anniversary Edition. New York: HarperCollins, 1995.

Lyman, Rick. "In the Arms of Memory." *New York Times* 1 February 2002: E1.

Martelle, Scott. "New Look at 'Mockingbird.'" *Richmond Times-Dispatch* 22 June 2000: A2.

Mulligan, Robert, dir. *To Kill a Mockingbird*. Universal Studios, 1962.

Sundquist, Eric J. "Blues for Atticus Finch: Scottsboro, Brown, and Harper Lee." In *The South as an American Problem*, edited by Larry J. Griffin and Don H. Doyle. Athens: U of Georgia P, 1995. 181–209.

Twain, Mark. *Adventures of Huckleberry Finn*. 1884. Edited by Walter Blair and Victor Fischer. Berkeley: U of California P, 1988.

———. "The United States of Lyncherdom." In *The Complete Essays of Mark Twain*, edited by Charles Neider. Garden City, NY: Doubleday, 1963. 673–679.

Williams, Michael Paul. "Building Bridges Life's Work for Richmond's New Mayor." *Richmond Times-Dispatch* 2 July 1998: A19.

Weeping or Wanting:
Post-Death Dislocation in Moral Constructs in Faulkner, Twain, and Zola

In 1925, through the diligence of a state legislator and in support of the teaching of creationist beliefs in the public school system, Tennessee passed the Butler Act, forbidding the teaching of Charles Darwin's 1865 *Origin of Species*.[1] After high school biology teacher John Scopes agreed to put the law to the test, a court case emerged, primarily from a challenge by the American Civil Liberties Union. Known as the *Tennessee v. John Scopes* case, the dispute went to trial in Dayton, Tennessee. The trial caught the eye of fundamentalist powerhouse William Jennings Bryan, two-time failed presidential candidate, author, and self-appointed messiah for religious fundamentalism. At the same time, H.L. Mencken of the *Baltimore Sun*, later to become the politically-minded editor of the *American Mercury*, defended Scopes via his typewriter while Clarence Darrow defended Scopes in the courtroom. The influence of the Scopes trial extended well past the boundaries of Tennessee, indeed throughout the United States.

What made the Scopes trial such a sensation? Why would America care if some small-town Southern schoolteacher taught biology from a popular textbook with a smattering of the concept that man descended from a lower order of animal? Yet America did care. In August of 1925, the Scopes trial began—only to be sent to a higher court a year later. Scopes's own counsel aided in his guilty verdict, convincing Scopes to accept the jury's guilty ruling so the case could be appealed. After the trial, Scopes left high school teaching to become a scientist, Clarence Darrow receded into history, and Bryan died in his sleep at the peak of his religious fundamental revival. The Tennessee Court of Appeals threw the case out, yet the Butler Act remains on the books in Tennessee to this day. Why all the fervor?

The debate over evolution in the public schools galvanized both the religious and the scientific communities, opening the door for moral discourse about human nature and behavior. Any discussion of evolution caused the fundamentalist Christian believers and the scientific community to take up intellectual arms. Ironically, such a battle concerns not only the past and the present but also the future. Thus, it is also a battle about what occurs at death and in an afterlife. It deals strictly with the physiological aspect of man while ignoring the psychological aspect—an aspect that may tell more about man than any intellectual battle over bone structure.

While there is no direct link between evolution and social behavior, in terms of a direct cause and effect, the strong contributions of American authors dealing with naturalism as a literary approach certainly influenced the connectivity and emotionalism within the issue of Darwinism versus creationism, especially within the American arena. This form of naturalism, seen in Frank Norris, Theodore Dreiser, Sinclair Lewis, Sherwood Anderson, William Faulkner, and Erskine Caldwell, addresses what Joseph Karaganis describes as a condition whereby "[n]aturalism found its coherence in new theories of psychology and emerging scientific doctrines of determinism, predominantly Darwinism and its social and Spencerian varieties" (154).[2]

From this perspective, the *Tennessee v. John Scopes* case was not simply a battle of religion versus science but a battle of human identity—of behavior viewed as something of glory and behavior viewed as a reduction to animalistic greed and expansion. Many writers address the topic and prove their engagement with naturalism and extended fatalism. Most notably, William Faulkner, Emile Zola, and Mark Twain engage with the topic in their treatments of the dead—for it was truly the future of the dead that underlay the naturalistic view of humanity with its primary question of where physical man would go after life. Was the human future one of heavenly reward or one of decomposition in the earth? Even more importantly, how did the treatment of the dead by the living reflect humankind's true perspective? In essence—if a moral construct dictates that the dead are to be venerated—this suggests a creationist approach to the value of human beings after they pass away. However, if practical accessibility to economic or personal gain occurs upon one's passing and is accepted by the living, then this denotes an evolutionary possibility in that the individual will pursue survival, regardless of any moral construct.

One strong psychological indicator of the latter argument as accurate is our process of dealing with our dead, the truly dispossessed. It can be argued that mourning the dying may be nothing more than a biological drive to achieve benefice and costs that are acceptable, to come to an understanding of grassroots mortality, thereby escaping the legal positivism of the courtroom but demonstrating that Darwin's analysis of human design may be uncomfortably close in terms of our animalistic behavior as we divide the spoils of the truly dispossessed.

To draw such a conclusion—that the moral construct of respect and service to the dead is nothing more than a biological need to acquire vacated resources—stands in the way of how human moral constructs exalt the value of human life. To suggest that funerals and the ritual that surrounds them are little more than recognizing the personal gain of the survivors from the emotional, mental, and fiscal estate of the deceased seems harsh. However, to assume that there is no gain upon a position vacated in life seems to avoid the issue of what the deceased mean to the living, beyond the emotional attachment created within a narrow sphere of life. Such a limitation belies the apparent human desire to support life if the only qualifier is that one must be emotionally attached to a deceased individual in order to mourn his or her passing.

This distance is precisely what Faulkner achieves in *A Fable*, what Zola heralds as representing the grassroots citizens of rural France in *Earth*, and what Twain injects with humor in "A Curious Dream." Each of these writers demonstrates that the claim of biological evolution can be supported by the side effect of funerals and the disposal of the dying as social duties that generate gain for the living in terms of resources no longer being shared, thereby providing evidence that evolution occurs by the elimination of those processes which do not provide resources for the living. This latter statement is a primary support of the naturalistic platform or behavior dictated by resource and scarcity.

Certainly, deeper explorations into these various time periods in American and European literatures in which funeral scenes play a central role would reveal a multitude of writers who discovered the same evolutionary understanding: that service after death occurs only when resource conditions are positive. When conditions for disposing of the dead are not positive, the American and European process appears to allow compromises to the duty contract between the living and the dead. Such evidence is most noticeable in Faulkner and Zola, and although less so in Twain, nevertheless, is still present. All three of these writers demonstrate within their writings that human behavior and its ensuing moral discourse and ritual are influenced directly by the availability of shared resources. Such a position supports Richard Alexander's studies regarding the human condition in *The Biology of Moral Systems*, in which the perceived morality and the biological human psyche must achieve complete cooperation in order for conflict to be eliminated. Such cooperation corresponds to Alexander's fifth hypothesis in which he states that:

> Consciousness and related aspects of the human psyche
> (self-awareness, self-reflection, foresight, planning,
> purpose, conscience, free will, etc . . .) are hypothesized
> to represent a system for competing with other humans
> for status, resources, and eventually reproductive suc-
> cess. More specifically, the collection of these attributes
> is viewed as a means of seeing ourselves and our life

situations as others see us and our life situations, so as
to outguess, out-maneuver, out-do those others—most
particularly in ways that will cause (the most and the
most important of) them to continue to interact with us
in fashions that will benefit us and seem to benefit them.
(113)

Within this hypothesis, Alexander maintains that all social ritual may be understood as a competition for resources, but in such a way that will provide us with the most direct benefice, or nepotistic results if we receive nothing for ourselves, "nepotism" being defined as where or when copies of our genes reside in collateral (non-descendant) relatives.[3] In terms of our discussion of post-death dislocation and moral discourse, represented through the writings of Faulkner, Zola, and Twain, we are given evidence that Alexander's hypothesis is accurate through specific narrative examples. This evidence occurs in both the legal field and the philosophical arena, which together most influence moral discourse. When we address these two areas, and then apply the narrative constructs of these writers, we find that Faulkner, Zola, and Twain corroborate Alexander's hypothesis of the rituals toward the dead as not being a genuine moral deliberation but rather a negotiation of the physical and social resources made available by the vacancy created by the dead. Such negotiations are hidden beneath the subtle conventions of prescribed behavior.

The concept of social negotiation becomes important, especially within legal and philosophical avenues, and must be explored as an area of moral discourse prior to providing evidence of behavior toward the dead within cultural frameworks. Within the legal framework, Howard Kahane,[4] in his analysis of evolutionary biology in relation to moral sentiments, terms the balance between the two as social contracting or contractual ethics (54). Within this contractual ethics paradigm, a multitude of implied contracts are developed, all with the intent of furthering resource availability and social benefice. For example, a husband and wife or a legally recognized union may employ "Until death do we part" as one of the rules of the marital contract. At the point that one of the two in the union die, the marital contract is immediately voided. Such a nullification of the contract occurs against the backdrop of an additional implied contract between the living and the larger society. If the society allows for circumstances to alter the contract with the living members in terms of how the dead are to be treated, then the society agrees that only under certain circumstances must the funeral ritual be carried out to the terms of the contract: whatever society deems as appropriate behavior for dealing with its dead. In this sense, funeral rites and associated rituals are contractual obligations which are dissolved in the first case between the living and the deceased, and rendered negotiable a second time through revision in the second case; the affected living and the larger society modify the contractual agreement under varying circumstances by making behavioral allowances in times of emotional distress or resource scarcity. This aspect is important because while a contract is an agreement that only human beings use within daily interactions with other human beings, these same contracts can be nullified in any given situation, thereby reinforcing the idea that, in times of stress, the affected living may be released from all interpersonal contracts instantaneously and with short- and long-term cost benefice to themselves, generally indicated through economic inheritance and sympathy extended to the bereaved by the larger society.

William Faulkner, in both *A Fable* and in *As I Lay Dying*, demonstrates both extremes of the social contract and models contractual ethics structure regarding the treatment of the dead. In *A Fable*, we are spectators in a macabre psychological setting where almost all social contracts have been abrogated within a setting of war. Within the novel, moral discourse on both sides of the battlefront have been reduced to a pragmatic survival discourse where the moral construct no longer represents the strength and courage of men but a harsh reality of resource allocation and fatalism as we see in the French division commander's understanding of his role in the war:

> to reap every hope save glory, and every right save the chance to die for it. He could desert of course. But where? To whom? The only people who would accept a French failed general would be people so far free of the war. (687)

Even within this fatalistic understanding that war does not necessarily award the brave or clever, the division commander comes to a wry understanding of the actual value of the war in noting:

> War and drink are the two things man is never too poor to buy. His wife and children may be shoeless; someone will always buy him drink or weapons, thinking more than that. The last person a man planning to set up in the wine trade would approach for a loan would be a rival wine dealer. A nation preparing for war can borrow from the very nation it aims to destroy. (688)

Lothar Honnighausen's analysis of Faulkner's treatment of war and values in *A Fable*, especially against a backdrop of what is attributed as the German understanding of biological negotiation in times of resource scarcity, reflects Faulkner's French commander's understanding of the human consciences' ability to borrow resources while at the same time plan the destruction of the benefactor.[5]

> [There is] relativising of victory and defeat in regard to the distribution of resources. A nation insolvent from overpopulation will declare war on whatever richest and most sentimental opponent it can persuade to defeat it quickest, in order to feed its people out of the quartermaster's stores. (Honnighausen 133)

Faulkner demonstrates that the motives for the war are no longer the same motives as the rationales that might begin a war—moral discourses on subjects like freedom and oppression and other lofty moral constructs. The Commander has had his awakening in understanding that war takes on many evolutionary concepts, including the use of a pack mentality to take over a territory, the irrelevance of each individual member of that pack should the individual member be killed, and the recognition that using the enemies' resources in times of peace does not negate or make unjustifiable an immediate call to violence against the provider of earlier resources.

As *A Fable* continues, Faulkner's characters regress to an even more evolutionary process of competition and survival. Faulkner reduces whatever moral reasoning the soldiers used for engaging in the war to a basic naturalism, a regressed bewilderment, as he evokes an analogy of cave dwellers emerging from the ground in relation to the war-torn soldier, evidenced in his description of the troops as they:

> Would be creeping in the darkness out of the savage bitter fatal stinking ditches and scars and caves where they have lived for years now, blinking with amazement and unbelief, looking about them with dawning incredulous surmise . . . (775)

Faulkner's use of naturalism in conjunction with fatalism, demonstrates a shift of power from moral constructs to the mere act of environmental survival. War becomes a social condition where all moral discourses—except the value of procreating life—are abrogated in favor of biological survival[6] including the treatment of the dead. Such an outcome offers support to Darwin's representation of evolutionary man using regression as a means of discarding traits which he no longer needs even if they were once moral-discourse staples,[7] and engaging in what would be considered, in a more modern psychological format, forms of social deviancy stemming from stress,[8] indicating a return to a more animalistic behavioral pattern. Such a condition supports Alexander's overall conclusion that all moral discourses arising from biological needs are simply rationales instead of actual embodiments of human truth. This power-shift from moral constructs to evolutionary behavior during Faulkner's war is clearly represented throughout the novel even by the daily headings of the week that guide the novel's progress, suggesting that a man could regress within days.

As additional evidence, we can see how Faulkner offers us another scenario relating to the idea of rejecting the social contract through his design of the narrative voices in *As I Lay Dying*. In this novel, the moral discourse regarding the disposal of the dead overrides biological needs. The contract made between Addie and her family is unbreakable, even as the family is virtually destroyed and every resource is made available for the carrying out of that promise; a promise now compromised by the self-interested motive of returning to Jefferson besides that of burying Addie. In the dialogue between Jewel, Vernon, and Pa, the disastrous outcome of living up to this social contract of burying Addie in her family plot in Jefferson is foreshadowed but never questioned by Pa. Vernon understands it, taking an almost neutral position about the outcome while Jewel rages about the coffin being built outside of Addie's window. Pa has already made up his mind that regardless of the cost of the resources, he'll honor his contract with the dying Addie.

> She wanted that like she wants to go in our own wagon," pa says. "She'll rest easier for knowing it's a good one, and private. She was ever a private woman. You know it well . . . .
>
> "Sho," Vernon says. . . . "She'll hold on till everything's ready, till her own good time. And with the roads like they are now, it wont take you no time to get her to town."
>
> "It's fixing up to rain," pa says. "I am a luckless man. I have ever been." (13)

Pa's statement of his luckless nature reeks of resignation, as if he knows the disaster that awaits his family, but there is no question that he'll see Addie's burial through, regardless of the consequences. When Jewel challenges Pa about doing everything the way Addie wants it done, Pa becomes angry as he tells Jewel how things would turn out if the doctor came tomorrow and told Addie it was time to die.

"I know her. Wagon or no wagon, she wouldn't wait. Then she'd be upset, and I wouldn't upset her for the living world. With that family burying-ground in Jefferson and them of her blood waiting for her there, she'll be impatient. I promised my word me and the boys would get her there quick as mules could walk it, so she could rest quiet." He rubs his hands on his knees. "No man ever misliked it more." (13)

When Jewel carries the argument further, still angry that Cash is building the coffin in the yard instead of buying one in town, Pa tells Jewel:

"It was her wish," pa says. "You got no affection nor gentleness for her. You never had. We would be beholden to no man," he says, "me and her. We have never yet been, and she will rest quieter for knowing it and that it was her own blood sawed out of the boards and drove the nails. She was ever one to clean up after herself." (14)

Pa's description of his and Addie's life serves as a eulogy to Addie even before she passes away. Within that eulogy, the finality of the decision to see all contracts through to the last detail is made by Pa, and it sets the course for the destruction of the family and its resources.

Faulkner's ability to show the polarities of social contracts being ignored in situations of scarcity, often sponsored by war, and social contracts being honored to a point of biological destruction can be labeled as more than incidental. In *A Fable*, the work takes on a more global understanding of human nature in the face of biological deprivation. In *As I Lay Dying*, Faulkner returns to his Southern moral discourse sub-system of a man's word, his binding contract, being even more important than poverty or physical death.

The question that arises in *As I Lay Dying* as it regards this discussion of moral discourse and resource availability and accessibility, is one of whether or not man is able to perform a moral act without an altruistic motive. If man can do a good moral deed with no expectation of reward, including the reward of satisfaction itself for doing the deed, then pure altruism can exist. However, since a man does achieve some form of personal gain for conducting a moral deed, then there is no such thing as an altruistic motive.[9] Alexander refers to this condition as nepotistic gain, whereby moral discourse "deeds" will benefit those either biologically close to the one performing the deed or, in the absence of bloodline, will benefit those whose environment, beliefs, and intellect are deemed related to those who commit the moral deed.[10]

Faulkner recognizes both the absence of the altruistic deed in the midst of conflicting rationales for going to Jefferson, as well as providing character evidence that, under periods of resource duress, the living are allowed to deal with the dead in whatever means are acceptable to that immediate society. The recognition of duty or obligation cannot be made without recognition of personal gain for an individual or that individual's immediate nuclear group.

Faulkner, Zola, and Twain, through their respective dealings with the dead, lead us to a point where we can show what the Scopes courtroom could not prove in terms of physical evolution or spiritual creationalism. These writers, within their literary developments, demonstrate that where man and the dying are concerned, the degree of attention to ritual and pre-established social contracts is directly proportionate to the availability of goods and resources available within the settings of each writer's reality, quite possibly making a statement for all of mankind through fiction. Not only do we find that social contracts are nullified or modified within periods of resource scarcity, or that not to nullify them, as in the case of *As I Lay Dying*, leads to destruction of the living nuclear group—we can also find ample evidence that the processing of the dead actually provides resource gain for the living, representing what Kant[11] referred to as self-interest. What becomes interesting to note is that the fewer biological resources available within an environment, the more society approves the nullification of social contracts and the awareness of personal-resource gain provided by the vacancy of the dead. This condition demonstrates that the moral construct regarding the treatment of the dead is little more than an extension of biological resource availability or scarcity. This viewing of the dead as creating a vacancy for more resource gain and pure self-interest of the living is clearly shown in two separate burial scenes in both Faulkner's *A Fable* and Emile Zola's *Earth*.[12] How is it that two authors writing at different time periods could portray nearly identical scenes dealing with the disposal of the dead in circumstances of scarcity if both did not have some understanding of the social contracting and self-interest motivations of man? While the characters are different, the settings and the contractual behaviors of the characters are nearly identical. Both scenes share economic periods of resource shortage that modify these nearly identical reactive behaviors.

As noted earlier, Faulkner chooses war for the placement of his setting. Zola chooses the poverty of the French peasantry for his. Regardless, the same outcomes emerge in terms of dealing with the dead. What becomes reinforcing to Alexander's overarching premise that moral constructs are purely biologically driven are those elements within naturalism writings that constantly demonstrate that under perceived resource duress, identical social nullifications are allowable regardless of the immediate cultural setting, be it war or provincial rural existence.

Zola's peasantry in *Earth* emerges from the French-Prussian war (Bakker 62) in no better or worse condition than when they entered the battle. The war is almost peripheral, another condition of life that deserves no more attention than a failed crop or a vindictive business arrangement. In the absence of education, wealth, and growth, Zola's characters become the living dispossessed, a form of the economic dead, and therefore can respond in any manner to a social contract that they choose. Zola demonstrates the simple casualness of dealing with the dead by people who have little more themselves. This occurs when Palmyre, a female peasant woman in the field of her village in the French Lior Valley, dies from heat stroke while Lise and Jean are copulating beneath a haystack and others are scything a field of standing corn nearby:

> LaGrande, [Palmyre's grandmother], who had renounced her and never spoke with her walked forward at last.
> "I think she's really dead. . ." She prodded her with her stick. The body, with its eyes staring vacantly in the bright light, did not move. The stream of blood was drying on the chin. The grandmother, bending lower, added. "Yes, she's dead, no doubt of it. And better dead than living to be a burden on others." (203)

Later, after Palmyre's grandmother vents her distaste for her granddaughter, the people in the field gather around the body, the value of a few stalks of corn almost overpowering the need to make a funeral bed for the corpse, as if the corn sustains more value. This is demonstrated when the peasants want to take some harvested sheaves of corn from a nearby field to make a bed for the corpse:

> Buteau, the owner of the corn and one of the wealthier peasants, objected.
> "You'll get your corn back!" [LaGrande]
> "I should hope so."
> Lise, somewhat ashamed of such miserliness added two bundles as a pillow and Palmyre's body was laid on top. . . (203)

Even then, when they are moving the body to the edge of the field, the dispute over the few corn sheaves used to make the bier is only marginally decided: "Not one of the tired harvesters spoke as they followed the [littered] corpse with heads lowered in resignation like a flock of sheep" (204).

Palmyre's disposal is overshadowed by Buteau's concern for his few corn sheaves, coupled with the tiredness of the men who carry "her stiffening body on the sheaves with their heads bowed, not in social grief but in tiredness and resignation" (204). In the casualness of the disposal of the dead and dispossessed Palmyre, social contracts are nullified in favor of self-interest. The entire funeral scene at the corner of the French field echoes the biblical stories of casting lots. As the scene of Palymre's death concludes, the peasants are "paid their scant share by the landowner and divide Palmyre's belongings amongst themselves" (204).

This could be said to be an incidental scene, but when compared to Faulkner's scene in *A Fable* of the burial of a dead brother, once again at the side of a French field, we see the same mood on the occasion, the same offhanded disregard toward the implied social contracts of proper burial rituals. In this scene, the brother, killed in the war, is brought home to his peasant roots. His two sisters, his widowed wife, and a husband to one of the sisters are in attendance.

> The [husband] getting down from the cart . . . to go stand looking at his ruined land . . .
> "Come now, let's finish this first." So he returned and entered the house. Apparently he had brought some of the tools back with him yesterday too because he reappeared at once with a spade and mounted the cart again. Though this time she had the lines, as though she knew exactly where she wanted to go, the cart moving again, crossing the field now, rank with weeds and wild poppies; skirting the occasional craters, on for perhaps half a kilometer to a bank beneath an ancient beech tree which had also escaped the shells. The digging was easier here, all of them taking turns, the girl [wife] too, although Marthe tried once to dissuade her.
> "No," she said. "Let me. Let me be doing something." Though even then it took them a long time until the excavation was deep enough into the bank to contain the coffin, the four of them now shoving and sliding the box back into the cave they had made.

"The medal," the husband said. "You don't want to put that in too? I can open the box." But Marthe didn't even answer, taking the shovel herself first, until the husband relieved her of it and at last the bank was smooth save for the shovel marks; afternoon then and almost evening when they returned to the house and the three women entered it while the husband went on to the stable to put the horse up for the night. (1034)

In this scene, we once again see parallels to Zola's indifferent characters; the withholding of the soldier's medal for the few pennies it might bring mirrors the perceived value of the corn sheaves that hold Palmyre's body as profit or as a social honor resource benefice. The jostling "sliding and pushing of the casket" in *A Fable* recalls Palmyre's body "stiff on the corn sheaves, some corn ears, hanging down behind the head [swinging] to and fro at each jolt in the measured pace of the bearers" (203)—both indicate a casual disposal of the dead bodies. We can also interpret LaGrande's statement regarding her granddaughter being better off dead as akin to Marthe's dogged silence and attention to "the shovel until her husband relieved her of it" (1034), as if processing the dead is nothing more than a duty to be fulfilled, especially under times of resource scarcity. Within both of these works we see work-worn characters who face a loss, not emotionally or with staunch ritual in line with social contract but, rather, characters who view the dead as direct access or impediments to resource availability.

With this evidence could we then say that the premise for suggesting that dealing with the dead identifies humans with animal behavior, an evolutionary marker of animal instinct that responds to a dying herd member in direct proportion to the availability of resources, is reserved only for the poor and not all humans in general? Does this evidence allow us to say that Alexander is incorrect in his biological assumption of all social contracts formed from biological rather than moral needs? Can we offer a theory of self-interest and duty as applying only to the economically deprived? We cannot, as Mark Twain's "A Curious Dream" is quick to tell us. Twain brings out the treatment of the dead within a setting that is described as economically comfortable, a township that is prospering, and hence, the individuals within that township living in a better resource-availability period than either Faulkner's soldiers or Zola's peasantry.

"A Curious Dream," upon first read, may appear to be nothing more than a Halloween story where a living man has a conversation with a dead man, a skeleton no less, on the march with his fellow-dead from the local town cemetery to take up residence in a new cemetery.

However, what disabuses the simplicity of "A Curious Dream" as a mere Halloween bedtime story is that it was originally subtitled "Containing a Moral" and was written during a period when several of Twain's works were engaging moral discourse and moral issues (Anderson, Frank, and Sanderson). Whether or not Twain intended the piece as entertainment or to chide local citizenry for their lack of upkeep of the abandoned cemetery, several components of the "sketch" deal directly with the speed in which the living forget the dead, indicating a survival mechanism that Alexander alludes to in his work regarding his theory of lifetimes, whereby:

> Lifetimes are evolved to be composed of (a) somatic effort and (b) reproductive effort. Somatic[13] effort increases reproductive value (if, in evolutionary terms, appropriately directed; reproductive effort leads to reproduction and lowers residual reproductive value). Reproductive effort is divisible into mating, parental, and extra-parental nepotistic effort. (140)

If Alexander is correct in this theory of lifetimes, then making the dead peripheral to the thoughts of the living over time, what we might more commonly call "healing over time," is a natural progression because the dead no longer participate in either the somatic or reproductive effort and cannot contribute to perceived altruistic or nepotistic gain after the initial settlement of the resources following internment, thereby becoming nothing more than benchmarks within individual memory. This theme of remembering and of participating in lifetime theory reproduction becomes the dominant focus of Twain's living character and his skeletal counterpart. The skeleton emphasizes this point as he speaks about how things once were in his cemetery, but now:

> Our descendents have forgotten us. My grandson lives in a stately house built with money made by these old hands of mine, and I sleep in a neglected grave with invading vermin that gnaw my shroud to build their nests withal! I and friends that lie with me founded and secured the prosperity of this fine city, and the stately bantling of our love leaves us to rot in a dilapidated cemetery. (93)

Following the conversation between the migrating skeleton and Twain's living character, a first-person narrator likely to be Twain himself, this moral tale is summarized within an act of tongue-in-cheek accusation that ends the story: "If the cemeteries in his town are kept in good order, this Dream is not leveled at his town at all, but is leveled particularly and venomously at the *next* town."

This conclusion puts a humorous slant on the story through a sardonic summary of the problems always being in the next town. Each town may maintain its cemeteries and its collective memories at varying levels, but certainly all of them relegate the cemetery and associated placement of the dead to a peripheral physical and mental position in daily activities within the town. This relegation, reducing the dead to memory whereby the poignancy of the passing is experienced in its severity based on the former relationships and recent proximity of the passing of the dispossessed, indicates that Alexander's life theme may be correct—that once a human dies, resources used by that person in life are made available. The dead serve neither somatic nor nepotistic reproductive processes, thereby allowing them to become peripheral figments within individual memory but collectively dismissed under a biologically-driven survival platform of resource acquisition and reproduction.

In conclusion, one has to recognize that, while these scenes may be incidental and localized to writings of European descent, multicultural literary analysis will yield the same results in varying stories. In each culture, parallel stories may be found that demonstrate contract mutability and acceptable rejection of unwritten moral behaviors regarding the treatment of the dead within times of resource scarcity, regardless of what rituals surround the treatment of the dead during times of plentitude.

These three writings all lead to the same place and associated conclusions that moral constructs—especially in dealing with the rituals applied to the dead—are contracts that a man can choose to keep or deny, while the biological outcome is not negotiable. The moral discourse can change, but biological resource scarcity or plenty does not move with moral-discourse decisions to adhere to, or reject, any moral-discourse pathway.

William Faulkner, Émile Zola, and Mark Twain all sought to describe geosomatic drives[14] within their works, and each writer sought to discover, invent, or illustrate human drives as inherent components of his characters. There is no motive for the writer to attempt to arrive at any definitive conclusion regarding human behavior, yet, inevitably, the issues of resource abundance and evolutionary survival mechanisms clash with the moral discourse of appropriated spiritual, ethical, and social beliefs tinged with moral-discourse issues ranging from individual dignity to perceived post-death mysticism. This clash invites the management, imagination, and drive of the creative writer to explore human motivation. Therefore, perhaps the courtroom argument within the Scopes trial should not have been a discussion of man's physical evolutionary traits, but a discussion of man's moral-discourse traits that provide rationales for any number of behaviors—behaviors that are socially sanctioned and reduced from the original declared moral duty to a lesser moral expectation to no moral expectation whatsoever when biological needs cannot be met through resource availability. Should this be proven true, then man can clearly be relegated to animal behavior wherein the only "evolution" in man is his ability to cast resource-gain rationales as moral constructs. Through this ability to create moral constructs, we may rationalize a perception that we are apart from the animal when, in fact, we may have simply created a series of elaborate artifices known as moral constructs to obscure the randomness of being biologically and instinctively driven to perform precisely like the animal, especially in terms of disposing of our dispossessed in both years of plenty and years of scarcity.

Notes

1. Charles Darwin's *Origin of Species* (1859–1865) forms the argument that man descended from animals physically but ascended in intellect as his primary weapon since, structurally, man was inferior to compete against other animals in terms of speed, claws, teeth, and instinct, an ascension attributed to regression of both physiological components and social traits. Ginger's (1958) work demonstrates that the *Tennessee v. John Thomas Scopes* trial was billed as an argument of evolution vs. creationism, but the case itself was a trigger to generate a power struggle between the ACLU and the Conservative Right of the broader issue of who would control content within the public schools.

2. Joseph Karaganis's work defends the traditional naturalism view of the individual in harmony or, more often, in conflict with his or her environment. Through a focus on Theodore Dreiser's *An American Tragedy*, he suggests that traditional naturalism is only one of two primary shifts, that naturalism without a social history is one which does not truly address the overall concept of naturalism. Karaganis and Alexander agree; naturalism is never a single battle between man and environment but is always affected by social history, culture and ethnic blend, race dominance, and socio-economic wealth within the overall societies demonstrated through *geosomatics*.

3. The traditional definition of *nepotism*—the providing of benefice to family members with the intent of generating residual benefice for the giver, if not receiving direct benefice for himself or herself, is taken further by Alexander's own nepotism premise. Alexander suggests that nepotism within a society will extend by kinship degree. According to Alexander, this

indirect benefice will continue until the giver finds a suitable outlet for his or her ability to provide benefice, unless offering the benefice will cause long- or short-term damage to the giver in which case giving benefice will not occur.

4.   Howard Kahane defines the negotiations of moral sentiments and physical benefice as "contractual ethics," whereby negotiations allow for opting out of a contract or allow for modifications within an existing contract. Much like the legal constructs of contract law, the ethics portion is modified as to which contracts are negotiable and which ones are not and under what conditions such contracts can be abrogated or modified.

5.   This concept of receiving benefice from the giver, while simultaneously plotting his or her destruction, is considered one of the more difficult social contract negotiations. During periods of resource plenty, this social contract generally leans toward the moral-discourse position of gratefulness to the giver, but during times of resource scarcity, this social contract may be purposefully abrogated in favor of physical survival. In many historical representations involving war, the ability to outsmart both one's own group, friend groups, and the enemy groups is often viewed as a positive social contract representing honor, which generates benefice. This surface-contradiction is one of the strongest arguments toward the recognition of an evolutionary path for mankind.

6.   Crader and Belcher's study of the relationship between fatalism and fertility in areas of resource scarcity demonstrates the relationship of fatalism to naturalism by reducing it to a degree of perceived powerlessness. Their study demonstrates that fatalism is in operation at the point one perceives oneself as unable to share in nepotistic gain, receiving resource benefice only by coincidence. However, such fatalism does not lower birth rates within a resource-depressed area, thereby lending strength to Darwin's and Alexander's evolutionary platform of reproduction as biological imperative in Darwin's profile and somatic effort in Alexander's explanation.

7.   See note 5.

8.   Merton's study serves as a bulwark to the concept of identifying social deviancy through developing a system for classifying norm violations which he terms as the conformist, the innovator, retreatism, ritualism, and rebellion, resulting in social deviance causality—"that when cultural goals exceed structured opportunities, people experience a discrepancy between their ends and means, a stressful psychological state, and that norm violations are a resolution to this stress" (36). Both in the situation of war, or

in the situation of extreme resource scarcity, social-norm violations (non-negotiated social-contract negation) emerge in order to ease the stress between the lack of structured opportunity and the perception of personal goals.

9.   Prichard's discussion of duty and self-interest engages the Kantian philosophic approach of whether true altruism can exist. For our study, the focus is on self-interest, a primary component of the naturalism form, which, in conjunction with Alexander's perspective of benefice, demonstrates that no moral discourse that results in a moral deed is purely altruistic as even a sense of having done a good deed is a benefice unto itself. Within their own narrative constructs, Faulkner, Zola, and Twain address the question of altruistic existence.

10. See note 3. Writer John Irving's examination of plot echoes Alexander's expression of nepotism by offering that "plot" is simply a condition of interaction where: "Everyone of emotional importance to you is related to everyone else of any emotional importance to you; the relationships need not extend to blood, of course, but the people who change your life emotionally—all of those people from different places, from different times, spanning many wholly unrelated coincidences—are nonetheless 'related'" (372). The concept of literary plot being formed by the actions of various 'nepotism families,' explains one approach to addressing plot structure in various works where naturalism is an underlying condition and plot design is not purposely formulaic.

11. See note 9.

12. In *A Fable* and *Earth*, the two burial scenes share a striking resemblance to each other in terms of setting. Both take place at the edge of a field. Both occur at the end of a war (*A Fable*) or the geographical aftermath of a war (*Earth*). Both involve immediate family in the processing of the body. The families of each are poor, both lands are war-shocked. Both the soldier and the peasant girl are carried by rudimentary means, each host a burial party that is divided by many different wants, from the value of the medals in *A Fable* compared to shocks of Buteau's corn that represents yield that cannot be counted as profit since it serves as a woven deathbed for the dead Palmyre in *Earth*. While there is no question that Faulkner is aware of French tradition, there is no evidence that places Faulkner as being directly influenced by Zola, and yet these two specific scenes share many of the same qualities, suggesting a shared understanding of contractual ethics negotiation when dealing with the dead.

13. The evolutionary platform relies on two separate entities: operations of the somatic and operations within the reproductive. *Somatic* addresses the needs of the body, what we term biological necessity in order to live. Maintenance of the somatic allows for an increase in the *reproductive,* which includes fertility and nepotistic relationship development. In terms of the literature discussed within this work, we find the somatic deprivations or excesses affected the reproductive capacities of all characters within the treatment of social contracts that serve to reproduce positive benefice for those who adhere to the social contracts. Naturalism within literature is required to address both of these functions although it more commonly focuses upon the struggle of the somatic.

14. The term *geosomatic* takes on a more deliberate definition in that it defines the somatic condition as directly related to or enhanced by geographic location, implying that even in an area of resource accessibility, one who is transferred from his or her familiar geography will not fare as well within the somatic and reproductive areas. We see this occurrence in Faulkner's *As I Lay Dying.* Even though Jefferson is a familiar place, the further the family gets away from their homestead (geographic area of maximum somatic comfort), the less capable they are of maintaining or accessing resources and maintaining bodily strength.

Works Cited

Alexander, Richard. *The Biology of Moral Systems.* New York: Aldine De Gruyter, 1987.

Anderson, Frederick, Michael Frank, and Kenneth Sanderson. Introduction to *Mark Twain's Notebooks and Journals, 1855–1873.* (2 vols.). Berkeley: U of California P, 1975.

Bakker, Bard H., ed. *Naturalisme Pas Mort: Lettres Inedites De Paul Alexis À Emile Zola, 1871–1900.* Toronto: U of Toronto P, 1971.

Butterworth, Nancy, and Keen Butterworth. *Annotations to* A Fable *by William Faulkner.* New York: Garland, 1989.

Crader, Kelly, and John Belcher. "Fatalism and Fertility in Rural Puerto Rico." *Rural Sociology* 40.3 (1975): 268–283.

Darwin, Charles. Forward. *Origin of Species.* 1859. Edited by Gillian Beer. New York: Oxford UP, 1996.

Faulkner, William. *A Fable*. 1954. In *Novels 1942–1954. Go Down, Moses / Intruder in the Dust / Requiem for a Nun / A Fable*, edited by Noel Polk and Joseph Blotner. New York: Library of America Series, 1985. 665-1072.

———. *As I Lay Dying*. 1930. New York: Vintage, 1990.

Ginger, Ray. *Six Days or Forever?:* Tennessee v. John Thomas Scopes. 1958. New York: Oxford UP, 1974.

Honnighausen, Lothar. "Imagining the Abstract: Faulkner's Treatment of War and Values in *A Fable*." In *Faulkner and War*, edited by Noel Polk and Ann Abadie. Jackson: UP of Mississippi, 2004. 120–137.

Irving, John. "The King of the Novel." In *Trying To Save Piggy Sneed*. New York: Arcade, 1996. 351-380.

Kahane, Howard. *Contract Ethics: Evolutionary Biology and the Moral Sentiments.* Lanham, MD: Rowman, 1995.

Karaganis, Joseph. "Naturalism's Nation: Toward *An American Tragedy*." *American Literature* 72.1 (2000): 153–180.

Merton, Robert. "The Structural Functional Perspective." In *Perspectives On Deviance*, edited by Allen E. Liska. New Jersey: Prentice, 1987. 28-58.

Prichard, H. A. "Duty and Interest." Inaugural Lecture. University of Oxford. In *Morality and Rational Self-Interest*, edited by David Gauthier. Englewood Cliffs, NJ: Prentice, 1970.

Twain, Mark. "Sketch of A Curious Dream: From the Morality Period." In *Mark Twain's Notebooks and Journals, 1855–1873*, (2 vols.), edited by Frederick Anderson, Michael Frank, and Kenneth Sanderson. Berkeley: U of California P, 1975.

———. "A Curious Dream." In *100 Hair-Raising Little Horror Stories*, edited by Al Sarrantonio and Martin Greenberg. New York: Sterling, 2003. 91–98.

Zola, Émile. *Earth*. Translated by Ann Lindsay. London: Elek, 1954.

Swinks and Snopeses:
The Germ of the "Global Provincial" in Twain and Faulkner

When I was a human being, and recognized with complacency that I was of the Set-Aparts, the Chosen, a Grand Razzledazzle, The Whole Thing, the Deity's Delight, I looked down upon the microbe; he wasn't of any consequence, he wasn't worth a passing thought; his life was nothing, I took it if I wanted to, it ranked with a mark on a slate—rub it out, if you like. Now that I was a microbe myself I looked back upon that insolence, that pert human indifference, with indignation—and imitated it to the letter, dull-witted unconsciousness and all. . . . Once more I was of the Set-Aparts, the Chosen, a Grand Razzledazzle, and all that, and had something to look down upon, be indifferent about. I was a sooflasky; oh, yes, I was The Whole Thing, and away down below me was the insignificant swink—extinguishable at my pleasure—why not? What of it? Who's to find fault?[1] (Clemens, Three Thousand Years *255)*

At first glance, Faulkner's Snopes trilogy, which begins with *The Hamlet* (1940) extends through *The Town* (1957) and ends in *The Mansion* (1959), would appear to have little in common with Twain's oft-neglected, unfinished manuscript of 1905, *Three Thousand Years Among the Microbes*. Faulkner's novels of the rapacious local yokels, the Snopes clan of Frenchman's Bend, appear to pursue an opposite trajectory from the quasi-science-fiction story of Huck who, as a result of a scientific experiment that goes awry, finds himself turned into a cholera germ. This Huck, after all, is not coasting down a bucolic Mississippi River on a raft—as in that earlier, more famous Huck Finn story that most major American writers have admired, including Faulkner—but rather travels in the rank and fetid bloodstream of Blitzowski, a homeless, drunken tramp not unlike Pap Finn (Tuckey xv–xvii).[2] If nodes of intersection do exist between these two authors and their texts, despite social, historical, and generic gaps, it will require a kind of double vision to see them.

This double vision, then, is precisely the object of this essay's experiment in reading. Seemingly oppositional and yet conjoined, "global provincial" is the oxymoronic term I use to describe it. As both adjective and noun, the global provincial is a constellation of attributes that diverge and at times overlap in characteristic ways, and it serves as a heuristic device for exploring these texts by Twain and Faulkner, in particular. It consists of: (1) a double-vision perspective with an inherent blind spot, a sort of mote (or microbe!) in the storyteller's eye/I; (2) a structure figured as worlds embedded within worlds, but usually made up of inhabitants both ignorant of that contingency (hence, the blind spot) and arrogant about their central place in the cosmos; and finally, (3) the literary persona of the "down home" regionalist storyteller who is, despite himself, also modernist or even worldly, and therefore a writer who belies the provincial pose by virtue of being in dialogue with a broader worldview. This last criterion readily speaks to the lives and respective personae of Faulkner and Twain, as we shall see in the final section of this essay.

The first attribute of double vision refers to the perspectives among storytellers in these authors' texts. While more concrete examples of how their points of view are doubled will emerge in the pages ahead, for now, suffice it to say that this doubling is less a mirroring than a paralleling, an act that produces simultaneously a sense of what is held in common and yet profound awareness of the gaps that separate the different storytellers across time and space. Endemic to the global-provincial double perspective, then, is its blindness, a sort of mote in the eye. This expression, you will recall, derives from Matthew 7:3: "And why beholdest thou the mote that is in thy brother's eye, but considerest not the beam that is in thy own eye?" It is most humorous and instructive in its variant form, however, as I.O. Snopes's dissembling riff in *The Hamlet*; here, he discusses with Ratliff Ike Snopes's love affair with the cow in response to Ratliff's demand that he stop his profitable peep show:

> "Sholy," Snopes said. "That ere wont do. That's it. Flesh is weak, and it wants but little here below. Because sin's in the eye of the beholder; cast the beam outen your neighbor's eyes and out of sight is out of mind. A man cant have his good name drug in the alleys. The Snopes name has done held its head up too long in this country to have no such reproaches against it like stock-diddling." (222)

Comically and aptly enough, I.O. is blind to who has the mote and who has the beam in the eye, and in the end that distinction itself flies conveniently "out of sight, out of mind." In the rush to judgment, what one sees in the other, the original proverb implies, is judged disproportionately, indeed, more harshly thanks to one ignoring those same faults in oneself. In Snopes fashion, however, what we cannot see cannot be judged, and more specifically, what one cannot see *is* oneself. The slapstick of I.O.'s malaprops and proverbial chatter serves less as an example of the global-provincial perspective, per se, than magnifies quite literally the ideas of relative perspective and the blind spot itself. Moving from the relative subjectivity of sin being in the eye of the beholder to the conclusion that what you cannot see cannot hurt you ("out of sight is out of mind"), I.O. expounds a theory of enlightened ignorance while illustrating it in his very character.

The double-vision perspective of the global provincial also could describe the methodology of reading I employ here, where close reading of texts by Twain and Faulkner yield productive questions at the level of the texts first, but then require a more bird's-eye view to see at levels beyond them, to a vista regional, national, and global in scope. The "global provincial" concept and perspective enables us to see what Faulkner and Twain share in these seemingly disparate texts and in the historical concerns that shaped their regional literary production in a global frame. However, such an attempt to see it all, both near and far, a regular feat of omniscience, is not only impossible, but also, well, full of itself. Still, it is a way of "seeing," if an ambitious one with potentially fatal blind spots. Such a heuristic, progressing by juxtaposition and alternation between Twain and Faulkner, will emphasize the blind spots and gaps in this and any reading, even as its blind spots enable re-visions by others. The mobility of the global-provincial perspective across distances depends on an eye/I that cannot see something at all times, a sort of Heisenbergian dilemma and first principle of sight, of knowledge, itself.

As the second criterion indicates, structures of worlds within worlds—nations within world power structures, or empires, or structures of kingdom/phyla/class/order/family/genus/species—are paradigmatic for the global-provincial viewpoint, and these structural blind spots are usually located precisely in illusions of independence and self-knowledge. In Faulkner, for example, we look down on the Snopeses from the vantage point of the community of Jefferson, represented by three respectable and somewhat self-righteous narrators of different generations and positions, and while each level is portrayed as if from other worlds or even other species, they contaminate and shape each other, too. And in Twain, such structures operate between the "nations" of microbes in their worlds in and outside of Blitzowski, each contained within each other in hierarchies, each looking down on the other in turn, all the way down to the swinks at the bottom of the food chain. As Twain's microbe Huck puts it in the epigraph that opens this essay, each microbial worldview blinds itself best and most precisely in seeing themselves at the center of "a Grand Razzledazzle, The Whole Thing."

I. Biological Agents: Huck and Snopeses

Faulkner's Snopeses are consistently referred to in terms that Twain's cholera germ Huck would have immediately understood: they are an invasion and a disease that infects Yoknapatawpha's Jefferson, themselves described in the general terms of vermin and plagues. In *Father Abraham*, an early version of *The Hamlet*, for example, we find this choice description:

> Cunning and dull and clannish, they move and halt and
> move and multiply and marry and multiply like rabbits:
> magnify them and you have political hangerson and
> professional officeholders and prohibition officers; reduce
> the perspective and you have mold on cheese, steadfast
> and gradual and implacable: theirs that dull provincial
> cunning that causes them to doubt anything that does not
> jibe with their preconceived and arbitrary standards of
> verity, and that permits them to be taken in by the most
> barefaced liar who is at all plausible. (20)

If we take together the characteristic macro and micro view emphasized by this description, we see that the Snopeses are a specific class unto themselves, like mold, a self-breeding spore-like corruption; and yet, this is a more capitalistic variety of human mold, one that specializes in crass commercial deception and profit in money matters. The names of the different Snopeses alone are instructive in this regard: to note just a few, we have Montgomery Ward and Watkins Products Snopes (named after mail order catalogs and home medicines); I.O. and Wallstreet Panic Snopes (suggesting escalating deferrals of debt and the Great Depression to come, as well as the economic panics of 1903 and 1907[3]); Mink Snopes (rodent-like, vicious and beaten down by poverty, he is a comically pathetic cold-blooded murderer); Ike, or Isaac (the family idiot who is not only in love with a cow—in the biblical sense, of course—but serves as a sacrifice on the altar of his cousin's rise to success); and there are Lump, Eck, and Flem, whose names do nothing if not evoke unwanted images of tumors, proliferating TB bacilli, or involuntary expulsions of germy sputum. Faulkner's Snopeses deliberately conjure forth a corrupted animalistic side of humanity, or rather, suggest a failure in the evolution of the species. Significantly, they are almost always described and narrated *about* from the judgmental vantage point of narrators in the more "civilized" community instead of from any possibly humanizing Snopes viewpoint.[4]

Huck, the cholera germ, on the other hand, narrates a story of humans from the doubled micro and macro perspective of a simple germ who used to be an educated man, actually a scientist. Twain originally called this story "Adventures of a Microbe" (Letter from SLC), more than satirizing the earlier *Adventures of Huckleberry Finn* in having Huck's new "home sweet home" be not unlike the place he tries to escape from in *Huckleberry Finn*, the trap of his father's alcoholic, abusive custody. There are similarities between Twain's Hucks, as Beverly Hume observes:

> Both Hucks are in a diseased body, both are boyish and naïve but clever narrators who inadvertently reveal the absurdity of their situations through Twain's manipulation of their narratives, both lie in order to survive in their respective worlds, and both often seem victims of circumstance or training. (73)

Further cementing a relationship between the two texts, John Tuckey has drawn our attention to Twain's notes on a draft of *Huckleberry Finn* in August 1884: "I think we are only the microscopic trichina concealed in the blood of some vast creature's veins, and it is that vast creature whom God concerns Himself about and not us" (xv). Huck, whose name before he became a germ was "B.b. Bkshp" also suggests the abbreviation for "Blankenship," a reference to the likely model from Twain's Hannibal boyhood days for the fictional Huck Finn.[5] But in other concrete details, Blitzowski is less like Huck Finn's poor white father, the almost Snopes-like Pap Finn who is decidedly provincial; after all, Blitzowski is an urban immigrant, a global nomadic Hungarian tramp who, according to microbe Huck,

> . . . was sober once, but does not remember when it was; he never shaves, never washes, never combs his tangled fringe of hair; he is wonderfully ragged, incredibly dirty; he is malicious, malignant, vengeful, treacherous, he was born a thief, and will die one; he is unspeakably profane, his body is a sewer, a reek of decay, a charnel house, and contains swarming nations of all the different kinds of germ-vermin that have been invented for the contentment of man. He is their world, their globe, lord of their universe, its jewel, its marvel, its miracle, its masterpiece. They are as proud of their world as is any earthling of his. When the soul of the cholera-germ possesses me I am proud of him: I shout for him, I would die for him; but when the man-nature invades me I hold my nose. At such times it

is impossible for me to respect this pulpy old sepulchre (Clemens 164–165).

Blitzowski, a literal "tramp abroad," travels the globe and is a globe himself for the organisms that inhabit and traverse his body. Huck the cholera germ, living for the first time as an opportunistic germ in this rich cesspool of paternalistic flesh, resourcefully learns to speak microbial, to tell time in microbe years, and to get along cheerfully with other germs and survive in his new environment, actually becoming a teacher to the other germs about World History and the world of and outside of Blitzowski. As the narrative progresses, however, this unfinished manuscript becomes increasingly fragmented as Huck's memory itself becomes less and less dependable as his microbial lifespan nears its end, and both manuscript and Huck seemingly break down at one and the same time. By the conclusion, the steady cheerful Huck of earlier pages has begun to change in character, become single-minded and greedy in persuading his germ buddies to go with him on a gold-digging expedition in Blitzkowski's teeth, specifically the molars, as he needs the capital to keep alive his pet teaching project, the "Institute of Applied Morals." The newly selfish and greedy Huck wavers in the last pages whether to share the gold or keep it all for himself. The adaptive and opportunistic cholera germ Huck degenerates and devolves, morally speaking, rather than evolves, finally confused and obsessing over a get-rich-quick scheme to survive at the end of a dying, fragmented manuscript. Indeed, such an ending implies Huck's own germy and malignant, perhaps even fatal, contribution to the dying body of his host, Blitzowski.

Although the Snopes trilogy ends rather patly with the death of its chief villain, Flem Snopes, just as *Three Thousand Years* appears to end similarly in the forecast demise of either the germ Huck or his host Blitzowski (although it may also have been simply that the "oxygen" in this germ of an idea dissipated for Twain), both stories are "unfinished," literally and aesthetically. The architecture of both fictions ends in ruins, the antebellum Frenchman's mansion becomes mausoleum for the murdered Flem Snopes, and Huck's narrative home in Blitzowski becomes inseparable from his own decay, as Twain the "translator" at the start of the tale foreshadows in calling Huck's narrative style "corpsy" (Clemens 162).

II. Snopesism: The Germ of an Idea

Although the Snopes trilogy begins with the 1940 publication of *The Hamlet*, in fact, Faulkner's career as a writer and a Modernist was inaugurated with the germ of the Snopes idea. In 1926, Faulkner apparently began work on the unpublished story *Father Abraham*, which contains many of the main themes of the Snopeses,[6] while in a 1957 interview he claimed that it was around then that "I thought of the whole story at once like a bolt of lightning lights up a landscape and you see everything but it takes time to write it (Gwynn and Blotner 90)."[7] And indeed, from his earliest writings through his later novels, Faulkner would revise story after story before trying to get the Snopes story out of his system in a proper trilogy over the more than twenty years spanning the late 1930s through the 1950s. The three-volume trilogy issued by Random House was entitled simply *Snopes*, according to Faulkner's plan, but even then it did not reach its formal trilogy shape until 1964, two years after Faulkner's death and five years after the last novel of the series had been published. We might say that the Snopes trilogy succeeds best by Faulkner's own famous criterion of success for it: failure. It is as if Faulkner could not quite get the Snopes works right. By the final novel of the trilogy, for example, Faulkner's story apparently got away from him somewhat. James B. Meriwether and Albert Erskine traced discrepancies of various sorts between the final volume and the first two, and in his preface to *The Mansion*, Faulkner acknowledges that in thirty years of writing his Snopes story, understandably, things had changed, and indeed his own perspective as writer had changed. In this way, Faulkner justified some of the remaining inconsistencies readers might encounter.[8] Critics, however, did not and continue not to esteem very highly the last two novels of the trilogy in particular, noting the seventeen-year gap in publication between *The Hamlet* and *The Town*, and decrying the diminished powers of a once-powerful author now simply reworking former stories.[9] ("Spotted Horses," "Lizards in Jamshyd's Courtyard," "Centaur in Brass," "Fool about a Horse," and "Barn Burning" are some of the stories revised and later incorporated into the body of the Snopes fiction.) In a sense, the Snopes trilogy shares a publishing and reception history with Twain's neglected *Three Thousand Years*, the latter also considered a minor late work and incomplete, appearing only after the author's death in an excerpted form in A.B. Paine's 1912 biography of Twain. It would not be issued in its entirety until Tuckey's edited collection *Which Was the Dream?* in 1967,[10] long after both authors' deaths.

But my main point is not this parallel—one which many late, unfinished works and their authors might share—but rather that storytelling, and its breakdown, have more than a little to do with Faulkner's Snopeses and Twain's cholera germs. The Snopes stories are told mainly through the gossip and wandering interpretations and misapprehensions of the lawyer Gavin Stevens, the twelve-year-old boy Charles Mallison (who has grown to manhood by *The Mansion*), and the itinerant sewing-machine salesman, V.K. Ratliff. Down-home anecdotes and comical tall tales shape the stories that get passed around, retold, and mistold from person to person.

In the second preface to Huck's story, Twain the translator bemoans the narrator's writing, saying that "His style is loose and wandering and garrulous and self-contented beyond anything I have ever encountered before, and his grammar breaks the heart. But there is no remedy: let it go" (162). Rendered as local and provincial in dress and voice, the Snopeses as well as Huck have their stories mediated by "translators." In the case of the Snopeses, the story is told by narrators each with his own limited viewpoint, investment, and role in the stories, and in the case of Huck, by a translator who has given up the attempt to standardize Huck's style: "It seemed best to put him back into his shirt-sleeves and overalls, and let him flounder around after the fashion that he was used to" (162). This already "loose and wandering and garrulous" narrative structure of what Gavin Stevens calls "Snopeslore" is further complicated at the level of plot by the lying and tale-telling and confidence games of the Snopeses and Huck, too (Faulkner, *The Town* 146).

"Snopesism" is a derogatory term used abstractly to refer to any invasion of the corrupting forces of expediency, modernity, and capitalist profit that perversely succeed over quality, tradition, honor, or morality. In more concrete terms, though, Snopesism is simply embodied in the invasion and subsequent proliferation of poor, white Snopeses—they are all "cousins" apparently—into Frenchman's Bend and Jefferson. As Gavin Stevens puts it, ". . . they none of them seemed to bear any specific kinship to one another; they were just Snopeses, like colonies of rats or termites are just rats and termites" (*The Town* 40). Yet, as we can see in the Snopeses' loose familial ties based more on convenience than blood and in the cases of Eck and Wallstreet Panic in particular, Snopeses are not even necessarily Snopeses, and non-Snopeses can be snopes-like, too.[11] In *The Town*, Stevens describes Wall Snopes's wife and her "fierce Snopes antipathy," summing up her determination to keep herself and her husband free of "that morass, that swamp, that fetid seethe" that represents Snopesism (146). The cases of Eula and her daughter Linda, as well as Wall Snopes's wife, make clear long before Gavin Stevens explicitly tells us, women are biologically precluded from being real Snopeses:

> So this was not the first time I ever thought how appar-
> ently all Snopeses are male, as if the mere and simple
> incident of woman's divinity precluded Snopesishness and
> made it paradox. No: it was rather as if *Snopes* were some
> profound and incontrovertible hermaphroditic principle
> for the furtherance of a race, a species, the principle vested
> always physically in the male, any anonymous conceptive
> or gestative organ drawn into that radius to conceive and

spawn, repeating that male principle and then vanishing; the Snopes female incapable of producing a Snopes and hence harmless like the malaria-bearing mosquito of whom only the female is armed and potent, turned upside down and backward. (136, emphasis added)

Here, *Snopes* as idea is not something human, per se, so much as an atavistic, destructive principle of race-species, a genus or class or phyla whose males have a certain malignant prerogative that overrides even their quality of impotence. The destiny of the Snopes male is to spread Snopesism like so many disease microbes of "the malaria-bearing mosquito." Snopesism, we see, is a germ of an idea, one conceived in storytelling and run rampant in Snopeslore, threatening to infect the whole community. Faulkner creates its epitome in the specific form of Flem Snopes. That Flem—that most dangerous of Snopeses, moving up from tenant-farmer origins to horse trader to store owner to become president of the Jefferson Bank, usurping the positions of others—is finally revealed to be sexually impotent only underscores the ideological stamp of the class to which Flem Snopes lends, with interest, his name. That women cannot be Snopeses in this fundamental sense, according to Stevens, hints at their own Manichean and stereotypical representations: as "mammalian," that Faulknerian principle of fecund femaleness, or alternately, as mannish; either feisty spinsters or outsider-reformers and radical resisters to Southern and patriarchal norms. Eula and Linda Snopes, respectively, fall into these categories, and while the former is destroyed by Snopesism, it will be the latter who deals the fatal blow to its patriarchal figurehead, Flem: Linda Snopes Kohl manipulates Gavin Stevens to pit Snopes against Snopes and thereby destroy Flem.

When critics do not describe Flem and his ilk in terms of vermin and parasites, they invoke instead the mechanistic and imitative, the adaptive principles of Darwin's natural selection and evolutionary theory.[12] It seems hardly an accident that the germ of the Snopeses arises with the 1925 Scopes monkey trial in Tennessee, the date for their conception mentioned by Faulkner in his preface to *The Mansion*.[13] Even their names (Snopes/Scopes) resonate, as Gail Mortimer has noted. Most recently, however, critics recognize Flem Snopes as merely a gear in an economic system larger than himself. As a member of a social class in furious resistance to staying put in his "place," he therefore adapts and displaces others ruthlessly to achieve social mobility, regardless of social ritual or morality.[14] Flem becomes the idea of a rapacious market economy that locates value in the cash nexus and profit, his negative representation dramatizing how exploitative edges in trade are preconditions of success, as the principle of surplus implies. Money and the market economy displace barter and use-value trade in kind, creating competitive conditions to which some Snopeses more easily than others learn to adapt, but out of which the Snopeses as Snopes emerge.[15] Flem's father, Ab Snopes, for example, was not born a Snopes and a barn burner but was made one, according to Ratliff (*The Hamlet* 31–33).[16] He loses everything in his downhill trading with the shrewd Pat Stamper, whose brand of horse-trading entails tricking Ab, who is a "fool about a horse," into buying one that he had painted and blown up with a bicycle pump to make look healthy. When the paint wears off and the air leaks out, Ab and his family are left without the cow needed for the milk separator, his wife furiously separating the same borrowed milk over and over again in a vicious mechanical repetition that suggests the vicious cycle of poverty that the Snopes family has entered into. In becoming a barn burner, Ab Snopes puts into play the only currency he has to up the ante in exchanges with those who have contaminated good old-fashioned horse-trading with the abstraction of cash, what Ab Snopes calls the "loose" dollars somewhere in the trade.[17]

It is Ab's son Flem, though, who best represents full-fledged Snopesism: He learns to beat the system at its own game, going to school on the less than scrupulous methods of his father as well as improving upon the ways of more genteel Varners and de Spains and Sartorises who casually foreclose a mortgage on a struggling family as easily as they take their evening meal. Deliberately described in blurry terms, Flem's features stress his malignancy and his ability to change shape and adapt as required, even to materialize as if out of the blue:

> One moment the road had been empty, the next moment
> the man stood there beside it, at the edge of a small
> copse—the same cloth cap, the same rhythmically
> chewing jaw materialised apparently out of nothing and
> almost abreast of the horse, with an air of the complete
> and purely accidental which Varner was to remember
> and speculate about only later . . . His eyes were the color
> of stagnant water . . . His face was as blank as a pan of
> uncooked dough. (*The Hamlet* 24)

With his predatory little beak of a nose, and at times wearing a black planter's hat, Flem begins to sport a little bow tie in imitation of Will Varner, the prosperous country landowner he first mimics and then displaces, gradually taking over his store, the old Frenchman's mansion, and even marrying his daughter Eula.[18] And yet, we cannot really visualize Flem because, in the end, he is less a man and character with depth than

208

an opportunistic, adaptive principle, a warning and allegory of economic forces in a New South, where indentured servitude in the form of tenant farming and sharecropping is alive and well into the twentieth century, made more rapacious because rationalized and therefore invisible in the terms of a competitive market economy. With the Snopeses, and of course early on with the Bundrens of *As I Lay Dying*, we can see Faulkner's concerted deromanticization of the conditions of poverty under rural depopulation and tenant farming, and his demythification of Southern aristocracy in a fashion W. J. Cash appreciated; and yet, as with the perennial questions about the "truth" of race and women for Faulkner, there is little doubt that the man Faulkner had his own strong bourgeois-class allegiances and felt keenly the threat of lower classes out of their "place."[19] This too, ironically enough, is Snopesism, that built-in class bias, exposing how much any Snopes needs a paternalistic protector of the status quo such as Gavin Stevens or V.K. Ratliff against which to come into being in the first place. Indeed, at the same moment as the aristocratic Sartoris family, the Snopeses too appear in Yoknapatawpha, infecting the former and making the two less oppositional than mutually, if uneasily, constitutive in their evolution from the same cracker stock: stemming from *Father Abraham* but developed further in *Sartoris* and then matured in the *Snopes* trilogy, what Faulkner called "the germ of my Apocrypha," quickened into life with a double vision of contesting classes.[20]

III. Twain's "Stories of Germ Life"[21]

Most of the scholarly criticism (and there is precious little of it to date) that has bothered to take up *Three Thousand Years Among the Microbes* explains it in terms of Samuel Clemens's intense interest in science and medicine. After all, Huck is himself a scientist and we are told his nickname in the tale, "Huck," derives from Huxley, his middle name, referring in all likelihood to T.H. Huxley (1825–1895), an advocate of Darwinian thought and scientific rationalism whom Twain admired.[22] Twain's ire was often directed at people who opposed science and rational thought with what he deemed superstition, ignorance, or blind religiosity. Targets of his satire included Elizabeth Stuart Phelps, whose *Gates Ajar* (1868) described a materialistic heaven far too much like earth's home sweet home, while Mary Baker Eddy's Christian Science creed, embodied in the 1875 *Science and Health, With Key to the Scriptures* gets lampooned as "Science and Wealth, With Key to the Fixtures" in *Three Thousand Years*.[23] Twain's story stresses biology and evolutionary science, we may safely say, as does Faulkner with his Snopeses.

Clemens goes so far as to compare God to a scientist, giving the scientist no greater place of honor, while locating that of humans in a, shall we say, less ambiguous place, as microbes. In his 1898 notebooks, Clemens describes a God of Nature who has created all of the world, and all of it beautifully and perfectly, as an "artisan" and "artist." God is, and sees as artist and as scientist simultaneously, two mindsets that are not at all incompatible for Twain's notion of Superior Intelligence.

> The materials of the leaf, the flower, the fruit: of the insect, the elephant, the man: of the earth the crags & the [sea] ocean; of the snow, the hoar-frost 'the ice may be reduced to infinitesimal particles & they are still delicate, still faultless; they may be further reduced till only the most powerful microscope can reveal them;—they are still faultless, still delicate, still beautiful. The materials of a rotting animal are delicate & beautiful—the microscope proves it . . . The diatom which is invisible to the eye on the point of a needle is graceful & beautiful in form, & in the minute & exquisite elaboration of its parts it is a wonder. The contemplation of it moves one to something of the same awe & reverence which the march of the comets through their billion-mile orbits compels.
>
> This is indeed a God! He is not jealous, trivial, ignorant, revengeful—it is impossible. He has personal dignity—dignity answerable to His grandeur, his great- ness, His might, his sublimity; He cares nothing for men's flatteries, compliments, praises, prayers—it is impossible that He should value them, impossible that He should listen to them, these mouthings of microbes. He is not ignorant; he does not mistake his myriad great suns, swimming the measureless oceans of space for tallow candles hung in the roof to light this forgotten potato which we call the earth & name His footstool. He cannot see it except under his microscope. The [hand do] shadow does not go back on His dial—it is against His law: His sun/moon does not stand still on Gideon to accommodate a worm out on a raid against other worms—it is against His law. He does not degrade himself to a microbe & suffer death to save other microbes. He cannot die. He would not if He could—for microbes . . .
>
> The Bible of Nature tells us no word about any future life but only about this present one. It does not promise a

future life, it does not even vaguely indicate one. It is not intended as a message to us, any more than the scientist intends a message to surviving microbes when he boils the life out of a billion of them in a thimble. The microbes discover a message in it: this is certain—if they have a pulpit.

The Book of Nature tells us distinctly that God cares not one rap for us: nor for any living creature. It tells us that [He enjoys] His laws inflict pain & suffering & sorrow, but it does not say that [the intent of this is to afford Him] this is done in order that he may get pleasure out of this misery. We do not know what the object is, for the Book is not able to tell us. It may be mere indifference. Without a doubt He had an object, but we have no way of discovering what it was. The scientist has an object, but it is not the joy of inflicting pain upon the microbe. (Clemens Notebook 40) [24]

Clemens here derides the Bible as a man-made fiction, even suggesting that the very idea of Christ is wrong, as he could not have been God and also a mere microbe man ("He does not degrade himself to a microbe & suffer death to save other microbes. He cannot die. He would not if He could—for microbes. . ."). Clemens exhorts himself and/or his readers in these notes to read the Book of Nature to get close to God and His laws, in order to approach an understanding of his beauty and his power. It is God as a scientist using a microscope that thrills Clemens with awe, and for him this is not at all the scene of an experiment by some sadistic Mind, the objection that Clemens clearly anticipates in his example of the boiled microbes, but rather a scene of detachment. The image of a Greater Power boiling microbes in a thimble is one repeated not only in *Three Thousand Years* but also in *The Mysterious Stranger* stories in different ways, as if it were such an irrefutable argument of real power for Clemens that he could not help but repeat it.[25] In *Three Thousand Years*, Huck and his fellow sooflaskies boil alive a family of swinks, those micro-organisms damned to existence at the bottom of germ hierarchy, a scene that on the surface is very like Satan's destruction of a tiny family in a display of his power before two boys in *The Mysterious Stranger*. Satan does this to demonstrate his power, of course, but also to provide the boys with a new perspective, one of God's detachment from, if not cosmic indifference to, natural catastrophe and large-scale destruction and death. In *Three Thousand Years*, however, Huck has the double vision to realize that he and the sooflaskies are wrong, that they killed the swinks for no good reason, in short, only because they could. In these discrepant takes on the same scenes, then, we see Twain exploring the meanings, and abuses, of Power itself, whether in the name of God, Satan, or their hybrid human avatars in Christ or evil men.

In 1904 and 1905, Twain was composing the *Mysterious Stranger* stories and "Adventures of a Microbe" at the same time, and it is not surprising that these texts should infect one another. What *is* surprising is the dearth of sustained critical attention to this connection. The tendency has been almost to dismiss this period of Twain's writing as his darkest and most pessimistic, one resulting from new stresses and griefs in his life that included the deaths of his daughter Suzy in 1897 and his beloved wife Olivia in 1904. The pressures of being more outspoken on controversial political matters such as colonialism and imperialism in Africa and Asia could not have been insignificant. And yet, in 1898, when the above notebook entry ends with a reference to Satan, it is not to posit Satan as a rival but rather to suggest that Satan does not compare to God, that he has no Bible to show for himself like God has the Book of Nature. Ending on a humorous note, Clemens asks "If Satan is around, & so much more intelligent & powerful than God, why doesn't He write a Bible? There is much more evil than good—he might claim that as his—another evidence of superior power" (Notebook 40, 25)." At first it appears that Twain offers Satan some advice to advance his goal of proselytizing evil, but in the context of this entry, the evidence of Satan's not yet having written a Bible comparable to Nature actually proves God's superiority. In fact, the Satan that Clemens challenges here sounds considerably like microbe Man in the rest of the entry, one eager to flatter and usurp the law of God's superior power in the pulpit; Clemens intentionally conflates the two. Perhaps this version of satanic humanity is closest to Huck and the other sooflaskies in *Three Thousand Years*, a description of human abuse of powers that rightfully belong only to God, including the taking of life. To sum up, Twain's God has the double vision of artist and scientist, but his Satan is seen doubly as rival to God, a fallen angel, or else as God's inferior opposition. Microbe-man and Huck, however, while able to see with a double perspective nonetheless have a blind spot: they think they are made in God's image, but they are actually viewed through the double lens of, and aligned with, Satan.

Man as a microbe, then, Clemens has little patience for, be he a Bible-thumping microbe or merely a potato inhabitant. In another notebook entry from 1897, Clemens puts it even more bluntly:

> He said, "The globe is a living creature, & the little stinking human race & the other animals are the vermin that infest it—the microbes. We dig into its skin to suck

its blood (water) & we use its Niagaras & rivers (tears) for power. We sail its oceans (sweat) in fleets which it is not conscious of & cannot see. We dig deep into the thin outer gold-leaf layer of its skin 3000 feet (mining) & it is not aware of it. Nothing hurts it but a belly-ache, then it heaves with a trifling earthquake. It [breathes] catches cold at intervals of years (volcanoes). We lice die & are dust, our king-lice the same; & we put up statues so that we may not forget how they looked when they were living lice; & we honor them reverently [as becomes] as becomes the louse kind (Notebook 42, 37).

In describing the rivers as tears and catching cold as the eruptions of a volcano, Clemens here gives us an incipient vision of Blitzowski, a body who is the whole world to its microbe inhabitants, a world comprised of the various landscapes of different parts of the body. And while the body as a whole is admirable, like a planet in its complexity and diversity, it is clear that humankind is belittled as "the little stinking human race," "the microbes." The human race here is nothing but lice, oblivious to the wider worlds in which their globe moves in its orbit. Just as in *Three Thousand Years*, here the lice worship kings and think themselves the center of the world, exceptional among all life forms and not merely one group among many. On top of that, is it not instructive that Clemens puts himself in this same category, when "he" (or the narrator at least) says "we lice," as if suggesting that awareness of one's blindness is not the same thing as a cure for it; put another way, human ideology is itself critiqued, that thinking in which one is so immersed as one's "natural" habitat that one cannot see beyond it. In comparing these two notebook entries about God and Microbes, we can see how Twain could describe Huck with such sympathy and humor at the start of *Three Thousand Years*, and then swiftly begin to demonize him by the story's end, as the continuum between his human and cholera germ natures becomes more evident.

Once one begins to look for it, Twain's work appears rife with a fascination for germs, microbes, vermin, infestations, and contaminations, especially as they, literally and figuratively both, allow him to speak about God and science from many perspectives. It is with *Three Thousand Years* that Twain uses germs to express political ideas as well, finally finding a way to express the diversity, gradations in scale and power, and the relative dependency among political bodies for which he had been searching. But it is when Twain also uses germs to express more private experiences of the body and of growing old, as we can see here in one of Twain's unpublished poems, taken from his notebooks, that we might understand germs as carriers of more emotionally charged meaning.

> cohabit   bacillus dream
> The Microbe-God.
>
> From Cradle unto Grave I keep a house
> Of Entertainment where may drowse
> And feed & [swill] dis-ease germs—and
>   in a wild
> Their species procreate & carouse
>
> Think, in that battered Caravanseral
> Whose portals open stand all night & day
> How many a microbe with the
> Arrives in state & comes to stay
>
> Rheumatic [pain] gout! A moments taste
> Of being dipped in Hell up to the Waist
>   And to the District Messn has reached
> The Doctor he set out for—O make haste
>   & feed
>   All wandering [germ] bacilli
> the G of all of
> all G of maladies
> & feed bacilli & kindred germs
> Of maladay
>   dream & breed (feed)
> Bacillii & other germs & [hide]. (Notebook 40, 47)

"Eat, drink and be merry—enjoy life while you can!" is the message here. Humor and a gentle self-deprecation set the tone overall. In this poem, one would not be surprised to see the microbes meet the Snopeses (for example, Virgil Snopes and Fonzo Winbush from *Sanctuary*, or perhaps Clarence and Montgomery Ward Snopes in that scene's repetition in *The Mansion*) because described here is a place very like Miss Reba's whorehouse in Memphis, a stopping point on the Snopeses' and microbes' journeys for some sex, fun, food, and drink. As we see in the early pages of *Three Thousand Years*, too, Man's purpose in life is reduced merely to giving "all wandering" germs and bacilli a place to live, displacing the superior human from its rung or two above the germ. The "G" here likely refers to "God" in the possible poem title, "The Microbe-God," creating a parallel for the Microbe-God to Satan's role in *The Mysterious Stranger* manuscripts. As we noted earlier, Satan was a fallen angel perhaps but also like humankind, in Clemens's microbe terms, and both are conjoined here as "Microbe-God."

The humor in the Microbe-God poem is rich, and richer still in my view for being followed in the same 1898 notebook by another poem, a more melancholy one called "AGE—A Rubaiyat." where Twain again evokes the Caravan but this time as a metaphor for human life, not simply the nomadic journey of microbes.

AGE—A Rubaiyat.

In age we a feeble
        lack of confidence
With some uncertainty we

We think no more, we do but dream

And weakly throbs our failing heart

A moment's halt, a momentary taste
Of Being at the Well amid the Waste,
  And lo the phantom Caravan has reached
  the Nothing it set out from—
[The]
O, make haste!
                             I wiss
Ah now, in Age a feeble [ ] we
And maunder feebly over That & This
  Thinking we think—we do but dream—
                 moonings
And wonder shy our moundrings go amiss

Whether at Naishapur or Babylon—
Whether the Cup with Sweet or Bitter run—
 The wine of Life is oozing drop by drop
The leaves of life are falling one by one.
                     (Notebook 40, 47)

In this very rough draft of an unpublished poem, Clemens loosely adopts the quatrain form of the Persian rubaiyat, a verse form conventionally rhyming AABA after Edward Fitzgerald's early nineteenth-century translation into English of Omar Khayyam's *Rubaiyat*. Clemens's poem experiments with that form and takes for his philosophical theme Life and Death viewed while passing through that stage of life known as Aging. In this twin poem to the "bacillus dream," we find repetitions in the language of making haste, and images of Waste and Wells, the Caravan, the dream narrative. Here though, in contrast to the Microbe-God poem where the parasitic, commensal, or symbiotic life of the microbe is non-stop festivity thanks to human hospitality, the phantom Caravan distinctly represents life as a brief journey to and from the Great Dark, to and from "Nothing." Human life is summed up as one without a great motivating cause and concluding to no great effect. It is neither a great nor small experiment by God, and the setting does not matter: all is the same indifferent and universal world. Most moving here are the brackets standing alone and suspended, as if a figure for that brief span of human life, a miraculous exception in what counts as the rule—a vast void.

Twain's "bacillus dream" poem describes the body as Hell, a site of pain. There, Satan, as a fallen angel and God of all maladies, establishes his playground in the human body with hordes of nomadic, opportunistic germs; and yet, by means of that same title, "bacillus dream," the poem offers an escape from its own nightmare—which is reality, and which the dream?—a common question in these late works of Twain. Knowing and feeling these years as his last ones, Twain faced it with laughter at his body's failing by creating the bad germs of "maladay" to explain the bad days, as well as the good germs he hastens to save from the Doctor, perhaps saving "the G of all of" whose microbes might actually help to form the vaccine for aging, or death itself. Such conjoined optimism and despair often attended scientific discoveries about microbes and medicine in Twain's time, and Twain took great interest in such science, with all its new questions and hopeful possibilities.

H.W. Conn, professor of biology at Wesleyan University, wrote in his book *The Story of Germ Life* that germs can be deadly but their diseases can often be prevented. Twain's *Three Thousand Years* explicitly references Conn as an expert on germs and Twain is known to have read this book in particular.[26] It must be stressed, however, that the story of germ life that Conn tells is one in which germs are not merely destructive, but vitally constructive and useful in the arts (particularly in fermentation, cooking, and textile industries). For Twain, too, germs were useful for the storytelling arts, whether for depicting the private despair and humility of individual illness and aging as in the poems above, or in satirizing on a global scale the hubris and myopia of human history in *Three Thousand Years Among the Microbes*. In the end, he puts a microbe to good use, making Huck the cholera germ the narrator of his story.

IV. Continuity and Contingency: Over and Beyond the Imperial "I"

Rarely speaking, incessantly and mechanically chewing tobacco, and furtively involved in machinations to take over all business, Flem is a cipher that the talkative Ratliff tries to both explain and second-guess, the sign of a Snopish lawless and illegitimate class uprising with all its attendant terrors and comedies that it is his moral duty to thwart. Despite coming from tenant farmer origins himself, V.K. Ratliff acts as the Snopeses' most persistent opponent. As John E. Bassett puts it, "[Ratliff, the 'folk raconteur,'] is both foil to Snopes and generator of Snopes lore" (138). Refracted through the narrative lens of Ratliff, Stevens, and Chick Mallison, the Snopes story exposes unscrupulous terrorizing Snopeses but also usurious if genteel Varner-like complicity in the American nightmare on all sides. When democracy under unfettered capitalism gives freedom to the disenfranchised but no real home, opportunity but no social respect or dignity, financial gain and debt without social responsibility, then the American Dream threatens to approach something like totalitarianism as a form of capitalism. Accordingly, Faulkner's vision required that by *The Mansion*, Flem's ultimate ambition would have to shift from the amassing of fortune to the pursuit of the elusive abstraction: "respectability."

Snopesism highlights the contradiction in the American Dream between, on the one hand, democratic equality for all, and on the other, ruthless competition and ladder-climbing to gain at the expense of others. "American Dream" ideology lies behind Faulkner's Snopesism, thanks to the likely influence of Benjamin Franklin. Certainly, the Protestant work ethic and capitalist entrepreneurial spirit for which Benjamin Franklin is credited, thanks to his *Autobiography* and *Way to Wealth* (1758), feeds the satire in both Faulkner and Twain. In *Three Thousand Years*, Benjamin Franklin's name is given to the comically irascible yellow-fever germ at the start of the tale, while I.O. Snopes's proverb-riddled bluster is, one might argue, a comical and exaggerated twisting of Poor Richard's platitudes as they arm the egos of self-made men. It is not insignificant that the term "American Dream" was not actually coined until 1931 by James Truslow Adams;[27] in other words, this potent myth of social mobility came into the language in an era of economic depression, just when the reality most starkly contradicted the rhetoric.[28]

Robert Brinkmeyer has persuasively argued that the 1930s through the 1950s, the Snopes trilogy era, saw Faulkner received in a context of hot and cold wars, one with a "democratic crisis" that arose amidst growing suspicions that democracy and fascism might be on a continuum rather than in opposition; that is to say, radical egalitarian policies and social reforms intended to enfranchise the lower classes, women, and minorities could lead to a counterproductive mechanistic flattening of social classes, one which offered undeserved social gains and financial rewards without regard for tradition, individual morality, effort, or talent. In this scenario, the American Dream slides naturally into the American Nightmare unless vigilant Ratliffs and Stevenses divert its course. While such a vision is rife with reactionary and conservative motives, and such "Gothic fascism"[29] had been attributed to Faulkner throughout the 1930s and 1940s, as Brinkmeyer documents, what the Snopes/Sartoris germy fable also shows is that the American Dream could be Janus-faced (72). In other words, American freedom rhetoric was rather more trumpeted against fascism abroad and strikingly less practiced at home where "domestic fascism" in the form of Jim Crow, lynching, tenant farming, and sexual discrimination were sanctioned. The South, of course, was already strongly associated with violent and reactionary atrocities, so writers such as Faulkner stressing regionalism and resistance to modern society and its progressive reforms at the time of the more widely hailed "democratic revival" appeared to be simply further evidence of an unregenerate character. Brinkmeyer, however, contends that Faulkner's wartime letters, for example, demonstrate how thoroughly Faulkner recognized the hypocrisy of American Dream and democratic freedom rhetoric, particularly with regard to race, and that it was his location as a Southerner that enabled his better insight into it (73–74).[30] After noting Faulkner's letter to Malcolm Cowley in 1945 contending that he invented Percy Grimm of *Light in August* in 1931 as a proto-fascist before Hitler created Nazis, Brinkmeyer contends:

> It is this awareness of the dangers of extremist regionalist thinking that separates Faulkner from most Southern traditionalists, who forthrightly stood by their logic that linked democracy—not the South—with fascism. Faulkner made this anti-democratic connection, but he also understood that such regionalist thinking had dark undercurrents—undercurrents every bit as potentially fascist as the abuses of democracy that Faulkner recognized in the political landscape of the South and America. (92–93) [31]

Whether one sees Faulkner as stuck in Lost Cause cynicism and anger over the encroaching modern world and Occupation by the North's imposed social and political reforms, or Faulkner in dialogue with a New South whose progress he mostly agreed with but which, in turn, failed to understand his particular brand of scandalous, literary dissent, it is clear that Faulkner's work emerges from a complex, ideologically loaded, historical matrix and takes it as his subject matter in the Snopes.

We should not forget that *Father Abraham* opens with lines that set the stage for Flem Snopes's appearance against a backdrop of Democracy:

> He is a living example of the astonishing byblows of
> man's utopian dreams actually functioning; in this case the
> dream is Democracy. He will become legendary in time,
> but he has always been symbolic. Legendary as Roland
> and as symbolic of a form of behavior; as symbolic of an
> age and a region as his predecessor, a portly man with a
> white imperial and a shoestring tie and a two gallon hat,
> was: as symbolic and as typical of a frame of mind as Bud-
> dha is today. With this difference: Buddha contemplates
> an abstraction and derives a secret amusement of it; while
> he behind the new plate glass window of his recently
> remodelled bank, dwells with neither lust nor alarm on
> the plump yet still disturbing image of his silkclad wife
> passing the time of day with Colonel Winword in front of
> the postoffice. (*Father Abraham* 13)

Flem Snopes is "the man" (14) compared here to the Asian deity, Buddha, but Flem does not worship abstractions of religious or moral thought but rather his own reflection in the pane of glass at his bank, the temple of money itself. His religion is the modern religion that thrives under Democracy, Faulkner implies; the money motive is the real American Dream.[32] Twain too, of course, pursues this theme in *Three Thousand Years*, where America is denoted as the "the Republic of Getrichquick."

At this point, we might reconsider Faulkner's modernist and regionalist reception as a critique of Democracy, by comparing it to Twain's contemporary reception. In recent years, in particular, there has been growing interest in Twain's anti-imperialism, including texts such as "To the Person Sitting in Darkness," *Following the Equator*, and the *Nightmare of History* fragments. Scott Michaelson, for one, has argued against the New Americanism represented by critics John Carlos Rowe and Amy Kaplan in particular, contending their analysis is flawed by overarching theoretical constructs and an agenda that is blinded by its own pro-agency approach to historical actors, analyzing imperialism from a "cultural" rather than a social, economic, or political perspective. For Michaelson, this kind of reading, while intended to highlight superstructural ideologies of race, gender, class, and nation often obscured by attention to base economic structures, does so at the cost of all-important details of history, politics, and social change that do not fit into the "cultural theory" framework. In their desire to figure "culture-as-agency," they situate "everything else" in opposition to that project, seeing historical actors' engagement with imperialism in the simple terms of subjugation or liberation, contribution or criticism.[33] Ultimately, Michaelson reminds us that economies and societies are structures and, as such, entail constraints as much as freedom, even if agency sometimes emerges in surprising places. While one might take issue with Michaelson's full frontal attack on New Americanists' ahistorical "cultural" approach, their "misreading" of literary texts, and what he deems their false choice of structure versus agency (and indeed, there does seem to be something of a polemic motivating this essay's sharp edges), it is hard to dismiss his respectful reading of Twain, and the force of his argument that replacing the state as system with a version of the state as an agent figured as "I" has well-recognized dangers.

Calling on the work of Carl Schmitt and his contemporary interpreter Giorgio Agamben, Michaelson stresses that the nation-state form has always been, and continues to be, inherently troubled by questions of sovereignty (limited "I" power that is prone to abuse) and of constitutionalism (power distributed so as to check and balance as well as enable democratic participation). To ignore these eddies and traps in state structure and political and economic workings—the "ragged blanket full of holes" that Twain called the Constitution in 1901—is to position oneself, as do the New Americanists, in Michaelson's view, outside of the system and to inadvertently advocate the unlimited power and freedom of agency, itself a rather privileged and imperialistic stance. Twain, in "The Stupendous Procession" (1901) and in numerous other anti-imperialist writings that Michaelson examines, attacks kings and czars with such vehemence precisely because their abuses arise from investing a sovereign with the "character" of the state, the rule of which belongs to a system enfranchising the people and not celebrating a charismatic or powerful individual. Michaelson compares Twain's writing through these issues to Hannah Arendt, both writing about the imperial character of sovereign power to issue decrees and thereby create by fiat new classes of the stateless—the refugee, the derelict, and, we might add in today's context, the "terrorist." Brinkmeyer's attention to anthropologist Margaret Mead's 1942 *And Keep Your Powder Dry*, wherein she posits a wider "American culture" with an attendant "character structure," one founded on the exception of the anti-democratic, racially antagonistic, and non-normative South is instructive in this context (Brinkmeyer 76). In other words, the South did not fit into the real "identity" of "America" and consequently had to be excluded.

Three Thousand Years has something to say about all this sovereignty business as well. Turning things inside out, Twain makes Blitzowski, a derelict and tramp, in effect, the sovereign himself; after all, he is the whole world for the "nations" of microbes that inhabit his body. His derelict and drunken and thieving character finds its reflection in the character types of germs in his body, such as Franklin, the irascible and highly oxygenated yellow fever germ. As Huck points out, and before long unwittingly falls prey to himself, self-deception characterizes both Man and Microbe, each ensconced in his world and looking down on those below. Structured as dependent worlds within worlds, though, Blitzowski is as dependent on the microbes for life and death as they are on him. Huck, with his peculiar double vision of microbe and man, can see this at times, especially earlier in the narrative, recognizing that Blitzowski in his own world is likewise misapprehended as what Agamben calls "bare life," the disposable life, just a germ within the social body.

At the end of the narrative, in bringing up the history of nations and contemporary events such as China's partition into "spheres of interest" by Western missionaries leading to the Boxer Rebellion and the Russo-Japanese war, Twain reminds us that the American national character and image depends on the exclusion of such germs as Blitzowski even as he satirically makes Blitzowski and Huck the cholera germ the main characters, sovereign only in their respective and dependent little stagnant ponds, so to speak. Huck's criticism of Franklin for his self-deception shares echoes with Michaelson's critique of the New Americanists' methodology and standpoint:

> You notice that? He did not suspect that he, also, was engaged in gnawing, torturing, defiling, rotting, and murdering a fellow-creature—he and all the swarming billions of his race. None of them suspects it. That is significant. It is suggestive—irresistibly suggestive—insistently suggestive. It hints at the possibility that the procession of known and listed devourers and persecutors is not complete. It suggests the possibility, and substantially the certainty, that man is himself a microbe, and his globe a blood-corpuscle drifting with its shining brethren of the Milky Way down a vein of the Master and Maker of all things, Whose body, mayhap,—glimpsed partwise from the earth by night, and receding and lost to view in the measureless remoteness of Space—is what men name the Universe. (182)

Referring here to the incomplete "procession of known and listed devourers and persecutors," Huck reminds us of Twain's 1901 "The Stupendous

Procession" wherein each nation is characterized relative to others in the historical train. The "nations" of microbes are like the "nations" in the historical procession in being complacent in their self-deception, myopically seeing themselves as sovereign and independent of others, always the "good guy," incompatible with ever being also at times the "bad" one. To get this perspective, though, Twain finally has to take an impossible leap out of the Milky Way galaxy, as only then can he gain the necessary distance to see his own nation's germy complicity and dependence on others; in doing so, he is able to connect this kind of viewpoint with a sovereign, God-like one. In other words, here we see Twain dramatizing the paradox of national sovereignty, at once *dependent* on a context of other nations and *independent* in claims to a singular, self-determining power.

The global provincial structure we see here has more than a little in common with the "dependency theory" of Immanual Wallerstein. Wallerstein's theory shapes the critical perspective of Susan Willis in a well-known essay on Faulkner's "The Bear," and illuminates how modernization and capitalism meet the lesser-developed, backward South. In Willis's formulation, Wallerstein contends that the "underdevelopment of the third world is a direct result of contact with capitalism. Dependency is a global system where different modes of production define degrees of dependency and constitute a synchronic dialectic" (174). For Wallerstein, the key is the semi-periphery and how it functions to oscillate between and destabilize, when not bridging, center and periphery. Finally, for Willis, Faulkner's cosmos creates hybrid characters and liminal spaces that overlap in degrees of dependency, thereby transcending oversimplified oppositions. In "The Bear," for example, the bear Ben is as hybrid a figure as is the poor white Boon Hogganbeck. That is, Ben is not just Nature but a liminal figure invoked in terms of the modern, as a charging locomotive for instance, so that he represents simultaneously the modern encroachment and obliteration of wilderness by railroads and that wilderness itself in demise.

Huck's microbe world might be viewed through the lens of Willis's reading of Wallerstein's dependency theory, since in *Three Thousand Years* we have a narrative viewpoint that is de-anthropomorphized as microbe and yet in the same moment positioned as human, a hybrid and liminal perspective. We should also mention its Chinese puzzle box narrative structure of worlds within worlds, which create overlapping structures in hierarchies of dependence and independence.[34] The larger payoff of dependency theory when applied to Faulkner and Twain anticipates that the slide from democracy to fascism, as well as from sovereign nationhood to nationalism, might be diverted at just such semi-peripheral nodes where mutual dependence and self-interest peak and collide most productively.

The greater risk is ignoring, or oversimplifying, these complex, dense sites of history, economy, society, culture, and politics in our hurry to complete "The Stupendous Procession." To put this in the terms of the global provincial, then, the risk is a double vision refusing or ignorant of its blind spots (semi-peripheral nodes, liminal spaces, hybridity) even as the solution too might lie in a double vision capable of imagining the blind spots that structurally have to exist.

V. The Global Provincial Goes to Japan

The notorious modernist complexity in Faulkner's work, just what Willis describes as difficult but rich in semi-peripheral figures and spaces that aid our understanding of the South, has also made it difficult to understand historically, particularly in terms of his literature's circulation and reception. A persistent debate among scholars has been Faulkner's relative obscurity in the decade preceding his winning the Nobel Prize; many of his works were out of print and his reputation was most identified with the scandal of *Sanctuary* before being saved by Malcolm Cowley's *The Portable Faulkner*. Another aspect of this is Faulkner's work as cultural ambassador for the State Department's United States Information Service (USIS) in the 1950s, and, indeed, his visit to Nagano, Japan, in 1955 was under government auspices. As part of the U.S. Cold War agenda, American culture was to be disseminated around the globe through representative cultural figures, book publications and translations, and radio broadcasts. But Faulkner? The author of corncob rape scenes, love affairs with cows, the shame of lynching and Jim Crow—*that* Faulkner as America's cultural representative? Even with the Nobel Prize, it still gives one pause.

Lawrence Schwartz takes up this problem and explains it most persuasively by tracing Faulkner's public relations creation into a national figure soon after WWII. He credits Cowley, the Rockefeller Foundation, and the unlikely alliance of the New Critics and the New York intellectuals for this.[35] Brinkmeyer, too, succinctly describes their mutual interests in promoting Faulkner:

> Faulkner's difficult and tortuous prose, once typically
> considered as decadent as his subject matter, now came to
> be seen, like abstract art, as embodying the artist's heroic
> quest for self-expression in a democratic society that
> encouraged such endeavor. The protofascist artist before
> the war became the democratic hero after, global hero and
> Nobel laureate. (78)

It is here that we see most starkly what I call the "global provincial" persona of Faulkner. It was Faulkner's stress on rugged individualism in the face of mass production and mechanization under modernity that cultural and government groups touted for global distribution, as Helen Oakley points out, citing along the way Harvey Breit's 1951 *Partisan Review* essay on Faulkner's representative Americanness. No longer merely regionalist and Southerner, Faulkner had become American and thereby "worldly." Who is to say how much of this went into the Snopes trilogy, whose traveling and worldly narrators move beyond Yoknapatawpha borders (going to war and going to New York) and incessantly discuss the world around them to locate in time or make sense of their community (New York, Europe, the Germans, the Pearl Harbor attack, "the Japs")? The least we can assert is that Faulkner's emphatic international presence and the Cold War context cannot be ignored.

Journals like *Partisan Review* and various cultural organizations supported the arts and also government efforts to spread American culture abroad, but in doing so they also abetted the Cold War propaganda of "information" in the title of USIS. The Cold War context in which William Faulkner participated in the conference at Nagano as cultural ambassador was complex: one in which the State Department's propaganda-through-culture focus was through the USIS; the CIA supported "cultural warfare" through organizations such as the American Committee for Cultural Freedom, founded in 1951; the U.S. government sponsored journals such as *Jiyu* in Japan or *Encounter* in England and other countries aimed at intellectual elites; and a government-and-industry joint effort was made to flood book markets all around the world with translated "Overseas Editions" (Oakley 409–411).[36]

Perhaps none of this would have been so bad if the USIS had been more like the British Council, John McCormick argues in a sarcastic and humorous essay entitled "The United Snopes Information Service." In this 1962 *Kenyon Review* piece, McCormick blasts the incompetence and bureaucracy of the USIS, which filled its posts with individuals who had no "cultural" bent at all, in other words, creating posts for provential philistines, veritable "Snopeses," who, undeserving of their high positions, rode the bureaucratic escalator to promotions and success at teas and toasts for cultural affairs about which they knew nothing and cared less. For McCormick, the main problems were bureaucrats and politicians displacing "culture" for ideology's utilitarian purposes. In classic anti-intellectual American style, they emphasized culture as propagandistic "information" that could combat Communism and the Cold War instead.

Taking its title and text from Faulkner's naïve and wandering sketch of Japanese ways and culture on his short visit to Nagano, the State Department film *Impressions of Japan* depicts a revered Faulkner among Japanese students and academics, a pipe-smoking American serviced by a "geisha" in his hotel room in Kyoto, all narrated in the measured grandiose tones of what McCormick might call a "Snopes" bureaucrat of the USIS. It reeks of Occupation-era propaganda, and Faulkner's own voice is never heard even if the narration ventriloquizes his fragmentary notes. Indeed, Faulkner may have become increasingly uncomfortable with being thrust into the role of representative of America by the State Department and others. According to Helen Oakley, this is best evidenced perhaps when, in the year before his death in 1961, he instructed the William Faulkner Foundation to take steps to translate Latin American fiction for Americans, a move against the USIS Snopesian tide that unilaterally translated American works for specific overseas distribution (414–415).

We would do well to recall at this juncture that it was just at Faulkner's visit to Japan that he often mentioned being at work on a manuscript about the American Dream. Indeed, what he left from this project, essays entitled "On Privacy" and "On Fear," both followed by "The American Dream: What Happened to It?" in parentheses, echoes lines Faulkner wrote in "To the Youth of Japan." In particular, he tells about the need to face the disaster, even shame, of conflict and war as a means to rise above it, and the necessity of living out one's individual freedom without regard for hierarchy in racial or other castes. Although Faulkner's American Dream project was never realized, in response to Faulkner's own subtitled question, "What Happened to It?," we might respond that it appears to have become the Snopes trilogy. In the mid-1950s, Faulkner was traveling and thinking beyond both Yoknapatawpha and U.S. borders to other "regions," parts of a world larger than his micro-cosmos. We might wonder how Faulkner's international travels at this point in his life, particularly his visit to a recently "occupied" and "defeated" Japan, made him rethink the "splendid failure" of the utopian American Dream in a global frame of capitalist expansion, and how that shaped the Snopes.

Just after Faulkner's visit to Japan, his letter from Rome, Italy, on September 5, 1955, to the *New York Herald Tribune* regarding the Emmett Till murder evoked the dependent worlds-within-worlds structure such as described in Twain's *Three Thousand Years*, and mentions Japan in the process.

> When will we learn that if one county in Mississippi
> is to survive it will be because all Mississippi survives?
> That if the state of Mississippi survives, it will be because

all America survives? And if America is to survive, the whole white race must survive first?

Because the whole white race is only one-fourth of the earth's population of white and brown and yellow and black. So, when will we learn that the white man can no longer afford, he simply does not dare, to commit acts which the other three-fourths of the human race can challenge him for, not because the acts are themselves criminal, but simply because the challengers and accusers of the acts are not white in pigment?

Not to speak of the other Aryan peoples who are already the Western world's enemies because of political ideologies. Have we, the white Americans who can commit or condone such acts, forgotten already how only 15 years ago, what only the Japanese—a mere eighty million inhabitants of an island already insolvent and bankrupt—did to us?

How then can we hope to survive the next Pearl Harbor, if there should be one, with not only all peoples who are not white, but all peoples with political ideologies different from ours arrayed against us—after we have taught them (as we are doing) that when we talk of freedom and liberty, we not only mean neither, we don't even mean security and justice and even the preservation of life for people whose pigmentation is not the same as ours.

And not just the black people in Boer South Africa, but the black people in America too.

Because if we Americans are to survive, it will have to be because we choose and elect and defend to be first of all Americans to present to the world one homogeneous and unbroken front, whether of white Americans or black ones or purple or blue or green.

Perhaps we will find out now whether we are to survive or not. Perhaps the purpose of this sorry and tragic error committed in my native Mississippi by two white adults on an afflicted Negro child is to prove to us whether or not we deserve to survive.

Because if we in America have reached that point in our desperate culture when we must murder children, no matter for what reason or what color, we don't deserve to survive, and probably won't. (Press Dispatch 222–223)

In the opening of the letter, Faulkner moves from a single county in Mississippi where Emmett Till was murdered to the state of Mississippi to America and outward to the world with its various nations and "races" of people denoted by colors. He begins and ends by proclaiming each world's dependence on the other, asserting that the world is as accountable to that county in Mississippi as it is to the world. In mentioning Japan's Pearl Harbor attack, Faulkner is doing something rather similar to Twain in his well-known championing of Japan's side in the Russo-Japanese War; that is, Faulkner, like Twain, uses Japan as a cautionary tale of the nonwhite "nation" or "race" who will fight back and destroy the white race—deservedly so—if the U.S. continues its repressive regimes of violence and apartheid, be it in Africa, Asia, or back home in the U.S. South. It is as if both Japan and the South as regions were smaller occupied worlds whose fascism was being conquered, within the larger world dominated by the "democracy and freedom" of the U.S.[37] These two "countries" have much in common in this international letter home from Faulkner.

Strangely enough, the blind spots, not the hubris of omniscience, most illuminate these nodes of convergence in Faulkner and Twain. Faulkner telescopes Japan into the purview of the South to condemn the South from a global perspective, even as he exposes his provincial belief in U.S. "freedom and liberty," advocated overtly here as the best means for saving the South; and yet, such salvation must be carried out covertly in acts of cultural imperialism, such as these Faulkner had himself participated in in Japan. In Twain's case, the satirical rhetoric was often polemical, and in explicitly political, anti-imperialist works it could be high and mighty in its angry didacticism. We can locate his blind spot in *Three Thousand Years Among the Microbes* in the absence of concern for the colonial plight of Korea over which Japan and Russia largely went to war in the first place.[38] Historian Andrew Gordon sheds some light on the background and events of the Russo-Japanese War and the war's resonance not only for Twain's time but for Faulkner's with the start of World War II. Faulkner's emphasis on Pearl Harbor and Twain's on the Russo-Japanese War have something in common:

> The Pearl Harbor attack has become enshrined in American memory as an immoral "sneak attack." The Japanese apparently intended to provide minimal advance notice, although not enough to allow the United States to prepare defenses in Hawaii. In any case, American policymakers by late 1941 had ample evidence that the Japanese were considering war and were likely to launch

an attack soon, someplace in Asia. In addition, at the time
of the Russo-Japanese War in 1905, Japan had made good
use of a surprise attack at Port Arthur. American military
strategists in 1941 might have anticipated a similar tactic,
but the United States commanders in the Pacific were
complacent and ill-prepared. Ironically enough, Western
observers in 1905 praised the Japanese military for its
brilliant strategy. (210)[39]

Here, Gordon clarifies the relation between the Russo-Japanese War,
which so engrossed Twain, and the events of Pearl Harbor, that placeholder
for a momentous spot in time before and after which everything changed,
one mentioned repeatedly in the final pages of Faulkner's *The Mansion*. In
the Emmett Till letter, Pearl Harbor is not only a figure of the past but of
the future: Even as Faulkner the American was provincially blind to the
historical continuum between the Russo-Japanese War and Pearl Harbor's
"sneak attack," after his visit to Japan he had developed enough of a global
perspective to imagine U.S. inferiority and weakness from other countries'
perspectives.

   Which brings us now to Clemens/Twain as global provincial with
Three Thousand Years Among the Microbes. First of all, Twain himself, unlike
Faulkner, was long considered a representative American writer. Arguably,
his pen name gradually usurped his real one as best representative of the
man. Yet, despite his cultivated regionalist and provincial reputation as an
American tall-tale spinner and common man spouting common sense,
Twain was a world traveler many times over and used to looking at the U.S.
from both inside and outside of itself, becoming increasingly involved in
international politics and anti-imperialism in his late years as he criticized
U.S. foreign policy. Indeed, Twain risked this same representative American
reputation in speaking out and trying to publish anti-imperialist satires and
opinion pieces. His letters and notebooks are full of his thoughts in this
vein.

   At the time he was writing *Three Thousand Years*, Twain was engrossed
in the Russo-Japanese war of 1904–05, supportive of the Japanese as a
non-Western, non-white nation in their victory over the Russian Czar
Nicholas II.[40] He shared similar sentiments to African-Americans such
as W.E.B. Du Bois for whom the Russian defeat signalled real progress
in race as well as international relations, suggesting that oppressed and
colonized nations in fighting back could compel European nations to deal
with them as equals. Twain's "The Fable of the Yellow Terror" and "Flies
and Russians" tell just such a historical allegory by endowing Japan with
real "civilization" and poking fun at the colonizing and missionary efforts of

U.S. and other Western countries as "backward."[41] Twain criticizes the hysteria of the "yellow peril" in his fable, but he also indulges in the rhetorical usefulness of this discourse, as we perhaps best see in Huck himself, who after all was not just any cholera germ but specifically an *Asiatic* cholera germ (*Three Thousand Years* 261). The outbreak of cholera that began in Asia and quickly spread across the globe to Europe in 1882–1883 caused international alarm. It reminded nations of their global interdependence even as it created a metaphor used against Asian countries to evoke their inferiority as origin of the contaminating spread of disease, producing yet another version of the "yellow peril" (Kruif 134–139).[42] Consequently, when *Three Thousand Years* ends with a reference to the Russo-Japanese War as it would interest a microbe, it can hardly be coincidental.

In this snatch of conversation in *Three Thousand Years* between Huck and his student germs, he explains the war by noting that the Japanese had far fewer casualties than did Russia, and, moreover, the latter's dead came not from combat but from their doctors. It did not hurt Twain's satirical and political cause, of course, that this was also a historical fact reported widely at the time. In stressing, however, that more Russians died at the hands of Russian doctors than at the hands of Japanese soldiers—in effect, their backward civilization and lack of medical knowledge and progress result in "natural" self-destruction—Huck actually implies that it was his own nation, the microbes, who won the war, the war over man and over medicine. After all, it was the doctors' blind spot, ignorance of the power of small nations—that is, of germs and bacterial infection—that led to so many deaths. Once again, Huck dramatizes Twain's larger point humorously and sharply: we tend to see our own kind as the hero of every story and place our nation at the center of history, blinding ourselves to the more complex stories of interdependence we should know better. Twain depicts the contradictions of the sovereign nation as an imperial "I" and yet simultaneously interdependent within and among other nations. So to put it in Snopesian terms and echo a Faulkner passage cited earlier, in always making oneself the big cheese, one risks revealing (unwittingly of course) one's own mold. Politics in the future will reveal these limits of nation-states and move away from them, Twain's critique implies; and in that he was, in understanding the significance of the Russo-Japanese War at the time, prescient.

Twain's *Three Thousand Years* is a satire largely indebted to Swift's vision of Gulliver tied down by Lilliputian forces,[43] and in a recent *Japan Focus* article, Joyce Appleby, too, makes recourse to Jonathan Swift to discuss the limits of nation-states. She invokes the image of Gulliver tied down by the Lilliputians to describe how large, powerful countries like the U.S. might find themselves surprisingly constrained by smaller countries and perhaps even smaller international "bodies" of various sorts. Appleby argues that the role of supranational bodies such as the U.N. and international organizations or military coalitions that go beyond nation-state borders and have the power to invade or go into countries without their permission is both a more appropriate trend in recent decades, and a more dangerous one. In noting that nationalist growth peaked after WWII and that that was when nations freed from colonial bonds established themselves, she reminds us that although nation-states are still very new, from a world-historical perspective, that their failures are already apparent on the global stage:

> The United States stands poised between wanting to write its own ticket and wishing to speed efforts to solve the world's problems. Conspicuously first among equals, it is going to have to get used to the idea that national sovereignty belongs to the past.
>
> Before the invasion of Iraq, it was possible to imagine American power as unbounded. Today the United States evokes images of Gulliver tied down by hundreds of Lilliputian concerns. Whether subduing Iraq and Afghanistan, combating sex trafficking, restricting nuclear weaponry or establishing order in the Middle East, it's obvious that the United States can't go it alone. Despite such an obvious reality, the Bush administration, intent on demonstrating hegemonic power, is unlikely to grapple with supranationalism in its remaining two years in office. ("Supranationalism")[44]

Appleby's supranationalism resonates remarkably with our concept thus far of global provincialism. Already, in Twain's Huck of *Three Thousand Years* and in Faulkner's Snopeses and letter home from Italy, the idea had been made clear: if the dominant and hegemonic Gulliver-like nations were not more careful, they might just find themselves tied hand and foot by the "invisible" forces of the Lilliputian and disenfranchised nations they thought they had well-contained but had thoroughly overlooked. Twain openly castigated Roosevelt's "big stick" diplomacy and McKinley's imperialist policies during the Spanish-American and U.S.-Philippine wars, and his *Three Thousand Years* offers an alternative view, a more complex picture of global interdependence surprisingly similar to the one Appleby configures for today's globalized political economies. One cannot help but wonder what kind of satirical imperial soliloquy Twain might have written for U.S. President Bush, just as he had done so famously for Russia's Czar and King Leopold of Belgium.

In concluding his adventures of Huck the microbe with a celebration of both microbes and Japan in their victory over Russian imperialism, all the while overlooking the colonial plight of Korea subject to Japanese imperialism, Twain reminds us of Huck's point at the start of the tale: The arrogant sovereign "I" is more often blind than insightful about matters of power, failing to see how his sovereignty as "the state, it is I" is always constrained from both below and above by constitutive relations and interdependence with other "worlds," worlds whose size—no matter how microbic—and "character"—no matter how Snopesian—hardly determine each one's ability to shake up the order of things in "the stupendous procession" of nations.

Notes

1.   This study is indebted to the generous and invaluable assistance of Neda Salem and Victor Fischer at the *Mark Twain Project* of the University of California, Berkeley. I also extend my gratitude to Robert Hamblin at Southeast Missouri State University who welcomed our Japanese panel (including my co-panelists Takayuki Tatsumi, Kazuhiko Goto, and Fumiyo Hayashi) for the Faulkner and Twain conference sponsored by the Center for Faulkner Studies. Special thanks go to the American Literature Society of Japan, Tokyo, for allowing me to present a longer version of this talk in November 2006. This essay is dedicated to my father, Grant D. Knighton (1942–2007), who encouraged me in this idea in the late summer of 2006. The title is "Swinks" because, like the Snopeses, the swinks have no voice and they make up the bottom of the microbe food chain just as the Snopeses do that of the human one.

2.   Tuckey notes, "Huck Bkshp, who exists within Blitzowski" is actually "a Huckian germ adrift in the Mississippi-like veins of a cosmic Pap Finn!" Also cited in Hume, 80–81.

3.   The Snopes trilogy extends in historical time from 1902 until 1946, almost half a century, encompassing the financial panics of 1903 and 1907 and the Great Depression, through the end of WWII, as Andrea Dimino points out in "Why Did the Snopeses Name Their Son 'Wallstreet Panic'?: Depression Humor in Faulkner's *The Hamlet*" (334, 350).

4.   Some scholars see Mink Snopes, especially, as having a voice that poignantly speaks to the disenfranchised and the ignorance of his impov-

erished, betrayed state, and Faulkner appears to give him a voice beyond that granted other Snopeses who are mostly narrated about or quoted in dialogue. However, even Mink Snopes's voice is thoroughly mediated by the free-and-indirect narrative voice that dominates these texts, indeed, in such a heavy-handed manner that it squelches more effectively than it does the Bundren voices in *As I Lay Dying* or Benjy's in *The Sound and the Fury*.

5. Tuckey also points out this possible connection. See his "Introduction" (ix–xx).

6. James B. Meriwether's "Introduction" to *Father Abraham* reveals this, noting, "In a 1957 letter, [Phil] Stone recalled that the idea for the Snopeses, and their book, had been his, and that he had given it to Faulkner after *Mosquitoes* (his second novel, published in April 1927) was written but before the writing of *Sartoris*. 'The core of the Snopes legend,' explained Stone, was 'that the real revolution in the South was not the race situation but the rise of the redneck, who did not have any of the scruples of the old aristocracy, to places of power and wealth.' And he recalled that 'Bill once wrote fifteen or twenty pages on the idea of the Snopes trilogy which he entitled "Father Abraham" but I think that has disappeared.' Stone's recollection seems accurate, both for the date and for his own attitude, at least, towards the lowly origins of the Snopeses. In a piece he wrote early in 1927, for the local paper, announcing the forthcoming publication of *Mosquitoes*, he mentioned a Faulkner novel in progress which, he said, 'is something of a saga of an extensive family connection of typical "poor white trash" and is said by those who have seen that part of the manuscript completed to be the funniest book anybody ever wrote." (n.p.)

7. James B. Meriwether documents Faulkner's incipient ideas about Snopes in 1925 in "Sartoris and Snopes: An Early Notice."

8. Names and dates or chronology are examples of such discrepancies. For instance, the name of Ratliff's partner in the restaurant business is his cousin Aaron Rideout in *The Hamlet* but becomes Grover Cleveland Winbush in *The Town* and *The Mansion*.

9. The most telling evidence of this fact is the degree to which critics apparently feel justified in dealing only with *The Hamlet* when writing about the Snopeses, not infrequently ignoring the last two novels of the trilogy.

10. It is interesting to note that even today while there is an entry for *Three Thousand Years Among the Microbes* in J.R. Lester and James D. Wilson's *The Mark Twain Encyclopedia*, there is no similar entry in R. Kent Rasmussen's *Mark Twain A to Z*.

11. For example, Ratliff and Gavin Stevens in conversation both describe them this way: ". . . It's that non-Snopes boy of Eck's, that other non-Snopes that blowed his-self up in that empty oil tank back while you was away at the war, wasting his time jest hunting a lost child that wasn't even lost, jest his maw thought he was—" (Faulkner, *The Town* 143). Meanwhile, a Snopes-like non-Snopes is Wilbur Provine in *The Town*, sent to prison not for making whiskey, which could not be proved at trial anyway, but for making his wife walk a mile and a half to fetch water.

12. See Gail Mortimer's "Evolutionary Theory in Faulkner's Snopes Trilogy."

13. Mortimer explores this idea briefly, building on an earlier note about this coincidence in Gerald Smith's "A Note on the Origin of Flem Snopes."

14. The work of Richard Godden and Mauri Skinfill in this area is representative. See, for instance, Godden's *Fictions of Labor: William Faulkner and the South's Long Revolution* and Skinfill's "Reconstructing Class in Faulkner's Late Novels: *The Hamlet* and the Discovery of Capital."

15. Ratliff points out that Eck Snopes could not survive because he was not Snopes-like enough (Faulkner, *The Town* 107): "Eck wasn't a Snopes. That's why he had to die. Like there wasn't no true authentic room for Snopeses in the world and they made theirselves one by that pure and simple mutual federation, and the first time one slips or falters or fails in being Snopes, it dont even need the rest of the pack like wolves to finish him: simple environment jest watched its chance and taken it.'"

16. Specifically, Ratliff describes Ab Snopes as having "soured" or "went curdled" beginning with the milk separator incident. He begins the telling of the Pat Stamper horse trade tale in this way: "'Sho now,' Ratliff said. 'Old man Ab aint naturally mean. He's just soured'" (Faulkner, *The Hamlet* 31–33).

17. *The Hamlet* describes the horse whose black paint washes off in the rain and the discovery of the bicycle pump valve (47–48) and the "loose dollars" in the transaction (37–38). Mauri Skinfill in "Reconstructing Class" first used the language of repetition/vicious cycle to describe so aptly the borrowed milk and its separator in this way.

18. If we could draw a picture of the idea of Flem, he might look like Felix Octavius Carr Darley's illustration of Simon Suggs (see the *Documenting the American South* archives online, especially the Frontispiece: http://www.docsouth.unc.edu/southlit/hooper/). It is more than likely that Faulkner's brand of tall-tale humor owes something to Johnson Jones Hooper's

Adventures of Captain Simon Suggs (1815), as we know it does to G.W. Harris's *Sut Lovingood* (1867), A.B. Longstreet's *Georgia Scenes* (1835), and T. B. Thorpe's "The Big Bear of Arkansas" (1841).

19. Mortimer cites Alfred Kazin's essay "Faulkner: The Rhetoric and the Agony," saying that Faulkner's bitter frustration came from "being a Sartoris (the southern aristocratic *manqué*) in a Snopes world" (Kazin 390–391; Mortimer 198).

20. It has been a staple of Snopes criticism to read Flem and the Snopeses as representative of the forces of evil (which take different forms, as suggested earlier in this essay) against which the Sartoris, or even Sutpen, and their force of goodness can be best measured. This dichotomous and even Manichean approach is not inappropriate but it does tend to flatten the connotative meanings generated by the texts, in ways similar to readings for Christian imagery and Biblical allusion as the bottom-line determinant factor in textual exegesis. See interview with Faulkner in 1958 at Washington and Lee University in *Faulkner in the University* (285). As cited in Watson, Faulkner responds to a question about where to begin reading his work in this way at the University of Virginia in 1958: "Probably . . . with a book called *Sartoris* that has the germ of my apocrypha in it. A lot of the characters are postulated in that book. I'd say that's a good one to begin with" (Gwynn and Blotner 285). Also see James Gray Watson's "'The Germ of my Apocrypha': *Sartoris* and the Search for Form." Even before W. J. Cash's groundbreaking 1941 *The Mind of the South*, we see the beginnings of this idea in his short piece for H.L. Mencken's *Mercury*, "Genesis of the Southern Cracker" in May 1935. Available online at http://www.wjcash.org

21. I adapt my section title here from W.H. Conn's book, *The Story of Germ Life* (1897), for reasons that will soon be apparent.

22. Beverly Hume, in "Twain's Satire on Scientists: *Three Thousand Years Among the Microbes*," argues that unlike Hyatt Howe Waggoner's important essay on the influence of Huxley on Twain's thought ("Science in the Thought of Mark Twain"), she finds more than a little satire of all scientists, including Huxley, in *Three Thousand Years*. She privileges the Swiftian impulse to satire over the almost inert reverence for science in Waggoner, finding that it best explains the vitality of Twain's work and the role of Huck himself.

23. Huck's secretary, Catherine, tells him that she read a book entitled "Science and Wealth, With Key to the Fixtures," a spoof on Eddy's 1875 *Science and Health, With Key to the Scriptures*. For more information, see

Yoko Arima's "Twain's Move Toward Fantasy: A Study of His Writings, 1905–1906." Working closely as assistant editor on *Mark Twain Studies* with Professor Arima on her article first inspired my interest in this work by Twain. Arima is also the translator of this story into Japanese: *Saikin Hakku no bouken/ Three Thousand Years among the Microbes*.

24. From the typescript of Samuel L. Clemens and with permission to cite it provided by the *Mark Twain Project*, Bancroft Library, University of California at Berkeley. Microfilm edition of Mark Twain's literary manuscripts available in the Mark Twain Papers. Prepared by Anh Quynh Bui, Victor Fischer, Michael B. Frank, Robert H. Hirst, Lin Salamo, and Harriet Elinor Smith.

25. No. 44 and Satan in these stories may also be read as fallen angels, which would suggest that their evil status is not absolute, just as God the scientist in the notebook passage is not evil in Clemens's eyes.

26. H.W. Conn is mentioned in *Three Thousand Years* in this way: "In the World, when I was studying micrology under Prof. H. W. Conn, we knew all these facts, because they were all true of the microbes that infest the human being; but it was new to me to find them exactly duplicated in the life of the microbes that infest the human *being's* microbes. We knew that the human race was saved from destruction in the beginning by the microbe; that the microbe was the protector and preserver and alblest propagator of many of the mightiest industries in the Earth; that he was the personage most heavily interested in the corporations which exploited them, and that his expert service was the most valuable asset such corporations possessed; we knew that he kept the Earth's soil from being covered up and buried out of sight and made unusable; in a word, we knew that the most valuable citizen of the Earth was the microbe, and that the human race could no more do without him than it could do without the sun and the air. We also knew that the human race took no notice of these benefactions, and only remembered the disease-germ's 10 percent contribution to the death-rate; and didn't even stop with that unfairness, but charged all microbes with being disease-germs, and violently abused the entire stock, benefactors and all! Yes, that was all old to me, but to find that our little old familiar microbes were themselves loaded up with microbes that fed them, enriched them, and persistently and faithfully preserved them and their poor old tramp-planet from destruction—oh, that was new, and too delicious!" (251–252)

27. The term "American Dream" was introduced by Adams in his book *The Epic of America* (1931). We see it in the language of de Crevecoeur's melting pot and optimism about the American race as a new race, as well

as in Franklin, Jefferson, and Horatio Alger stories. Critics have identified the Abraham of Faulkner's *Father Abraham* as the Biblical Abraham, Abraham Lincoln, Sherwood Anderson's idea for a work on Abraham Lincoln, and also of Franklin's *Way to Wealth* (Bassett 150).

28. See Dimino. She argues that it is "depression humor" that marks the Snopes tall-tale comedy written after the Depression began but set beforehand, during, and in its wake.

29. Alan Reynolds Thompson's "The Cult of Cruelty" (1932); Maxwell Geismar's *Writers in Crisis* (1942); Robert Penn Warren writing after *The Portable Faulkner* came out in 1946 that Faulkner had been largely represented as "a combination of Thomas Nelson Page, a fascist and a psychopath, gnawing at his nails. Of course, this picture is usually accompanied by a grudging remark about genius" (cited in Brinkmeyer 71; Warren, "Cowley's Faulkner").

30. Throughout his essay, Brinkmeyer points out the South's character as antimodern and regionalist (therefore partial and unrepresentative) in portrayals by contemporary reformers.

31. Brinkmeyer may be revising this more positive evaluation of Faulkner's "progressive" attitudes and thinking about matters of democracy and fascism in his most recent work.

32. Flem's wife Eula would make him a cuckold with Major de Spain (not Colonel Winword) in *The Town*, but that did not bother him, as it does not bother him here. Indeed, later, he will only make use of such information to blackmail his way into becoming president of the bank.

33. See Scott Michaelson's "'The State it is I': Mark Twain, Imperialism, and the New Americanists."

34. See Lindborg's "A Cosmic Tramp: Samuel Clemens's *Three Thousand Years Among the Microbes*," (653), which also describes the structure this way.

35. See Schwartz's *Creating Faulkner's Reputation: The Politics of Modern Literary Criticism.*

36. Oakley also cites much of this intriguing CIA-related information from Frances Stonor Saunders, *Who Paid the Piper? The CIA and the Cultural Cold War.* My quick examination of several early issues of *Jiyu* revealed prominent Japanese literary figures involved, with Kikuchi Kan, among others, writing articles for it. Richard Minear's *The Scars of War: Tokyo During WWII (Writings of Takeyama Michio)* discusses the cultural

cold war from both sides, American and Japanese. He stresses the secretive and problematic role of the CIA in funding *Jiyu* as part of the Congress for Cultural Freedom (CCF), by focusing on author of the WWII novel *The Burmese Harp*, Takeyama Michio, who worked closely on the journal's publishing.

37. This was an oft-repeated slogan, especially during the Occupation of Japan (1945–1952). See John W. Dower's *Embracing Defeat: Japan in the Aftermath of World War II*. Of course, Faulkner, among other regionalists, is well known for referring to his region as a "country."

38. "The Russo-Japanese War was brought about by the conflict of Japanese and Russian ambitions in northeast Asia and more directly by the Russian failure to withdraw from Manchuria, which she [sic] had occupied at the time of the Boxer rebellion. . . . The war gave Japan a dominant position in Korea and rights in Manchuria and had worldwide significance as the first defeat of a European power by an Asian country. It also stimulated Chinese nationalism and further weakened the tsarist regime" (Hunter 182–183).

39. Korea was gradually annexed by Japan from the end of this war, first in 1907 with the forced abdication of the Korean king, and then officially in 1910, and remained colonized through the end of WWII. Gordon notes the further irony that, while Japan inspired anti-colonial sentiments throughout the world and especially in Asia, it was the victory in the Russo-Japanese War that led Japan to expand its imperial ambitions such that it changed from "a force for Asian liberation to one of oppression" (177). See all of Gordon's Chapter 8, especially pages 121–123, for further discussion of the domestic and foreign factors that shaped Japan's engagement in the Russo-Japanese War.

40. This last czar of Russia and his family were executed at the hands of the Bolsheviks in the 1917 October Revolution.

41. Du Bois's final story in *Darkwater*, "The Comet," shares with Twain a fascination with comets, and Halley's in particular, in relaying a futuristic tale of the world's destruction.

42. Also see K. Patrick Ober's *Mark Twain and Medicine* regarding the cholera outbreak of 1849 in Hannibal, Missouri, and regarding Twain and his mother's fear of this disease in particular.

43. See Kathleen Walsh, "Rude Awakenings and Swift Recoveries: The Problem of Reality in Mark Twain's 'The Great Dark' and 'Three Thousand Years Among the Microbes.'"

44. Appleby's book is *A Restless Past: History and the American Public.*

Works Cited

Appleby, Joyce. *A Restless Past: History and the American Public.* New York: Rowman, 2005.

———. "Supranationalism and Mythologies of American Power." *Japan Focus* and *History News Network.* 2 October 2006. 15 October 2006.<http://www.japanfocus.org>.

Bassett, John E. "Yoknapatawpha Revised: Demystifying Snopes." *College Literature* 15.2 (1988): 136–152.

Brinkmeyer, Robert H., Jr. "Faulkner and the Democratic Crisis." In *Faulkner and Ideology: Faulkner and Yoknapatawpha 1992*, edited by Donald M. Kartiganer and Ann J. Abadie. Jackson: UP of Mississippi, 1995. 70-94.

Clemens, Samuel L. "The Fable of the Yellow Terror." In *The Devil's Racetrack: Mark Twain's "Great Dark" Writings*, edited by John S. Tuckey. Berkeley: U of California P, 1980. 369–372.

———. Notebook 40, ts. Mark Twain Papers. U of California, Berkeley.

———. Notebook 42, ts. Mark Twain Papers. U of California, Berkeley.

———. *Three Thousand Years Among the Microbes.* In *The Devil's Racetrack: Mark Twain's "Great Dark" Writings*, edited by John S. Tuckey. Berkeley: U of California P, 1980. 161–281.

Dimino, Andrea. "Why Did the Snopeses Name Their Son 'Wallstreet Panic'?: Depression Humor in Faulkner's *The Hamlet.*" In *William Faulkner: Two Decades of Criticism*, edited by Frederick J. Hoffman and Olga W. Vickery. 1951. East Lansing, MI: Michigan State College P, 1954.

Dower, John W. *Embracing Defeat: Japan in the Aftermath of World War II.* New York: Norton, 2000.

Du Bois, W.E.B. *Darkwater: Voices from Within the Veil.* New York: Harbrace, 1920. Mineola, NY: Dover, 1999.

Faulkner, William. *Father Abraham.* Edited by James Meriwether. New York: Random House, 1983.

———. *The Hamlet*. New York: Random House, 1940.

———. Press Dispatch Written in Rome, Italy, for the United Press, on the Emmett Till Case. In *William Faulkner: Letters, Speeches, and Public Letters*, edited by James B. Meriwether. London: Chatto and Windus, 1967. 222–223.

———. *The Town*. New York: Random House, 1957.

Gordon, Andrew. *A Modern History of Japan: From Tokugawa Times to the Present*. New York: Oxford UP, 2003.

Gwynn, Frederick L. and Joseph Blotner, eds. *Faulkner in the University: Class Conferences at the University of Virginia, 1957–1958*. Charlottesville: U of Virginia P, 1959.

Hume, Beverly A. "Twain's Satire on Scientists: *Three Thousand Years Among the Microbes*." *Essays in Arts and Sciences* 26 (October 1997): 71–84.

Hunter, Janet E., comp. "Russo-Japanese War (*Nichiro senso*)." In *Concise Dictionary of Modern Japanese History*. Berkeley: U of California P, 1984.

Kazin, Alfred. "Faulkner: The Rhetoric and the Agony." *Virginia Quarterly Review* 18 (1942): 389–402.

Kruif, Paul de. *Microbe Hunters: The Classic Book on The Major Discoveries of the Microscopic World*. 1926. New York: Harcourt/Harvest, 1996.

LeMaster, J.R., and James D. Wilson, eds. *The Mark Twain Encyclopedia*. New York: Garland, 1993.

Lindborg, Henry J. "A Cosmic Tramp: Samuel Clemens's *Three Thousand Years Among the Microbes*." *American Literature* 44.4 (Jan. 1973): 652–657.

McCormick, John. "The United Snopes Information Service." *Kenyon Review*, xxiv, 330-350.

Meriwether, James B. Introduction to *Father Abraham*, by William Faulkner, edited by James Meriwether. New York: Random, 1983.

———. "Sartoris and Snopes: An Early Notice." *Library Chronicle of the University of Texas* 7 (1962): 36–39.

Michaelson, Scott. "'The State it is I': Mark Twain, Imperialism, and the New Americanists." In *A Companion to Mark Twain*, edited by Louis J. Budd and Peter Messent. Malden, MA: Blackwell, 2006. 109–122.

Minear, Richard H. *The Scars of War: Tokyo During World War II: Writings of Takeyama Micheo*. Lanham, MD: Rowman, 2007.

Mortimer, Gail. "Evolutionary Theory in Faulkner's Snopes Trilogy." *Rocky Mountain Review of Languages and Literature* 40.4 (1986): 187–202.

Oakley, Helen. "William Faulkner and the Cold War: The Politics of Cultural Marketing." In *Look Away!: The U.S. South in New World Studies*, edited by John Smith and Deborah Cohn. Durham: Duke UP, 2004. 405–418.

Ober, K. Patrick. *Mark Twain and Medicine: "Any Mummery Will Cure."* Columbia: U of Missouri P, 2003.

Paine, A.B., ed. *Mark Twain, A Biography*. New York: Harper, 1920.

Rasmussen, R. Kent, ed. *Mark Twain A to Z*. New York: Oxford UP, 1995.

Saunders, Frances Stonor. *Who Paid the Piper? The CIA and the Cultural Cold War*. London: Granta, 1999.

Schwartz, Lawrence H. *Creating Faulkner's Reputation: The Politics of Modern Literary Criticism*. Knoxville: U of Tennessee P, 1988.

Smith, Gerald. "A Note on the Origin of Flem Snopes." *Notes on Mississippi Writers* 6 (1973): 56–57.

Tuckey, John S. Introduction to *The Devil's Racetrack: Mark Twain's "Great Dark" Writings*, edited by John S. Tuckey. Berkeley: U of California P, 1980. ix–xx.

———. *Mark Twain's 'Which Was the Dream?' and Other Symbolic Writings of the Later Years*. Berkeley: U of California P, 1967.

Twain, Mark. "Flies and Russians." *Fables of Man*. Edited by John S. Tuckey. Berkeley: U of California P, 1972. 421–424.

———. Letter from SLC to Clara Clemens. 16 July 1905. Mark Twain Project. U of California at Berkeley.

Wallerstein, Immanuel. *The Modern World-System*, vol. I: *Capitalist Agriculture and the Origins of the European World-Economy in the Sixteenth Century*. New York: Academic P, 1974.

Walsh, Kathleen. "Rude Awakenings and Swift Recoveries: The Problem of Reality in Mark Twain's 'The Great Dark' and 'Three Thousand Years Among the Microbes.'" *American Literary Realism* 21.1 (1988): 19–28.

Watson, James Gray. "'The Germ of my Apocrypha': *Sartoris* and the Search for Form." In *William Faulkner: Critical Assessments*, edited by Henry Claridge. Vol. II. New York: Routledge, 2000.

Willis, Susan. "Aesthetics of the Rural Slum: Contradictions and Dependency in 'The Bear.'" *Social Text* 2 (Summer 1979): 82–103. Rpt. in *Faulkner: New Perspectives*, edited by Richard Brodhead. Englewood Cliffs: Prentice, 1983.

Faulkner, Twain, and Just About Everybody
Not Currently Working in Washington

*"Barely a decade since their fathers and uncles and brothers just finished the one
which was to rid the phenomenon of government forever of the parasites—the
hereditary proprietors, the farmers-general of the human dilemma who had just
killed eight million human beings and ruined a forty-mile-wide strip down
the middle of western Europe. Yet less than a dozen years later and the same old
cynical manipulators not even bothering to change their names and faces but
merely assuming a set of new titles out of the shibboleth of the democratic lexicon
and its mythology, not even breaking stride to coalesce again to wreck the one
doomed desperate hope—."* (Faulkner, *The Mansion* 160)

I open with this epigraph so that you might be aware that I intend
here to deal with, as the quote notes, cynical manipulation of the
democratic lexicon, that is, with distorting the meaning of words for the
supposedly patriotic promotion of interests of the State, war being chief
among them.

Given my subject, I should tell you at the outset that I am here under
false pretenses. I know very little about Mark Twain, and I am convinced
no one knows much about William Faulkner. The more volumes on Twain
and Faulkner we produce, the more we realize we don't know.

But I do know this about both of them: they are cultural icons whose
iconic portraits often bear little resemblance to the writers themselves.

We have, of course, Mark Twain, the somewhat irascible but much
beloved wit whose sayings fill books of quotes, books whose covers often
portray the mane and mustache of the avuncular figure known as a humorist. And we have William Faulkner, variously dressed to ride to the hounds
or dressed fit for the doghouse, pipe in hand, kindly Mr. Bill whose books
are hard to read.

These portraits ignore the Twain tortured by personal loss, bankruptcy,
and the emerging imperialistic designs of racist America; and they ignore
the Faulkner who, while personally conflicted over everything from radios
to race, understood that both individuality and community were threatened
by the menace of fascist and communist collectivism, particularly as naively
parroted by mediums of popular culture.

Both Twain and Faulkner, therefore, by their selective celebrity, are victims of the art of misrepresentation that each fought as a writer.

Twain had, of course, regaled us with the loveable Tom Sawyer, and reading *Tom* is still one of the best reading memories from my youth. This Twain stands beside the likes of Alexander Dumas and Robert Louis Stevenson, writers who provided much of the enjoyment of my young life, enjoyments that found their way into the formulations of Hardy Boys mysteries, Edgar Rice Burrough's jungle stories, and Dr. Doolittle's talks with the animals. These are the joys we have taken away from our youngsters by robbing them of their literacy and socializing them instead.

But the same Twain who gave us Tom Sawyer as boy hero could lampoon Tom in *Huckleberry Finn*, the novel he had to stop writing (and then resume again) after he'd figured out how not to make it another Tom Sawyer book, after he'd thought through how racism had deprived America of the future that Emancipation and amendments to the constitution had promised. And this Twain, I'll venture for a moment to call this the "real" Twain, could give us the much neglected and forgotten "War Prayer." You won't see the prayer mounted on tablets outside Alabama courthouses. Written out of Twain's vehement opposition to the Philippine-American War going on at the turn of that century, Twain's text places the prayer at a Sunday service, shortly after "a war chapter from the Old Testament was read" and an "organ burst . . . shook the building." "An aged stranger" pushes the preacher aside, and prays:

> O Lord our Father, our young patriots, idols of our hearts,
> go forth to battle—be Thou near them! With them in
> Spirit—we also go forth from the sweet peace of our
> beloved firesides to smite the foe. O Lord our God, help
> us to tear their soldiers to bloody shreds with our shells;
> help us to cover their smiling fields with the pale forms
> of their patriot dead; help us to drown the thunder of
> the guns with the cries of the wounded, writhing in pain;
> help us to lay waste their humble homes with a hurricane
> of fire; help us to wring the hearts of their unoffending
> widows with unavailing grief; help us to turn them out
> roofless with little children to wander unbefriended
> through the wastes of their desolated land in rags and
> hunger and thirst, sports of the sun flames of summer and
> the icy winds of winter, broken in spirit, worn with travail,
> imploring Thee for the refuge of the grave and denied
> it—for our sakes, who adore Thee, Lord, blast their hopes,
> blight their lives, protract their bitter pilgrimage, make

heavy their steps, water their way with their tears, stain the
white snow with the blood of their wounded feet! We ask
it, in the spirit of love, of Him Who is the Source of Love,
and Who is the ever-faithful refuge and friend of all that
are sore beset and seek His aid with humble and contrite
hearts. Amen.

Sardonically Twain adds that "It was believed afterward that the man was a
lunatic, because there was no sense in what he said."[1]

Fishkin notes, "Twain tried, but failed, to get this piece published in
his lifetime" (5).[2] Twain is an inconvenient presence: he was inconvenient
to have around in his own day and has become much more inconvenient in
ours.

William Faulkner is Mark Twain's inheritor. His own iconic portrait
bears traces of Twain's; he noted Twain's importance in American literature, and his novels reference works of Twain's. Of course, others could
also claim inheritance from Twain, and there were others besides Twain
who influenced Faulkner, but one could fairly argue that it is Faulkner on
whom Twain's mantle most rests. Faulkner shares with Twain the traditions
of Southwestern humor, the tall tale, the art of capturing local dialect in
the orthography of print, and the penchant for using boys' adventures as
the site of the pursuit of serious themes. Scholars have noted the parallels
between Faulkner's story of Chick Mallison in *Intruder in the Dust* and
Twain's story of Huck Finn, and someone should pursue the possible
parallels of *Roughing It* and *The Reivers*.

But if Faulkner inherited something of the iconic presence of Twain,
he also inherited a great deal of the truer inconvenient, acerbic, iconoclastic
Twain, as is readily apparent in the themes and characterizations found in
the novels.

Indeed, although Faulkner appropriated Twain's attitudes in a manner
individual to Faulkner's own style in the projection of his Yoknapatawpha,
Faulkner was by no means alone in focusing on the deceitful use of words
as the prime culprit in the criminal state of the world. This focus was so
widespread that one wonders why it has not gained more attention as a
cardinal tenet of both Modernism and its precursors.

Beginning with the growing imperialistic designs of America in the
post-Civil War period and continuing through each of the succeeding
postwar eras, writers at home and abroad saw how lies were the underpin-
ning of the twentieth century's penchant for collectivism. Because she has
put the matter so succinctly, let me quote at length Shelley Fisher Fishkin's
summary of the idea and the extended era:

The New York Times called World War I, "the first press agents' war;" to one historian it represented "the first modern effort at systematic nationwide manipulation of collective passions." "[I]t was the astounding success of propaganda during the war," wrote public relations magnate Edward Bernays, "which opened the eyes of the intelligent few in all departments of life to the possibilities for regimenting the public mind." John Dos Passos was one of those who found his eyes opened to "the possibilities of regimenting the public mind" during the war—but he was horrified by the prospect that cheered Bernays. As Martin Howe, the main character in his first novel, *One Man's Initiation: 1917*, complained, "What terrifies me . . . is their power to enslave our minds. . . . I shall never forget the . . . gradual lulling to sleep of people's humanity and sense by the phrases, the phrases. . . . People seem to love to be fooled. . . . We are slaves of bought intellect, willing slaves." His friend then interjects, "But Howe, the minute you see that and laugh at it, you're not a slave." As a novelist, Dos Passos would give his readers the tools to understand and thereby extricate themselves from propaganda that would enslave them. In Dos Passos' World War I novel, *Three Soldiers*, the character John Andrews says that "Men were more humane when they were killing each other than when they were talking about it." Andrews believes that the so-called ideals of civilization that led him into war—"[the] gigantic phrases that floated like gaudy kites above mankind" were, ultimately, just "contraptions of tissue paper held at the end of string, ornaments not to be taken seriously." As the writer Henry James had put it referring to World War I, "The war had used up words: they have weakened, they have deteriorated." Then, "As a result of lies of propaganda and the hyperboles of hate, language," James said, "suffers 'an increase of limpness.'"[3]

All of us here could add other sentiments of other writers. As I was listening to Fishkin's lecture at Yunnan University in Kunming, PR China, I was making notes in a small journal I keep with me, and I discovered in that journal that over many months I had also recorded similar sentiments, such as George Orwell's line, "In a time of universal deceit, telling the truth is a revolutionary act," and Wendell Berry's poetic evocation of the "tongue / set free of fashionable lies." In that journal as well was a quote from W. H. Auden (that Fishkin also uses): "All I have is a voice to undo the folded lie"; and, auspiciously for our topic today, there was Twain's own phrase, "The lie of silent assertion." And, of course, I have only to quote the opening, "I was always embarrassed by the words . . ." to call to our minds Frederic Henry's famous thoughts from *A Farewell to Arms*.

My point, obviously, is not that other writers have not concerned themselves with truth but that from Twain to Faulkner (and encompassing the writers of their eras), there seems an undeniable sense that the powers of mass media had catapulted lying into a new and more deadly potential for evil, especially the evils associated with war, and that this sense issued in both Twain and Faulkner in sentiments not only critical of war but in fact very complementary to the large body of pacifistic literature we associate with that other giant of their eras, Leo Tolstoy.

Twain's "War Prayer" will have to stand today for Twain's growing opposition to imperialism and warmongering. I want to turn in the final section of this paper to Faulkner's own sentiments as found in his novels, sentiments Theresa Towner characterizes as "Faulkner's own . . . ironic disparagement of [the] juvenile sentiment" expressed in unthinking acceptance of America's wartime rhetoric.[4] There will not be time to trace pacifist sentiments to the spreading of both pacifistic religious bodies (such as the Mennonites, Quakers, Hutterites, Doukhobors), the institutions that offered noncombatant roles (such as the Red Cross, AFS, and YMCA), and the peace-prone immigrants who had fled the wars of their British and European homelands and saw no reason for their sons to be embroiled in another of them.[5]

Faulkner readers will recognize that Faulkner's chronicle of his saga begins with a Compson forebear fleeing Scotland after the Battle of Culloden, and note the frequency with which Faulkner depicts the ravages of war on individuals, communities, and society. But, here again, we are faced with the difference between the iconic Faulkner and the Faulkner who emerges from the pages of his own novels. There was, to be sure, the "Count No 'Count" Faulkner, who had desperately tried to get into a British flying squadron, his Canadian training brought to an end by the spread of the flu epidemic, returning to Oxford in an airman's uniform and spreading tall tales of his exploits.[6] From this history, some of his later statements, and his continued overtures to join the military, it has been easy to assume that Faulkner was the would-be soldier, cheated out of his battle. Faulkner, however, appeared in many guises, each of them in some way a rehearsal for walking a mile in another's shoes; and it is the empathy he gained through these masquerades (and from his growing experience of the world) that pervades the novels and their portraits of war, soldiers, and public sentiments surrounding the Civil War, the Great War, and World War II. Emerging in his novels and stories is a scathing hostility to war rhetoric and sentiments in tune with pacifism's disparaging view of the empires at war.

Despite critics' and locals' assumptions about his soldier guise, Faulkner well understood how an increasingly powerful American myth, in this case the glamorous myth of the western cowboy, was helping to foster lies through the vehicles of popular culture. By the time Random House published Faulkner's *The Wild Palms* in 1939, the myth was becoming embodied in the figure of John Wayne, who, Garry Wills notes, "embodied [the] deep-seated American mythology." The traits championed by the myth, Wills claims, were "contact with nature, distrust of government, dignity achieved by performance, and skepticism toward . . . experts" (311).[7] Or as Paul Olson puts it, "the official head lawmen are not reliable, innocent women need protecting and avenging, and the Indian Territory needs civilizing through ritualistic and private violence" (3).[8]

Faulkner indicates the power of this myth, especially as it was conveyed in popular culture, in the case of the convict in the "Old Man" sections of *The Wild Palms*. Faulkner tells us that the "outrage" in the convict's eyes was "directed not at the men who had foiled his crime, not even at the lawyers and judges who had sent him [to prison], but at the writers, the uncorporeal names attached to the stories, the paper novels—the Diamond Dicks and Jesse Jameses and such—whom he believed had led him into his present predicament" (20). His "attempted train robbery" had "followed his printed (and false) authority to the letter" (21).

Faulkner's characters and their situations frequently suggest a sensibility quite at odds with this myth. Having lived through and seen through the era in which, as Malcolm Cowley put it, "death itself exerted a curious magnetism on young men . . . and became a romantic dream," Faulkner emerged as a writer capable of seeing the destructiveness of the war impulse and the verbal machines that powered it. In *Flags in the Dust*, he could see even the legendary Jeb Stuart's daring as "wild and self-consuming" (19), and young Bayard could retort (both to the Civil War and the Great War), "Takes damn near as big a fool to get hurt in a war as it does in peacetime" (45).[9] Speaking sardonically of the young men psychologically damaged in the Great War in general and more specifically of Bayard's brother John, killed in aerial warfare, Aunt Jenny can say, "John at least had consideration enough after he'd gone and gotten himself into something where he had no business, not to come back to worry everybody to death" (54–55).

Faulkner embeds this skeptical attitude into reflections on the Civil War as well as comments on the Great War. Picturing Bayard's grandfather, sitting in the room where his memories are stored, the narrative describes its furniture as "like patient ghosts holding lightly in dry and rigid embrace yet other ghosts—a fitting place for dead Sartorises to gather and speak among themselves of glamorous and old disastrous days" (93). While the violence of battle is described as "magnificent," it is also described as "needless" (94). And, describing Bayard "talking of the war," Faulkner describes him talking "Not of combat, but rather of a life peopled by young men like fallen angels, and of a meteoric violence like that of fallen angels, beyond heaven or hell and partaking of both: doomed immortality and immortal doom" (133).

Faulkner's view, so far as it informs the narrative of *Flags*, is decidedly skeptical about soldiers, armies, and war. When Bayard's grandfather asks old man Falls, "What the devil were you folks fighting about, anyhow?'" Falls replies, "damned ef I ever did know" (252).

In *Flags*, Faulkner waits for over a third of the book to bring young Horace Benbow back from the war where he has served as a noncombatant. In the train station, where he is met by his sister Narcissa, Horace encounters "a marine private with the Second Division Indian head on his shoulder"; the soldier "remarked the triangle on Horace's sleeve and made a vulgar sound of derogation through his pursed lips." Startled, Horace greets the marine, whereupon the marine "spat, not exactly at Horace's feet, and not exactly anywhere else." Walking away with Narcissa, Horace tells her, "'It's a good uniform . . . People will realize that in about ten years, when noncombatants' hysteria has worn itself out and the individual soldiers realize that the A.E.F. didn't invent disillusion'" (173).

The attitudes Faulkner came to are not isolated to this one novel. The stuff of which *A Fable* is made plays a prominent role from *Soldiers' Pay* to *The Mansion* as well. Nor does Faulkner come to any easy answers to the issues of war and peace, knowing that both pacifism and militarism are, after all, isms. Nevertheless, as early as *Flags*, it seems to me, Faulkner is examining issues of "war and peace," including in *Flags* lengthy reflections on peace and what it means, contrasting men's and women's attitudes toward war and peace, and registering in a variety of ways the alternatives to war and the myths that support it.

At the end of *Flags*, Miss Jenny visits the graveyard where the Sartorises are buried, where great-grandfather John Sartoris "lifted his stone back and his fulsome gesture" (426). There she muses on the difference in the tombstones:

> Bayard's grave too was a shapeless mass of withered
> flowers . . . the headstone itself sat nearby beneath a canvas
> cover. She lifted the cover and read the clean, new letter-

ing: Bayard Sartoris, March 16, 1893—June 5, 1920. That was better. Simple: no Sartoris man to invent bombast to put on it. Cant lie dead in the ground without strutting and swaggering. Beside the grave was a second headstone; like the other save for the inscription. But the Sartoris touch was there . . . and the whole thing was like a boastful voice in an empty church. . . . Old Bayard's headstone was simple too, having been born, as he had, too late for one war and too soon for the next one, and she thought what a joke They had played on him: denying him opportunities for swashbuckling and then denying him the privilege of being buried by men who would have invented vainglory for him. (426–427)

Sounds to me like the actual Faulkner who actually wrote books might just have read a little of the actual Twain who actually wrote books, too, the books of both of them voices against the deceitful use of words that perennially sacrifices the young and is busily doing so yet again.

Notes

1.   The most easily available text, the Harper Colophon, has no pagination. The portion I've quoted here is the latter half of the piece.

2.   Shelley Fisher Fishkin, "Wars of Words: American Writers and War," *The United States in Times of War and Peace: Conference Proceedings*. Foreign Language Teaching and Research Press, Beijing, 2005. Other commentators suggest Twain himself was reluctant to publish it, having some idea of the way it would be received.

3.   Fishkin's sources are these: Ray Eldon Hiebert, *Courtier to the Crowd: The Story of Ivy Lee and the Development of Public Relations* (Ames: Iowa State UP, 1966), p. 243; Jack J. Roth, *World War I: A Turning Point in Modern History* (New York: Knopf, 1967), p. 109; John Dos Passos, *One Man's Initiation: 1917* (Ithaca, NY: Cornell UP, 1969 [rpt.]), pp. 159–160; John Dos Passos, *Three Soldiers*, cited in Richard K. Pederson, *Hemingway: Direct and Oblique* (The Hague: Mouton, 1969), p. 121; Henry James, in a 1915 interview in *The New York Times*, quoted by John Brown, "The Anti-Propaganda Tradition in the United States." *Public Diplomacy Alumni Association*. <http://www.publicdiplomacy.org/19.htm> (accessed August 14, 2004).

4. Theresa M. Towner, *Introduction to William Faulkner* (Cambridge: Cambridge UP, 2008).

5. Gavin Stevens, as well as Horace Benbow, serves in the YMCA during the Great War. While neither should be taken as a spokesperson for Faulkner and both are portrayed as suffering limitations of mind and heart, both are portrayed as honorable men, Horace having foregone a calling as an Episcopal clergyman to serve as a noncombatant, and Gavin as something of a champion of justice. I treat Horace in the paper; for Gavin's service in the YMCA, see *The Town* (104) and *The Mansion* (180). Hemingway, too, it will be recalled served in the Red Cross as a noncombatant. First made ashamed of his fears by the ideals of the "strenuous life" championed by the man who had westernized himself, Teddy Roosevelt, Hemingway would later allow his characters (e.g., Nick Adams) to voice saner views. Even at the outset of the Great War, the high-school student Hemingway was spoofing the war rhetoric. For a fuller discussion see Michael Reynolds, *The Young Hemingway* (New York: Norton, 1986), 16–33.

6. For a brief account of Faulkner's charade, see Joseph Blotner, *Faulkner: A Biography* (New York: Vintage, 1991, one-volume edition), 60–61. Faulkner would have been parading about just about the time at which he depicts Anse bemoaning how the draft was "Talking me out of [Darl]" (*As I Lay Dying*, 36), a poignant description he could pen just a decade later.

7. See Wills's *John Wayne's America*.

8. Paul Olson, "Tolstoy and John Wayne in the Great Plains: The Conflict of Myths," a lecture for the Great Plains lecture series named for Paul A. Olson. As Olson notes, Wayne's "50 westerns from the 30s to the 70s" were performances of a genre that had long existed "in nucleus," beginning with Cooper's *The Prairie* and formulated in Owen Wister's *The Virginian*, a novel Wister dedicated to Teddy Roosevelt, who had "mythologiz[ed] himself as the western man" (2).

9. Cowley is quoted in Blotner's discussion of Faulkner's masquerading as soldier, p. 62.

Works Cited

Blotner, Joseph. *William Faulkner: A Biography*. New York: Vintage, 1974.

Fishkin, Shelley Fisher. "Wars of Words: American Writers and War." In *The United States in Times of War and Peace: Conference Proceedings.* Beijing: Foreign Language Teaching and Research Press, 2005.

Faulkner, William. *As I Lay Dying.* 1930. New York: Vintage, 1990.

———. *Flags in the Dust.* 1973. New York: Vintage, 1974.

———. *The Mansion.* 1959. New York: Vintage, 1965.

———. *The Town.* New York: Vintage, 1957.

———. *The Wild Palms.* 1939. New York: Vintage, 1995.

Reynolds, Michael. *The Young Hemingway.* New York: Basil Blackwell, 1986.

Twain, Mark. *The War Prayer.* 1923. New York: Harper, 1951.

Wills, Garry. *John Wayne's America: The Politics of Celebrity.* New York: Simon, 1997.

Contributors' Notes

Robert H. Brinkmeyer Jr., Professor of English and Southern Studies at the University of South Carolina, is an expert in twentieth-century Southern literature. His newest book, *The Fourth Ghost: White Southern Writers and European Fascism, 1930–1950*, has recently been published by Louisiana State University Press.

Françoise Buisson is Associate Professor at the University of Pau (France). A member of CLIMAS (Cultures et Littératures des Mondes Anglophones, Université Michel de Montaigne Bordeaux III, France) and AFEA (Association Française d'Études Américaines), she is the author of articles on Faulkner, Twain, Kaye Gibbons, T.C. Boyle, and Bret Easton Ellis.

Jason Cowan completed his bachelor's and master's work at Southeast Missouri State University, where he became interested in Twain and Faulkner studies while working as a research assistant in the Center for Faulkner Studies. He currently teaches composition at Jefferson College in Hillsboro, Missouri.

Laurel E. Eason is Leona Herman Fleming Professor of English at Catawba College in Salisbury, North Carolina. Her fields of interest include nineteenth-century American, English, German, and world literatures. She holds an M.A. in English from the University of Arkansas and an M.A. and a Ph.D. in German Language and Literature from Vanderbilt University.

Thomas Eaton is Assistant Professor of English at Southeast Missouri State University. He has published both critical essays and fiction in a number of periodicals. His short story, "Antelope," earned an Honorable Mention in the 2001 William Faulkner Short Story Competition.

Robert W. Hamblin is Professor of English and Director of the Center for Faulkner Studies at Southeast Missouri State University. The most recent of his several Faulkner volumes is *Critical Companion to William Faulkner*, co-authored with A. Nicholas Fargnoli and Michael Golay.

Fumiyo Hayashi, Professor of English and American Literature at the University of Tokyo, is the author of *Textual Labyrinth: William Faulkner's Cryptographic Design* and co-author of *Faulkner: After the Nobel Prize*.

M. Thomas Inge is the Blackwell Professor of Humanities at Randolph-Macon College in Ashland, Virginia, where he teaches courses in Southern literature, Faulkner, American humor, Walt Disney, animation, and Asian literature. His most recent publications include *William Faulkner: Overlook Illustrated Lives* and *The New Encyclopedia of Southern Culture, Volume 9: Literature*, and he is co-editing a new anthology of *Southern Frontier Humor*.

Mary A. Knighton is Associate Professor in English and the Program in Comparative Literature and Culture at the University of Tokyo. At the University of California, Berkeley, she earned an M.A. and a Ph.D. in English and an M.A. in East Asian Languages and Culture. She has written and presented on Japanese and American literature and serves on the editorial board of the *Journal of the American Literature Society of Japan*.

Leland Krauth is Professor of English at the University of Colorado at Boulder, specializing in American literature. Besides numerous essays on nineteenth- and twentieth-century American writers, he has published two books on Twain: *Proper Mark Twain* and *Mark Twain & Company*.

Gretchen Martin is Assistant Professor of American and Southern Literature at the University of Virginia's College at Wise. She is the author of *The Frontier Roots of American Realism* and has published essays on nineteenth-century American literature and Southern literature.

David M. Monteith is currently finishing his Ph.D. dissertation on child narratives of the South at the University of Western Ontario. He has worked extensively on the American South with a focus on William Faulkner and was awarded the William Faulkner Society Scholarship in 2005.

Charles A. Peek is Emeritus Professor of English at the University of Nebraska at Kearney. A former Fulbright Senior Lecturer in China and a current Fulbright Senior Specialist, he has published and presented nationally and internationally on Faulkner, Willa Cather, Ernest Hemingway, and the Harlem Renaissance. His poetry appears most recently in *Hurricane Blues*, and he is currently one of three performers in *Prayers for the People: Carl Sandburg's Poetry and Songs*.

Alisa M. Smith-Riel received her M.A. in English from St. Bonaventure University in 2006. She is currently enrolled in the Ph.D. program in American Literature at Northern Illinois University.

Melanie Speight teaches English at Ste. Genevieve (Missouri) High School. A former research assistant in the Center for Faulkner Studies, she helped coordinate the Faulkner and Twain Conference.

Matthew Sutton is completing his Ph.D. in American Studies at the College of William and Mary. His research interests include Southern Studies, popular music, and autobiography.